"Trust Me, Mom—Everyone Else Is Going!"

ALSO COAUTHORED BY RONI COHEN-SANDLER

"I'm Not Mad, I Just Hate You!"
  A New Understanding of Mother-Daugher Conflict

Roni Cohen-Sandler, Ph.D.

"Trust Me, Mom—

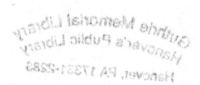

Everyone Else Is Going!"

The New Rules for Mothering

Adolescent Girls

VIKING

VIKING
Published by the Penguin Group
Penguin Putnam Inc., 375 Hudson Street,
New York, New York 10014, U.S.A.
Penguin Books Ltd, 80 Strand, London WC2R ORL, England
Penguin Books Australia Ltd, Ringwood, Victoria, Australia
Penguin Books Canada Ltd, 10 Alcorn Avenue,
Toronto, Ontario, Canada M4V 3B2
Penguin Books (N.Z.) Ltd, 182–190 Wairau Road,
Auckland 10, New Zealand

Penguin Books Ltd, Registered Offices:
Harmondsworth, Middlesex, England

First published in 2002 by Viking Penguin,
a member of Penguin Putnam Inc.

10   9   8   7   6   5   4   3   2   1

LIBRARY OF CONGRESS CATALOGING-IN-PUBLICATION DATA
Cohen-Sandler, Roni.
  "Trust me, Mom—everyone else is going!" : the new rules
for mothering adolescent girls / Roni Cohen-Sandler.
  p. cm.
  Includes index.
  ISBN: 0-670-03068-6
  1. Teenage girls. 2. Mothers and daughters. 3. Child rearing. I. Title.
HQ798 .C5645 2002
649'.133—dc21   2001026723

This book is printed on acid-free paper. ∞

Printed in the United States of America
Set in Adobe Garamond

For Jeff,
with much love

Acknowledgments

I am grateful to many people who supported this book in so many ways. Loretta Barrett is as fine a person as she is a literary agent; I am privileged to know her and to work with her. Also, many thanks to the ever-helpful Alison Brooks and Nick Mullendore. Janet Goldstein is an editor extraordinaire; at every step along the way, she works her magic while making the entire process gratifying and most enjoyable. It is a pleasure to work with the entire terrific team at Penguin Putnam, particularly Maureen Donnelly, Susan Hans O'Connor, Carolyn Coleburn, Cindy Hamel, and Ann Mah.

Everyone in my Wednesday morning study group—Caren Glickson, Lyn Sommer, Debra Hyman, Karen Alter-Reid, Allison Kravitz, and Debbie Eisenberg—is deeply treasured. With her expertise as a mother, psychologist, and writer, Lyn Sommer made thoughtful and incisive contributions to the initial manuscript. I am indebted to Barbara Vinograd, both for reading the first draft and, more important, for being my trusted comrade-in-arms throughout our daughters' growing-up years. Our solidarity has been precious to me. My other dear friends also have been wonderful, especially Jodi Susser, Victoria Schonfeld, Nancy Magida, and Dale Barcham. Susan Ault and Laura Van Wormer made excellent suggestions at the inception of this project. And special thanks to all the women and girls I have worked with over the years who have shared their stories and taught me so very much.

I am fortunate to have the love and support of my parents, Arleen and Larry Cohen, and my in-laws, Rose and Sam Sandler. My family's unwavering encouragement—even at the expense of home-cooked meals—has been much appreciated. My daughter, Laura,

made many insightful suggestions about the manuscript and gener-
ously allowed me to include anecdotes that could be helpful to other
mothers and daughters. My son, Jason, used his crack computer
skills to track down journal articles, and good-naturedly endured
countless inquiries about middle school in the interest of furthering
my research. Above all, I have been blessed with my husband, Jeff,
who helps make all my dreams possible.

—R.C.-S.

Contents

"Trust Me, Mom—Everyone Else Is Going!"

Chapter 1

Moms, Take Heart

A NEW OUTLOOK

"Somehow my daughter seems to be slipping away. I know she's growing up, but I'm still her mother. I don't want to wake up one day and think, 'What happened to her?' or 'Who is she?' And yet I'm not sure what I can do. There don't seem to be any road maps for bringing up girls today. I always wonder about what is going on in my daughter's life, but I don't seem to get any real answers. I just want to know that my daughter will be okay. I want to know that she'll make the right decisions when I'm not around. When I get nervous about all this and try to talk to her, she just gets angry, but I can't help it. I find that parenting is so much harder now that she's a teenager. Maybe this comes more naturally to other mothers, because nobody else seems to be as confused as I am. On especially awful days, I think, 'You're completely lost; you have no idea what you're doing.'" —Mary, thirty-four

"My daughter is only ten, but she's acting like a teenager. I guess I expected these sorts of problems when she was in middle school or high school, but I'm not ready for this now. In fact, I'm already at the end of my rope, and she's not even driving yet! My two older children were never like this. Sure, some of their friends weren't my favorites, but they were never consumed with all this social stuff like my youngest is. She's talking about issues that her siblings didn't mention until they were in their midteens. Even her language seems way too advanced for her age. Other than stopping the clock for a while, there doesn't really seem to be anything else I can do. Maybe I could use some help. My head is spinning!" — Francesca, fifty

"I had no idea that being a mother could be this hard! I guess I thought that if my daughter and I were always close, if I taught her the right

values and spent lots of time with her, that we would basically see eye to eye as she grew up. But she and I couldn't be less alike. In fact, sometimes I wonder where she's come from. Among other things, I've always stressed how important it is for her to be an individual, to think for herself. But she's completely swayed by what's in and, especially by what her friends do and say. We also have very different ideas about what's appropriate for girls her age. It really amazes me—and scares me—to think of how focused she is on boys, how eager she is to please them. How could this have happened? And how are we going to get through the next few years?"

—Gerri, forty-five

Nearly every time my telephone rings lately, it's the mother of a teenage girl who is confused, upset, or absolutely frantic about the state of her daughter's social life—her friends, her attitude, her boyfriend, her secrecy, her nightlife. Without exception, mothers are concerned about what exactly their adolescent daughters are doing, who they're doing it with and, especially, if they are safe. Whether your daughter is approaching or well into the teenage years, you too may question the quality of her friendships, worry about substances and sex, and have reservations about her romantic choices. Maybe you panic whenever you see a red flag that may signal trouble, making you wonder if you are completely crazy at times. If so, be assured that you are in good company. These days, no mother seems immune.

Perhaps because we have considered ourselves a more aware and progressive generation of mothers, we expected that our daughters would somehow make smarter decisions in their lives and bypass the typical teenage troubles. Unfortunately this turned out to be a fallacy. Mothers today share a nearly universal perception: Even girls who were once rational, reasonable, and levelheaded suddenly seem to be making stupid, frightening, or potentially dangerous choices.

These girls are not all troubled; these are difficult times. Since the publication of my first book, *I'm Not Mad, I Just Hate You!*, which dealt with conflict in the mother-daughter relationship, women have increasingly told me that their teenagers' social lives have become their number one concern. In fact, countless mothers have confided that they never could have imagined, much less predicted, their daughters' behavior. For example, some girls were caught using alcohol or drugs, sneaking out of their homes, and lying about their whereabouts. Others were found to have diaries or e-mail peppered with vulgar words or explicit sexual references. A few were even taken to emergency rooms or picked up by police or suspended from school.

These aren't evil girls from awful families but typical teenagers, some of whom are struggling, many with remarkable talents, who are nonetheless making worrisome choices. It may be difficult or even unthinkable to accept that your daughter, if she has not already done so, may soon join their ranks. Yet it is important to acknowledge from the outset that poor decisions, rash actions, and risk taking are as fundamental to adolescence as acne, braces, and the first kiss. It is just that you probably never thought you would have to deal with them.

Until now, it was always *other* teenagers who wove elaborate cover stories to elude parents who forbade them from certain peers and situations. You were sure that the open communication and trusting relationship you worked so hard all these years to establish with your daughter would eliminate her need for such subterfuge as a teen. The first time you discover that she has manipulated, deliberately misled, or outwardly lied to you, your whole foundation may be shaken. Is it possible that your daughter is being evasive, telling half-truths, or blithely ignoring your rules?

Similarly, some of you may gasp in shock and dismay when you discover that your daughters have not been victims but perpetrators of unkindness. Was it really *your* girl who started the vicious rumor, excluded the "loser" from the lunch table, or mercilessly used that lovely boy who had a crush on her? After discovering her thirteen-year-old's efforts to bad-mouth and ostracize a longtime pal, one mother maintained, "I never would have dreamed she would do anything like that. I thought my daughter would know better—and act better!"

Many of your daughters may make other, less serious but still self-defeating choices. While traveling across the country to speak to groups of parents, for example, I am frequently asked for advice about girls who develop unhealthy friendships and demeaning romantic relationships. Mira, mother to fourteen-year-old Phillippa, says, "I watch my daughter being excluded by her two so-called best friends, over and over, and yet she still lets them hurt her. Why can't she defend herself or, better yet, make more loyal friends?" Similarly, fifteen-year-old Loren's mother describes her daughter's pattern of "longing to be friends with girls in the popular crowd, who not only rebuff her but are often mean to her. It's heartbreaking." Norma, mother to seventeen-year-old Randy, is aghast at "the way her boyfriend seems to control her with his criticism, his emotional threats, and that awful pager."

Whether your daughter is placing herself in danger, tolerating harmful relationships, or engaging in behavior that makes your hair stand on end, you have probably found yourself, at various times, worried, frustrated, shocked, or disgusted. Confronted with her particularly bad decisions, you may even feel angry. As one mother put it, "After staying up half the night waiting for her to come home, I thought if she was still alive I was going to kill her!" You may have reacted similarly when your daughter was a little girl and wandered away from you. As you finally located her or pulled her from the street, your initial relief may have turned to rage as the enormity of what could have happened sunk in.

Even if your daughter is proceeding through adolescence in the slow lane, cautiously staying within the lines, you may be concerned because some of her friends appear reckless in their great rush to grow up. Or your daughter's shyness and preference for sticking close to home may make you concerned not about excessive socializing or harmful relationships, but loneliness and social inexperience. It is also possible that despite your own daughter's apparently good adjustment, you can't help but become alarmed as you look all around you. You may want to learn as much as you can about teenagers' social lives to avoid problems in the future.

It is the rare mother of a teenage girl, therefore, who feels she *doesn't* need help.

Skyrocketing Worries

These days the topic of your daughter's social life is likely to ignite instant contention between you two, along with a smoldering sensation in the pit of your stomach. Why is this happening? you might ask. It hasn't always been this way.

Since your daughter was a young girl, you have probably invested considerable thought and effort in teaching her to follow her heart while learning to get along with others. Still, despite your mindfulness, probably neither your daughter nor her life has been perfect. Perhaps her chattiness, possessiveness, or flair for melodrama has occasionally alienated others. Teased or disappointed by a close friend, she may have become furious, inconsolable, or vengeful. If your daughter acted without thinking, you may have helped her deal with the fallout of blurted nastiness or regretted self-disclosure.

Back then, however, the biggest social dilemmas were how she would handle a bossy friend, whether or not she should quit Girl Scouts, or whom she invited to (and could exclude from) her next birthday party. Sure, you may have been taken aback by the passion of her second-grade crush, but today the issues are far more serious, the stakes infinitely higher. You may be fearful about where she is headed, and worried that if she picks the wrong friends, she will be led astray or cave in to peer pressures with irrevocable consequences.

There are perfectly valid reasons for these fears. Though you may feel crazy, you are actually responding reasonably to a number of issues that are complicating your daughter's social life and therefore, your relationship with her. You may find it comforting that other mothers are struggling with these same concerns.

A Scarier World

If you have the sense that your daughter is growing up in a world different from the one in which you were raised, you are correct. Of course, the worries of undesirable friendships, traffic accidents, and teenage pregnancy have been around for generations. Similarly, despite the strong warnings you have issued, probably ad nauseam, your daughter could be one of the 52 percent of teenagers who admits to using an illegal substance by senior year of high school. But, without question, there are additional worries, wider choices, scarier dangers, and more intense pressures faced by contemporary teenagers, with fewer cultural protections in place.

As but one example, your daughter's use of PCs, cell phones, pagers, e-mail, and instant messaging makes it that much harder for you to monitor her social life, as well as to anticipate and resolve any difficulties that arise. In fact, you may be scrambling even to keep up with your daughter's knowledge of this technology, much less to establish guidelines that can limit or prevent its hazards. Similarly, unlike your own mother, you have to think about guns on playgrounds; angry, sexist lyrics inciting aggression toward girls at rock concerts; and the routine sex and violence in movies, television shows, and CDs. Even more alarming, there are the unthinkable possibilities: your daughter planning a rendezvous with a young man she met in a chat room, being raped after drinking a Roofie-laced soda, or contracting the fatal HIV infection. This new world requires a new approach, with new rules.

It may surprise you that it is not only mothers who perceive the world as scarier; daughters do too. A recent *New York Times*/CBS poll found that over 43 percent of teenagers surveyed believed they were having a harder time growing up than their parents had. These teens cited, among other causes, a faster pace of life, worries about a more dangerous world, and greatly increased peer pressure to use alcohol, drink excessively, and do other new drugs such as laced marijuana, ecstasy, and inhalants.

These data are consistent with a disturbing trend; although I have treated adolescents in psychotherapy for over twenty years, it is only during the past five years or so that girls have reported markedly higher levels of distress—and their mothers have dealt with correspondingly more distressing teen behavior. Interestingly, as I was finishing this book I came across a new study that corroborates this change. Psychologist Jean Twenge of Case Western Reserve University found that today's children feel significantly more anxious than did children in the 1950s. In fact, normal children ages nine to seventeen display more anxiety today than those who were treated for psychiatric disorders fifty years ago.

It is hardly surprising that your own apprehension slips so easily into overdrive. Perhaps on occasion you have extrapolated from your daughter's single bad decision to extreme or dire consequences. For example, the mother of a sixteen-year-old described that "after getting the inconceivable news that my daughter spent an evening at an unsupervised home with a boy generally regarded as trouble, I instantly became convinced that date rape, sexually transmitted diseases, pregnancy, and AIDS were just around the corner." Similarly, even the glimpse of a beer can or whiff of alcohol on her breath may result in panicky predictions of overdoses, addictions, and accidental deaths. Your memories of reading about tragedies involving teenagers and thinking, "That could be my daughter" are never far from consciousness.

Is it any wonder that whenever you are confronted with your daughter's poor judgment and risky behavior, you may think, "Has she lost her mind?"

Or just as likely, you fear you will lose your own.

She's Not Fully Mature

Because your daughter is still developing, you may have doubts that she is ready to handle a more dangerous world. It's not that she lost her mind, it's just not full grown yet. Techniques such as MRI (magnetic resonance imaging) and PET (positron-emission tomography) scanning have proven that your daughter's brain is still maturing through the teenage years and even beyond. Although this information may not reassure you that she is ready to take care of herself, it does clarify why the adolescent stage of development is, by definition, a minefield of impediments to good decision making.

For example, the corpus callosum, a structure that connects the left and right sides of the brain and is responsible for self-awareness, is not fully developed until the twenties. The temporal lobes, which facilitate emotional control and language, do not reach maximum maturity until age sixteen. Perhaps most important, the frontal lobes—the center of executive functions such as organization, planning, judgment, and the regulation of behavior and emotions—hit their peak growth spurt between puberty and young adulthood. Not only is the immature adolescent brain more vulnerable to trauma and drugs, but it also cannot manage stresses such as social pressures and sexual or aggressive urges as well as the adult brain. No wonder your daughter's tenuous impulse control has you worried!

There are other valid reasons for teenagers' poor judgment. Some have not yet developed sufficient abstract thinking to generalize from their experiences and benefit from their mistakes. Many have not learned good problem-solving skills. For example, teenagers' occasionally rigid, black-or-white thinking ("If I can't do it now, I'll never do it!") prevents them from considering several solutions to their problems. When one approach fails, they tend to give up ("Forget it, there's no way!"). Or often their adolescent veil of invincibility and immortality ("I'll be fine, nothing will happen") allows them to make choices without even considering the possible consequences of their behavior.

As if all this weren't enough to override teenagers' logic, the added ingredients of raging hormones and intense, unpredictable emotions are a surefire recipe for girls' unfortunate decisions. Adolescent daughters are all but infamous for mood swings. If your daughter is among the girls today who are experiencing the earliest signs of physical maturation by age eight or nine, this probably won't mean full-blown puberty or imminent menstruation. But she may be experiencing hormonal pulses long before her brain—not to mention her coping skills—are mature enough to handle them.

Of course, these developmental factors are not completely to blame; there are times when your daughter simply forgets to use her head. Caught up in the moment, she doesn't think. Or she deliberately chooses to ignore the wisdom you know she is capable of in favor of an appealing peer's influence or a tantalizing social experience. Among themselves, the teenage mantra seems to be, "Yeah, I know it was stupid . . . but I had fun." No wonder your fears have skyrocketed!

Yet it is important to remember that your daughter's unfortunate behavior, detrimental relationships, and even lapses of judgment do not suggest that she is a bad seed or terrible person. She has merely made unfortunate decisions. Although you might wish she would always use her head, you know this is hardly realistic. It also may be comforting to learn that your daughter and her friends are not unique in this regard. Not only are poor choices common during adolescence, but a survey by *Who's Who Among American High School Students* found that even academic superstars are not immune. For example, more than 75 percent of honor students nationwide have cheated, only half of sexually active teens use condoms, and 10 percent have driven a car while drunk. Obviously, being book smart doesn't make teenagers act smart.

Secret Social Lives

Just as the perils threatening your daughter appear to multiply, you probably feel it is harder to supervise her, let alone to protect her. The powerful developmental push to establish peer relationships—and ease away from intense emotional ties at home—is responsible for teen girls' developing private, almost secret, social lives. These days it is hard to miss the hints that your daughter prefers the company of her friends—if not the solitude of her room—to being with you. As Peggy, mother of fifteen-year-old Martha, put it, "She used to hang around and chat with me while I got dinner on the table, and sometimes we watched our favorite TV shows together. That's a distant memory now."

Other than to make requests, your daughter may be eager to communicate only one thing: that she is her own person and, therefore, no longer needs to rely on your opinions or advice. To make clear her independence, your daughter may adopt a perpetually bored demeanor around you, appearing so listless and apathetic that her typical response to your remarks or queries is a dismissive "whatever," or a barely audible, whispered syllable that sounds like "mumblemumble."

Until the phone rings, that is. Then you hear the delighted shrieks and peals of giggles reminiscent of her younger years. And if a boy happens to call, you may hardly recognize the charming, dulcet voice that answers the phone. With that all-too-familiar sinking sensation in your gut, it dawns on you that you no longer have the power to elicit this reaction from your daughter.

Even if your daughter is forthcoming about her social life, it is an illusion to believe you have *all* the information. Ask any mother who has wisely pretended to be invisible while driving a carload of her daughter's friends. When girls get caught up in conversation and forget to be guarded, mothers can overhear snippets of experiences they have had, names of people they know, and memories they share—none of which are remotely familiar. Once again, it may hit you that your daughter has her own social life, with its unique history separate from yours.

Your daughter may now be guarding this social life with a passion. Maybe she used to burst in the door from her elementary school bus, animatedly describing how Kendall's secret got spilled, why Dora and Marie got in a fight during recess, and what she is planning for tomorrow night's sleepover. But now you may find it difficult to obtain any particulars about what she and her friends are up to. She probably responds to even the gentlest of inquiries about her social life with retorts such as "What do you want to know?" or "Please, leave me alone!" Your more direct questions—should you have the nerve to ask any—are experienced as intrusions tantamount to brain surgery.

And heaven forbid you doubt her peers! Despite any misgivings your daughter herself may have, she will feel compelled to defend or even champion her friends to you or any adult who has the temerity to question them.

Although you may know full well that it is normal for teenage girls to prize their privacy, this developmental shift enormously affects your mothering. Needless to say, if your daughter classifies her thoughts, feelings, and activities as top secret, parenting her will be all the more challenging. Plus, if you cannot find out reassuring information, your maternal anxiety can run away with your imagination.

Your New Status (i.e., Demotion)

If your daughter is the eldest or only child in the family, you may be jolted by the realization that her strides toward independence are nudging—or, what is more likely, demanding—you to mother her differently. After all, during the past ten years or so there have been many moments when you felt reasonably confident; you have seen your daughter's adjustment and your relationship with her as an endorsement of the job you have been attempting to do as a mother. Now, suddenly, she may be telling you or showing you, "All that's in the past, Mom!" Her adolescent changes are increasingly causing you to doubt yourself.

At the same time, many women I speak to pride themselves on being more closely connected to their daughters and in tune with the teenage world than were their own mothers, whom they happily believe remained oblivious to their adolescent exploits. A modern mother's sense of being more in the know and involved with her daughter can lead, however, to a false sense of control. Thus you may be disappointed or even devastated in those moments when you feel helpless to make changes in your teenage daughter's social life. For example, even if you think the newest member of her youth group personifies trouble, your daughter may eagerly befriend her. Despite the poor reputation of a particular family, your daughter may spend considerable time in that home. This loss of control is not unlike when your school-age daughter became friends with children whose parents had different habits, rules, and expectations, some of which made you uneasy.

Now that she is a teenager, these fears are undoubtedly far worse. You realize that your daughter has stopped behaving according to your wishes, your guidance, and your wisdom. Not only have you been ousted from your long-held position as her ultimate authority and moral compass, but you have also been replaced by her peers as the litmus test of what is and isn't acceptable. Your daughter is making countless, daily social choices without your input or guidance, most of which you may never find out about.

Any lingering doubts about your status in your daughter's social life should be clarified by this rather humorous exchange I recently overheard between two sixteen-year-old employees of a clothing store:

"I met your mother yesterday," one said to the other, "and she was really nice."

"Yeah, she is," the girl replied. "There's only one problem."

"What's that?" the first girl asked.

"Well . . . she likes to talk to me."

Given this mentality, it is not surprising that even when you raise valid concerns about her life, your daughter is unlikely to be overly grateful for your interest. Instead she may be shocked by your accusations and eager to deny the existence of a problem ("I'm totally fine!"). Moreover, she probably tells you that it is not her but *you* who has the problem or, alternatively, that she does have a problem— and that her problem *is* you! If all else fails, teenage girls usually blame their mothers ("Why are you always overreacting?" or "You don't have to flip out!") whenever there is the slightest possibility they have erred.

Even when you have undeniable evidence of your daughter's foolish behavior or serious infraction of a basic family rule, she is likely to minimize the situation ("I just made one little slip; did you expect me to be perfect?") or defend herself ("Everybody else was much worse than me; you should be happy!"). Any efforts to correct her are not only rebuffed, but also intensely resented. Developmentally this makes sense. Because she is struggling mightily to establish a sense of who she is and who she will become, your teenager may cling to slivers of self-confidence that instantly chafe at the tug of your questioning. In fact, any advice you offer, no matter how cautiously, may be interpreted as an absolute demolition of her character.

Even if you realize this is normal, you can still feel discarded, rejected or abandoned by your daughter. In a somewhat wistful manner, the mother of a seventeen-year-old described her daughter as "kind of a boarder in my home. She sleeps here and eats here and that's about it." Bette, the fifty-one-year-old mother of a high school junior, put it perhaps most poignantly: "I anticipated losing my daughter when she went to college. She hasn't moved out yet, but she certainly has moved on."

An Evolving Mother-Daughter Relationship

So just what are you supposed to do? Of course, one of your main roles is to guide your daughter along the many pathways to becoming a young woman. You see it as your responsibility to step in when she faces hardship and trouble. It goes without saying that you would desperately like to keep her from becoming a teen in turmoil. But it is hard to know how to accomplish these and all your other goals, especially when your adolescent daughter seems to resist and resent your assistance.

Frustrated and discouraged, some mothers simply become resigned to their daughters' "doing whatever they want." Many conclude, in effect, that teenagers should take care of themselves because, "There's nothing I can do, anyway." It is not that these mothers are unloving or uncaring, but they withdraw from their daughters' lives because they don't know any other possible course. Perhaps it is agonizing helplessness that prompts some mothers' unconscious parenting philosophy: "If I don't see any problems, I don't have to deal with them" and its associated wish, "and then they will go away." Yet clinical experience proves over and again that this disconnection from mothers is the very last thing teenage girls need.

That is why I wanted to write this book: to offer an alternative approach that can help you to remain closely connected to your daughter while parenting her effectively through the adolescent years. This will require that your relationship with her evolve according to her age, skills, and needs. Essentially, you and your daughter will become a team—not as equal partners, of course, but as a mother and a teenage girl who, working together, benefit from both of your perspectives, desires, and expertise. This collaborative way of interacting with your daughter, as you will see throughout the chapters ahead, is guided by your BRAIN—that is, by the principles of Being flexible, Respectful, Attuned, Involved, and Noncontrolling.

Whether your daughter is nearing puberty, in the throes of adolescence, or getting ready to leave home, this approach will enable you to strengthen your relationship as well as your effectiveness as a mother. Of course you already have ideas about how your daughter is managing her life and assumptions about how you can help her to adjust well to adolescence. But as you read this book, these assessments may well change, especially as you become more aware of your own role in this relationship. Thus rather than jumping to conclusions or reacting automatically, you might want to consider these new rules for mothering.

Being Flexible and Attuned to your daughter, for example, helps you to adapt more precisely to her growing maturity and changing needs. You will learn to pay attention to your daughter's cues to decide when to pursue an issue, when to dig deeper, and when to let go. You will figure out more adeptly when to change a rule, make an exception, or stick to "Absolutely not!" When you are Respectful of your daughter's individuality, you can best convey your ideas about healthy relationships, solving interpersonal problems, and learning from mistakes.

Above all, this approach guides you to remain appropriately Involved, yet Noncontrolling. This delicate balance is key to successfully parenting a teenage girl. Being noncontrolling requires you to recognize that you cannot know everything about your daughter, make her decisions, or prevent her mistakes. Instead, you will learn to gauge when she is ready for the next step and support her age-appropriate autonomy. That way your daughter will get opportunities to practice thinking clearly, making smarter choices, and becoming more responsible for her own behavior. At the same time, however, it is equally crucial to stay involved with your daughter. When you monitor what is going on in her life, you can step in correctly when she oversteps a boundary, rushes ahead too quickly, or needs different limits. Remaining involved yet noncontrolling allows you to intervene appropriately and to prevent future problems.

Throughout these pages you will learn to use everyday situations as springboards for fundamental discussions about, say, expectations in friendship, limit setting, and personal values. The voices of real teenage girls will advise you about which of their mothers' approaches seem to work and, conversely, those they perceive as intrusive, condescending, or simply ridiculous. These tips will help you to communicate in ways that counteract the harmful cultural messages your daughter gets about self-esteem, romantic relationships, and sexuality.

In addition, to supplement what your daughter may or may not disclose, you will learn from other girls about the perils and pleasures of teenagers' social lives. As you read poignant accounts of the emotional roller coaster of the typical adolescent—the confusion, pain, elation, insecurity, enthusiasm, loneliness, self-consciousness, and discomfort—you will find yourself more attuned to your own daughter's feelings. As you are reminded of the devotion to friends and desperation to be cool that often guide teenagers' decisions, you will better understand your daughter's motivations. As you learn how these girls struggle and progressively learn to navigate their social world, you may become more sanguine about your own daughter's ability to do so.

Before you get into the nitty-gritty, however, I would like to share five basic premises that prove reassuring to other mothers raising teenage girls:

1. There Are No Perfect Kids—or Mothers

Unfortunately many women are operating under the false assumption that they alone are muddling through mothering, that everyone else has raising adolescent daughters all figured out. What usually promotes this way of thinking is the sighting of perfect girls—that is, those who refrain from wearing skimpy clothing, swearing, having tantrums, or doing whatever it is your own daughter is presently doing that most disturbs you. Eventually, you may find out that these seemingly ideal girls actually get drunk, have unprotected sex, develop emotional disorders, or accept rides from strangers. But until then, you may be convinced that your daughter is a disgrace—and that you have made her so.

Of course at least on some level, everybody knows there are neither perfect daughters nor perfect mothers. As Minna, forty-five, says, "It wasn't until my daughter had graduated from high school that my bubble was burst. I looked in her yearbook and was absolutely shocked at what her friends had written. The profanity! The sexual innuendoes! I realized then that I had known only a fraction of what they really did!"

Mothering is not only hard, but humbling.

Fortunately, whatever I failed to learn in graduate school or in nearly a quarter century of clinical practice, I was taught by my own two teenagers, who have been most eager to correct my deficiencies. A tendency to point out ideal peers was but one. When my son was in middle school, for example, I remember commenting that his friend had been a pleasure to have as a weekend guest because he was always so calm, had good manners, and used a respectful tone of voice. Without skipping a beat, my son replied, "You should know, Mom, that's because he wasn't home."

2. There Are No Perfect—or Permanent—Solutions

Because you have less knowledge about your daughter's social life than you used to and you are determined to be noncontrolling, it will be nearly impossible for you to solve her problems. If you are aiming for perfect solutions, you probably want to rethink that goal. In fact, if you are to be at all helpful, it will be because you are willing to put your head together with your daughter's, carefully consider and weigh all the issues, and come up with workable compromises. In other words, you'll collaborate with her. But even then, despite your finding this ideal solution, your daughter may decide on her own to take a different tack. Before you despair, however, remember that the most important social lessons are often learned not from your best conversations or most ideal strategies, but from your daughter's everyday experiences and mistakes.

In addition, your child-rearing solutions are neither perfect nor permanent because your daughter's social situations are in perpetual flux, your understanding is improving, and she is continuously maturing and changing. What this means, however, is that a parenting strategy that worked like a charm yesterday will fail miserably today. And by next week, you could well be chastising yourself, "Whatever could I have been thinking?" Therefore it is best to take mothering your teenage daughter one day and one situation or problem at a time. Now is the time to be flexible and creative.

3. Parents Can—and Do—Make a Difference

Regardless of what your daughter may be telling you, there is no doubt that she still needs you. When she claims, "I'm not a little kid anymore; I don't need your advice," you may offer a gentle reminder, "Yes, but I'm still your mom." Time and time again, whether working with parents and teenagers in my office or raising my own teenagers, I have seen the enormous impact that mothers— and fathers, of course—can have on their daughters' most important decisions. In fact, the pivotal role of fathers in girls' development, especially their social lives, could be the subject of a whole other book. Although this work focuses on the mother-daughter relationship, fathers may also find many of the principles and strategies useful.

Research corroborates that parents are a critical source of information teenagers get about the world, especially about close, committed relationships, values, sound decision making, and consequences of one's actions. For example, *The National Longitudinal Study of Adolescent Health,* the largest and most comprehensive study of American teenagers, found that feeling close to parents was one of the strongest deterrents to risky behaviors such as early sexual activity, substance use, and violence. According to a recent CBS poll, when one thousand girls aged thirteen to seventeen were asked whom they most admired, 40 percent said Mom. *The Roper Youth Report* found that the majority of adolescents cited parents as their number one influence—over friends, teachers, TV, and advertising—on issues such as drinking, decision making, and long-term planning.

4. Have Faith in the Learning Process

Having said all this about the importance of mothering, there are also undeniable limitations to your influence. Since you are rarely privy to all the information, won't be able to fathom many teenage social situations, and cannot control your daughter's decisions, how can you determine their outcome? You can't. That is why you must respect—albeit vigilantly—the process through which your daughter experiences and discovers certain things for herself as she goes out into the world.

I learned this purely by accident. For many years I had been concerned about one of my daughter's camp friends, who seemed particularly moody, remote, and self-deprecating. Fortunately, it was not until much later that I learned more about Tanya's problems. Had I known when the girls were younger about her tendency to binge when drinking, I would have worried more about Tanya's influence on my daughter and probably tried (undoubtedly without success) to discourage their association. What happened, instead, was far preferable.

Although for years my daughter maintained her friendship with Tanya out of loyalty and concern, she learned how to take better care of herself whenever they were together. Gradually, she distanced herself from Tanya. More important, perhaps, her own attitudes and decisions about drinking were apparently shaped, at least in part, by her observations of Tanya's sloppy and nasty behavior when drunk; essentially, she had learned from this friend what she did *not* want to do. My staying out of that process, however inadvertent, was a blessing.

5. The Mother-Daughter Relationship Evolves

When you are in the middle of a transition or in the thick of conflict, you may forget that circumstances can—and will—change. When you look into the future, it is hard to remember that someday things will be different with your daughter. Not only can't you be aware of what life will bring, but also you often cannot foresee how your daughter will mature and how you too will grow as a mother. It is hard to envision, in turn, how your mother-daughter relationship will evolve over time.

When my daughter started middle school, she suddenly began to protect not only her privacy, but also her entire territory, with a vengeance. Whenever I entered her bedroom, she went into a flurry, hastily closing her journal and stashing papers out of sight. Sometimes I felt like an intruder! In fact, I still recall a nearly visceral reaction, as if I were being forcibly evicted not just from her room, but also from her life. I longed to know her secrets, to touch the items most important to her, if only to stay in close touch with my daughter and her world. Several years later, however, I was shocked to discover equally abruptly that this situation had undergone a 180-degree turnaround.

In her rush to pack up and leave for a trip during her last summer of high school, my daughter's room was in unusual disarray. When I offered to straighten it in her absence, I was surprised not only that she didn't hesitate, but also that she was grateful! A few days later, eager for the project, I stood in the doorway of my daughter's room and thought, "Okay, where should I start?" However, I couldn't move.

I was immediately struck by the oddest sensation of discomfort: It was not my little girl's room anymore. In fact, I was conscious of feeling as awkward as if I were about to rifle through the possessions of another adult, perhaps some woman with whom I was sharing a home. It occurred to me that my daughter's maturation, my own growth, as well as the myriad changes our relationship had undergone during these years, had all contributed to this unexpected state of affairs. I left the room and closed the door behind me to await her return.

The road ahead with your own daughter may well seem confusing or overwhelming at times. But as you progress through this book, your insights will help you to build and maintain a trusting relationship, to encourage your daughter to develop a strong sense of self, and to enable both of you to tackle daily problems and crises that come your way. The first step, however, is actually to take a step back. Now that she is a teenager, it behooves you to reexamine and readjust, if necessary, your basic approach to parenting your daughter. The next chapter will lead the way.

Chapter 2

Revisiting Your Approach
TEEN PARENTING 101

"I'm not sure how strict I should be with my daughter. Parents I talk to have such different opinions about this. Since Leslie is pretty easygoing and it's not in my nature to crack down on her, I haven't seen the need to give her any ultimatums. But sometimes I worry when other mothers tell me about their seventh-graders getting boy crazy and spending all their time talking on the phone. When these girls act up and get into trouble, their mothers panic. I tell them that so far I trust Leslie, but they look at me as if I'm a fool and warn me about what will happen if I'm too lax. Maybe I'm naïve, but Leslie has had a fair amount of freedom already; she's home by herself after school, and I think she's handled that well. I don't know whether I should be giving her more rules to prevent problems down the line, or just continue the way we are. I guess I'm confused about the best approach with teenagers."

—Constance, forty-six

"I accidentally read my daughter's e-mail, and I'm not sure if I should be glad I did or not. She's apparently been going out with this boy—whatever that means. Now I know that Deirdre has been online with him for hours every night when I thought she was doing research. After all our discussions, I thought she would respect my wishes. But she is apparently very preoccupied with this boy and seems to have lost all reason. Now it also makes more sense why she quit her basketball team and cooled her relationship with her best friend. How can I help Deirdre to realize this isn't smart? Should I restrict her? Should I just ignore this phase she's going through and hope it passes quickly? Or, should I tell her how I feel? Maybe I should just keep quiet. I don't want her to get angry at me; it's not worth a tirade or days of silence."   — Tess, forty-two

"My daughter and I seem to be at a stalemate. Since she learned to drive, she acts as if she is in charge. But as long as she is living in my home, I think she should do as I say. Kellie doesn't seem to agree or to understand that. When I say that she can't go out, for example, she insists that she'll go anyway and I can't stop her. Every night I see her light on well past her bedtime. She leaves for school in the morning dressed in ripped jeans and cropped tops, which I've specifically forbidden. Kellie constantly tells me that I can't control her. Why not? She's my daughter! She used to get good grades and pitch in around here, but since we've been locking horns like this she seems hell bent on making everyone miserable. I'm at my wit's end." —Ruth, fifty-three

*A*ll too often, mothers struggle through one touchy conversation after another and make a seemingly endless series of difficult decisions without ever getting clearer about their goals for bringing up daughters. Some focus on the "trees" of raising teenage girls; that is, they deal with rock concerts, first dates, drinking parties, driver's licenses, and body piercing. But they rarely step back and get a good look at the whole forest, perhaps because they are too busy putting out daily brushfires. Others become overwhelmed, floundering without obvious parenting objectives, or adopt rather rote or unthinking responses. Still other mothers panic and lay down the law. Yet it is more pragmatic to think through what you are hoping to accomplish with your daughter, tailoring your mothering approach to your own values and expectations, as well as to her unique personality and needs.

That way, when you utter that detestable little syllable ("No!"), prompting her to protest that you are "totally unfair," that "nobody else's parents have these stupid rules," or that you are "completely ridiculous," all of your preparatory thinking will bolster you. You will be able to take a deep breath and calmly review all your reasons for that decision. Identifying and clarifying your own principles *before* your daughter challenges them is therefore like depositing money in the bank. In a pinch, you can rely on those reserves.

Down Memory Lane

The first task is reflecting on how your own past is influencing your mothering. That is because, unlike your daughter's father, at one time you too were a teenage girl. You probably had the experience of being raised by a mother and negotiating a relationship with her throughout the teenage years. This shared experience may offer you the advantage of being able to relate better to your daughter during her adolescence and perhaps empathize more easily with her. But with this comes the risk of attributing to your daughter your own thoughts and feelings about mothering and being mothered, without really learning hers. That is why it is so crucial to sort through your memories.

For example, how did your experience of being a teenage daughter shape your expectations about what happens between mothers and girls during these years? At various times in the course of your growing up, you may recall thinking that your mother babied you, seemed appropriately in tune with your needs, was too intrusive in your life, or gave you the breathing space you wanted. You may purposely emulate what you admired and enjoyed about your mother's style and, in an effort to avoid replicating unpleasant aspects of your adolescence, consciously try to be different in other ways. Of course, while finding the most comfortable approach for you, you must also consider what best suits your daughter. In fact, it is often the match between a mother and a daughter, especially their temperaments, that shapes the partnership they form. As you will see in the following stories, it is helpful to become aware of how your parenting tendencies have been influenced by how you were raised.

When Ingrid, forty-seven, was growing up, she felt removed from a mother whom she perceived as rather cold and distant. She says, "I think if my mother and I were closer, if we had more of a relationship, I would have wanted to please her more." Looking back, she attributes much of her teenage misbehavior to her mother's attitude. "As it was, I couldn't have cared less about being rebellious," she explains. "I did whatever I pleased." Ingrid is not gleeful when she says this, but somewhat sheepish and regretful. Determined not to repeat this sort of hands-off parenting style with her own daughter, who is now ten, Ingrid says, "I try to be open with her and very involved in her activities. I stress how much I want us to talk, and hope she will feel comfortable coming to me with any questions or problems she has."

- How did you feel about your own mother during your teenage years? Did you perceive her as understanding, loving, fair-minded, or knowledgeable?
- Looking back, how do you feel about your upbringing?
- How does this influence your mothering of your own daughter?

If you believe you were wild during your adolescence, you may now be bound and determined to prevent your daughter from having the same experiences you did. Heidi, now fifty, was a self-proclaimed hippie in the late '60s who is raising two daughters on her own. She says, "There's no way I want my daughters around the crazy stuff I was into. I'm going to keep track of what they're doing and who they're doing it with. They won't even go to the corner by themselves for a long time!" If you share this background, perhaps your greater awareness of the risks will make you stricter and more vigilant than if you had been sheltered as a teen.

- Were your parents strict, from the old school, relatively permissive, or inconsistent?
- Were rules established? Did you break them and, if so, how rebellious were you?
- How are these issues affecting your expectations for your daughter?

Maybe you were a goody-goody during your teenage years, rarely giving your parents any trouble. You may have conformed easily to your mother's expectations, reluctant (or even afraid) to venture beyond the boundaries. If you were timid or self-contained, you may have avoided testing the social waters. In this case, you may be astounded by having a daughter who is boy crazy at thirteen. Denise, fifty-one, says, "I'm appalled! I refuse to believe this is my daughter who is constantly calling boys. She's practically obsessed with getting a date to the eighth-grade dance. I've even heard from other mothers that she sits on boys' laps at youth group meetings!" Particularly when their girls' behavior seems alien, many a mother has asked, "Where did my daughter come from?"

- How different were you from your mother in terms of temperament and interests?
- Did you try to gain your mother's approval? Why, or why not?
- How aware and accepting are you of differences between you and your daughter?

If you were raised by overly restrictive parents, you may be inclined to give your daughter plenty of freedom. Remembering how trapped or angry you felt, you may bend over backward to avoid putting your daughter in that position. For some time, I worked with a woman who grew up with a harsh, critical, and occasionally abusive mother. Although Patrice had come to terms with her upbringing during a course of therapy in her twenties, when her own children became teenagers her distress returned. She could not bring herself to reprimand them, to set the mildest of limits, even to say no. As she described it, "I feel so mean if I disappoint my kids. I know it's bad, but I want to be so different from my mother that it's hard for me to discipline them." This is one of those instances when you must beware of the pendulum swinging too far in the other direction.

Does Your Parenting Need Fine-tuning?

Your evaluation of your own mothering is undoubtedly influenced by what the experts describe as ideal. You probably try as much as possible for a balanced approach, aiming for that middle spot on any parenting continuum that is considered best for raising children. As mentioned in the last chapter, however, no mother is perfect. Like Patrice, who sees herself as a pushover and knows she should be stricter, you are probably inclined to err at one extreme or another in your interactions with your daughter. Most girls recognize rather readily their parents' natural styles and learn to adjust to their quirks. With the stress of your daughter's adolescence, however, these less desirable tendencies may occasionally be exaggerated, interfering with your ability to maintain a healthy relationship with her.

These questions are offered, therefore, to guide you in assessing how you might monitor your parenting approach and make adjustments, if necessary, during your daughter's teenage years:

Am I Appropriately Involved in My Daughter's Life?

Each mother brings to the mother-daughter relationship ideas about how much participation is desired and expected. Partly, this will be based on your experiences with your own mother, as just discussed. For example, are both you and your daughter comfortable with how much you know about her friends, classes, and emotional life? Are you in sync around how much sympathy, advice, or homework help she wants? Perhaps you feel confident in this area. But when you go through difficult times or feel anxious, you may tend either to become overinvolved or, conversely, to withdraw from her.

Obviously, your participation in your daughter's life is one way you demonstrate how much you care about her. This loving concern not only helps her to feel comfortable exploring her environment, but also encourages her to develop sympathy, compassion, and emotional responsiveness and, therefore, to relate well to others. If your daughter is comfortable with your degree of involvement—that is, if she thinks you are neither too distant nor overly connected with her—she will perceive you as benevolent. Your daughter will then want to maintain your good opinion of her. To do so, she may be more eager to take your views and beliefs to heart and more motivated to embrace your ethical standards. Thus, your appropriate involvement also increases the likelihood of your daughter behaving according to your values.

At the other extreme, when mothers are indifferent, aloof, or even hostile, girls are uneasy around adults and less inclined to adopt parental values. Rowena, sixteen, says, "My mom and I have never gotten along. She's always criticizing everything I do. I know I can't please her, so I've just given up. Why bother?" Similarly, according to Lara, twelve, "My parents always lecture me and they think that'll get me to do better in school, but that just makes me mad. It's not like they're willing to help me. They say they'll get me the printer paper or foam boards I need, but then they don't."

Am I Using the Proper Degree of Parental Authority?

It is worrisome that young people in our culture seem to be disregarding the authority of parents, teachers, principals, police officers—indeed, just about all adults. A recent study by the Josephson Institute of Ethics found an 11 percent increase in cheating during the last decade; moreover, 78 percent of students surveyed had lied to their teachers. Some teenagers flaunt disobedience, daring their parents to have the audacity to impose restrictions. Their prevailing notion seems to be "It's okay to do anything, as long as you don't get caught." Mental health professionals speculate about why parents have lost their effectiveness. They often blame increased divorce and mobility, along with opportunities for youngsters to accuse adults of child abuse, which is thought to reduce their fear (and obedience). It is clear, however, that to be effective in raising teenagers, parents need some authority.

At one extreme, when parents are autocratic and cold, adolescents tend to contain both their anger and their behavior at home, but explode as soon as they are out of sight. Under this regime, your daughter might be superficially acquiescent to your demands, and then maintain complete secrecy about what is really going on in her life. Nell, sixteen, describes such a dynamic: "My best friend is always sucking up to her mom and dad, but then she goes out and is so, so bad."

At the other end of the continuum are parental laxness and inconsistency, which are associated with a lack of motivation and direction in children. Of course, asserting authority can be tough for many mothers. Because you love your daughter, you want to make her as happy as possible. Because you want to be giving and generous, it can feel downright unmaternal to withhold permission, resources, privileges, even your approval. It is also more expedient to say yes, especially when you can well imagine the painful consequences of saying no. At some moments, it may even be hard to muster the energy, both physical and emotional, to do what you know in your heart of hearts is right.

If you are too permissive with your daughter, however, she will come to believe that she is entitled to get whatever she wants. She will get the mistaken impression that she can have privileges, friendships, respect, successes, etc.—without effort, without having to earn them—simply because she wants them. If your daughter does not experience the negative consequences of her undesirable behavior, she will miss key feedback that can motivate her to learn from her mistakes and make necessary corrections.

When mothers are exceedingly warm and overly permissive, they create a family environment that, at least in some cases, blurs boundaries. Rather than collaborating as a mother-daughter team, mothers and daughters become equal partners with equal say in decisions. As Martina, forty-six, explained, "I think it's great that our family is a little democracy." Although this concept may initially appeal to you, especially if you were unhappy being raised in an authoritarian home, it is important to anticipate what might happen if you eventually assert your authority, either to establish rules, set limits, or enforce discipline: Your daughter may become confused and resentful. If you suddenly become sharply stricter during your daughter's adolescence, perhaps in response to uneasiness or concerns about her activities, she may rebel because she has not been taught to recognize, much less to respect, your authority.

Sherry, fifty-one, mother to fifteen-year-old Theodora, had always believed a teenage girl needs "freedom to make her own choices. I trusted her instincts and was committed to allowing her to learn things for herself." This philosophy worked well until Theodora started high school. When her grades took a nosedive and Sherry discovered drug paraphernalia in Theodora's room, Sherry "read her the riot act. I told her exactly what her life would be like until she could prove she was on the right track again. Only Theodora, instead of being contrite, was outraged that I had the nerve to tell her what to do. It felt like war."

Rather than these extremes of overly permissive or authoritarian parenting, you are striving for the middle ground. A parental approach that is highly accepting and moderately authoritative—that is, firm and age-appropriate—is associated with the best adjustment in children. When you are authoritative, you are attuned to your daughter's needs, reasonably demanding, and sensible in setting limits. Your daughter always functions best when it is clear to her what you consider out of bounds. From the time she was a little girl, you stepped in whenever her behavior was dangerous or improper. Knowing you would intervene this way if she crossed lines of propriety enabled your young daughter to feel more comfortable exploring her environment and trying out new skills.

It doesn't matter that your daughter has outgrown many of her childhood needs: She still feels more secure knowing that if circumstances—or she herself—get out of control, you will be there and jump in. Believe it or not, this is precious comfort when girls' impulses, urges, and wishes occasionally overwhelm them. In fact, in some cases girls unconsciously seek limits from parents that they are unable to provide for themselves. These teenagers wave ever-larger and louder red flags until their mothers take notice and take action. Provocative behaviors such as blatantly ignoring curfews, coming home intoxicated or high, and skipping school may be your cues that your daughter needs you to assert your parental authority.

Kassy, seventeen, who was in treatment for depression and self-mutilation, had been so gravely ill during infancy that her mother feared she would die and did not develop a strong bond with her. After her parents divorced when she was six, she mostly cared for herself while her mother traveled extensively for work. During her sophomore year of high school, Kassy began to get drunk at weekend parties, each night engaging in sexual behaviors with different boys. Although she reported feeling terrible shame afterward, week after week she drank excessively and was unable to stop herself from having sex with boys she barely knew, much less cared for. Her sister, who was two years older, was shocked and humiliated whenever she witnessed her behavior at parties or subsequently heard rumors about her in school. On some level, Kassy probably wanted her sister to know. Without a mother or father available, she needed her sibling to assert surrogate parental authority and initiate change within the family.

Am I Providing My Daughter the Structure She Needs?

When girls know what to expect from their world, when their parents create an environment that is predictable and consistent, they are best able to regulate themselves, anticipate the consequences of their decisions, and behave appropriately. In contrast, when mothers flip-flop from one position or parenting style or state of mind to another, girls are understandably adrift. Especially during adolescence, when girls' bodies, friendships, and emotions are in almost constant flux, they need mothers to be their predictable ballast.

Janel, sixteen, for example, spoke of never knowing how her mother would react when she came in after curfew: "Sometimes she gets so mad and says I'm grounded for like a year, and other times she doesn't even say anything. Once in a while, she doesn't even wait up, so I could come in at four A.M. and she wouldn't know." Given these mixed messages, Janel was unsure just what her mother really expected of her. More important, she was confused about how she herself wanted to behave.

This is not to imply, however, that structure requires rigidity. On the contrary! As we saw in the last chapter, the ability to be flexible, to make adjustments in your thinking and parenting responses, is one of the main ingredients for developing a workable partnership with your teenager. The structure you set in place for your daughter needs to be revised as she matures, her needs evolve, or her circumstances change.

What Methods Do I Use to Influence My Daughter?

At the extreme, parents are so determined to have their way that they are willing to maneuver daughters any way they must. Some rule with angry tirades, persuade with emotional manipulations, or induce anxiety or guilt. This tendency to be coercive is likely to be exacerbated in times of stress, such as when parents take issue with a daughter's attitude or behavior. Because this approach is neither attuned to nor respectful of a teenager's feelings and needs, however, it is likely to undermine a strong, positive mother-daughter relationship.

In addition, a coercive style of interacting with daughters often provokes the very rebellion parents most fear. A teenage girl who is desperate to feel independent will go to any length to demonstrate that her parents cannot control her. This, of course, may include cutting off her nose to spite her face. You can prevent this problem by deciding that you will refrain from using these tactics and learn healthier, more direct ways to guide and influence your daughter. While this may seem obvious, it is amazing how easily even the most well-meaning of mothers can land in this trap.

Consider the example of Resa, a thirty-nine-year-old mother who moved to a different part of town so that her daughter, Natalia, twelve, could attend a better middle school. Separated from her elementary school chums, Natalia was frantic to make new friends and to feel included by another group of peers. After struggling for some time to find her niche, she began to socialize again. However, as Resa admits, "I was horrified because my daughter wasn't making friends with the sorts of girls I had envisioned. These kids weren't the brightest, they didn't seem to care all that much about school, they ran around unsupervised and, quite honestly, they looked sort of weird. I didn't know what Natalia was doing hanging out with them."

Resa was a caring mother who wanted the best for her daughter. However, she reacted by monitoring Natalia's phone calls, forbidding her daughter from speaking to any girl she considered undesirable, and restricting her from activities that she thought would bring Natalia in contact with them. Moreover, Resa began to tell Natalia of the many sacrifices she had made so they could move, suggesting that the only way Natalia could please her and justify the expensive relocation was to be the social success her mother wanted. Refusing to capitulate to this emotional pressure, Natalia became even more determined to maintain the friendships her mother forbade. Yet without her mother's interference, there was a good chance Natalia would have tired of these girls or moved on to other classmates as the school year progressed. Resa's rigid attempts to control her daughter backfired because they redoubled Natalia's commitment to the very friendships her mother wanted to discourage.

Do I Have Appropriate Expectations for My Daughter?

Although you may imagine it would be best to have no particular expectations of your daughter, this is probably unrealistic. What mother, deep down, doesn't have basic standards she wants her daughter to uphold or dreams she would like her to fulfill? Perhaps you would love to see your teenager become a scholar, a stand-out athlete, or a progressive social reformer. More immediately, you may want her to be a leader of her high school, the yearbook editor, class council president, or one of the popular girls who always seems glamorous and surrounded by peers. Or maybe you want her to be above all the social shenanigans that typically take place in school hallways. You may prefer that your daughter remain her own person, an individualist who is unaffected by whatever happens to be the rage at any given moment.

If mothers and daughters have different expectations, especially when they remain unspoken, trouble often brews. When girls strive for the goals their mothers have for them, their achievements are empty and personally meaningless. As a consequence, these girls experience the despair and alienation that result from portraying a false self. They remain unaware of or disconnected from their own genuine dreams and desires.

Sheila is a sixteen-year-old high school junior who has been playing basketball since she was six. Currently on the varsity basketball team, she not only practices daily and plays in several games per weekend, but also participates in basketball camps during school vacations. Asked how she enjoys basketball, Sheila said, "It's okay, I guess. My parents are really supportive. They come to all my games. My father used to coach my teams, but now they just watch. Well, actually, they yell a lot too. I don't hear what they're saying, exactly, but I know they're telling me what I should be doing. My mom is head of the parents' association, so she raises a lot of money for our team jackets and stuff. They're hoping I'll get a scholarship to college, but I'm not good enough."

When you form realistic expectations of your daughter, you are attuned to and accepting of who she really is. You also convey accurate confidence in her abilities. This is an age when girls are becoming all too aware of how they stack up against their peers. Many can be brutally honest about their own lack of talent or potential—even when their mothers cannot. If you exaggerate or overestimate your daughter's abilities, in a heartbeat she will discount you ("You're my mother; you have to say that") and be dubious about your feedback in the future. It is key, therefore, to separate your hopes for her from her true potential. In truth, she may or may not have the endowments, interests, or opportunities to be what you desire.

If you want more from her than she can deliver, if your parental expectations are too high, your daughter will see the disappointment in your eyes and think of herself as a failure. Obviously, growing up convinced of one's perpetual shortcomings is devastating to any girl's sense of self-worth. This hardly inspires a teenager to challenge herself, to branch out beyond her comfort zone, and to experience the gratification that comes from hard work and eventual accomplishment.

At the other extreme, it is equally problematic if your expectations for your daughter are too low. When you communicate minimal hopes for her, she is likely to feel inadequate. If she has the impression you think she is incapable of accomplishing anything important or worthwhile, how can she believe in herself and reach for her dreams?

Seven Strategies for Successful Parenting

There are several general parenting strategies that can contribute to your ultimate goals in raising your teenage daughter: helping her to think more clearly, make smarter decisions, and assume greater responsibility for her own behavior. Admittedly, these suggestions may not be that easy to use consistently, particularly in the beginning. But like any skills, the more you practice them, the easier and more natural they will seem. In fact, each time you examine another facet of your daughter's development and social issues in the chapters ahead, you might want to review them.

1. Communicate Clearly What Is and Is Not Acceptable to You

For a variety of reasons, some parents are loathe to speak directly and straightforwardly about their standards with their daughters. In fact, even if they discussed values when their girls were younger, they often stop at puberty—yes, just when daughters most need to be reminded. Perhaps you too feel defeated even before you start a discussion ("She's not going to listen, anyway!"), get frustrated by your daughter's dismissive responses ("She just rolls her eyes or sighs when I try to talk to her"), or feel intimidated ("She acts like she knows more than me"). However, just because your daughter appears not to listen to or to welcome your input doesn't mean your efforts are in vain. Far from it! As an example, the Centers for Disease Control and Prevention (CDC) reports that campaigns to educate teenagers about the dangers of sexually transmitted diseases (STDs) are paying off: Teenagers are making positive changes in their sexual behaviors.

Make time to clarify what is most important to you in raising a teenage girl today. Unless you are clear in your own mind, you cannot communicate your ideas coherently and convincingly. For example, what family values do you and her father hold dear? When your daughter was younger, you may have noted that while some families emphasize togetherness at dinner and other rituals, others are content for members to do their own thing. Similarly, some families expect siblings to play mostly with each other at home; others promote frequent socializing with friends and classmates through play dates and sleepovers. As yet another example, while some parents expect girls to be somewhat quiet and blend in, others encourage daughters to speak up and stick out in the crowd. Now that your daughter is a teenager, you may have changed your views.

Whatever your opinions and preferences, how you convey them is crucial. Above all, be scrupulously honest, especially about controversial issues. Otherwise, your daughter will zero in on any perceived hypocrisy to justify ignoring your message. Describe your values clearly and concisely, without beating around the bush or apologizing. For example, unless you truly believe that all teenage sexual activity or alcohol consumption is wrong, don't issue blanket disapprovals in the hope of keeping your daughter safe. It is far better to differentiate the conditions under which these and other activities are and are not acceptable to you. Note that this is not the same as giving your daughter carte blanche to do as she pleases.

Speaking of sticky topics, don't think it isn't your job to educate your daughter about drinking, sexuality, relationships, drugs, and responsibility, or that you can leave these subjects to school health classes. Such discussions may never occur—at least not in the manner you would like. If you feel undereducated about these subjects or uncomfortable talking about them, find books in your local library or bookstore, or get information pamphlets from community agencies or physicians. A good, no-nonsense, fact-based resource for both you and your daughter is *Deal With It! A Whole New Approach to Your Body, Brain and Life as a Gurl* by Esther Drill and Heather McDonald. To desensitize yourself, practice discussing these subjects with a friend or spouse. When you feel ready, raise these issues in a matter-of-fact, natural way, when you believe your daughter will be most receptive.

NOT as she walks in the door:

> DAUGHTER: Hi, Mom, I'm home!
> MOM: Oh, good! I want to talk to you about sex.

NOT in anger or punishment:

> DAUGHTER: Mom, you have to sign my interim progress report, but don't worry, I'll do much better next quarter.
> MOM: You'd better, and there's another thing I've been wanting to talk to you about, young lady . . .

TRY

> MOM: Did you see this poll in the newspaper about what teens your age worry about most? What do you think about this?

OR

> MOM: What do you think this book said about girls and sex? How accurately do you think it portrayed high school students?

As you may well have already discovered, your daughter will often respond to your most earnest and important remarks with snippy or provocative retorts. Even when you hear her advocate an opinion that is diametrically opposed to your most fundamental beliefs, don't panic or punish or shut down conversation.

NOT

> DAUGHTER: I think it's perfectly okay for kids to experiment with drugs in high school.
> MOM: Oh really? Well, it's not okay for you. You're grounded until further notice.

TRY

> MOM: You think it's okay to experiment? Tell me why you think so.

OR

> MOM: Well, it's understandable to be curious. Let's talk about how drugs affect your body so you'll know what the consequences would be.

Because you want your daughter to live by her own standards even when faced with pressure to conform to her peers, this is something you have to model. Mention when your opinions are different from those of your close friends. Take an unpopular stand in a debated public issue if that is what you believe, even when that makes you uncomfortable or out of favor in your community.

Such an opportunity will undoubtedly be provided for you when your daughter complains that her friend's mother handled a particular situation far better than you. If you disagree, you can say so without fear of being overly judgmental or critical of the other parent. You can comment, "Well, I'm sure she has her reasons, but I disagree and here's why . . ." If you do this without defensiveness, you are communicating to your daughter that parents often have differing opinions, and that you are not afraid to stand by yours. You are clarifying the reasoning underlying your beliefs, and demonstrating that your daughter can count on you to give these matters your serious consideration.

Fortunately, you do not have to have answers for everything. It is perfectly acceptable (and often a great relief) to say that you don't know. Being unsure doesn't make you any less of an authority. Your daughter will learn that you are neither all-knowing nor perfect, and that dilemmas that are inherently complex will rarely have simple or black-and-white answers. As we all know, teenagers pay far more attention to what their parents do than to what their parents say, regardless of how eloquently they speak. So do some critical self-evaluation: Does your daughter see you rushing red lights, lying about someone's age to get movie discounts, or being dishonest to your friends? Does she see you making excuses when you don't fulfill your work or volunteer duties? The more you teach her about good behavior, the more goodness she will expect from herself and from others.

2. Make Distinctions Between Thoughts and Deeds

During adolescence your daughter may be flooded with new, intense emotions and urges that are difficult to sort through, much less control. For many girls this creates apprehension. It is important to distinguish what your daughter thinks and feels from how she actually behaves. She needs to know that having bad thoughts, sexual urges, or aggressive impulses does not make her a bad person. Parenting should therefore emphasize actions. Put another way, what your daughter thinks or feels is valid and important, but it is often what she *does* that matters more. Her choices count.

For example, your daughter is allowed to have negative feelings such as anger, frustration, and jealousy, but it is not okay for her to express them as she pleases. Recently I observed an incident in a park that illustrates this point. When a four- or five-year-old girl bit a playmate, her mother gently picked her up and said to the other parent, "Oh, sorry, she's just very tired because she's getting over an ear infection." I thought to myself, "So you're excusing her biting another child?"

Similarly, while you may understand your teenager's distress, insecurity, and fear when her two best friends get together without her, you don't advocate her being cruel, sabotaging their friendship, or starting rumors about them. When your daughter claims she torments her sibling because, "She embarrassed me in front of my boyfriend!" this may explain but does not condone her behavior. Part of her demonstrating emotional maturity is acknowledging and managing her own emotions so that she does not express them inappropriately or destructively. When she is taught that her actions are what matter, she learns to exercise appropriate self-control.

The corollary to this strategy is not to ignore but to take a stand on unacceptable behavior. Perhaps in fear of damaging their children's self-esteem, many parents have shied away from being critical or judgmental. This is usually a mistake. Dennis Prager, a contemporary theologian and popular talk show host, argues that contrary to popular opinion, people are not inherently good. He contends that children are not born knowing right from wrong, but need to be taught. In light of the cruel and violent actions of young people today, it ought to be apparent that good behavior merits parents' wholehearted attention. Among other qualities, girls need to learn that their mothers and fathers expect them to behave kindly, honestly, and with integrity and compassion.

When you are confronted with your daughter's undesirable behavior, part of taking a stand means choosing how to respond. You have to decide whether or not to give her consequences, as well as the nature and terms of that punishment (as discussed in Chapter 7). Your daughter is greatly influenced not just by what you do, but also by what you do not do. For example, it is important to consider how she is affected by your *not* giving her consequences for her poor decisions, or by your issuing punishments that you do not uphold.

3. Consider Your Daughter's Age

Girls today are often in a tremendous hurry to grow up. Many appear older than their chronological age because they adopt the language, styles of dress, and activities of more mature teenagers and even adults. Some desire social and emotional experiences before they can appropriately handle them.

It does not help that many girls today are showing signs of physical development, such as breast buds and pubic hair, earlier than they did generations ago. Because of better nutrition and public health (and, some say, obesity, hormones in our food, and chemicals in the environment), your daughter too may begin these changes as early as eight or nine. Of course, the media's sexualization of young girls compounds these biological factors. Witness, as but one example, the infamous Calvin Klein ads with half-naked preadolescents posed suggestively.

Along with faster physical maturation, girls today take on adult concerns far sooner than in years past. In part, this may be due to the changes in the typical American family, which will be described below, along with decreased parental supervision. Also, the population growth in this age group has led to increased competition for coveted spots in private schools, colleges, and jobs. Girls who have yet to hit high school describe intense pressures and efforts to excel that are truly mind-boggling:

- "If I don't get As, I start to cry and feel like the world is over." (A.J., twelve)
- "What if I have a boring, meaningless job and a boring life?" (Paula, fourteen)

- "Sometimes I stay up until two in the morning trying to figure out how to get my grades up when they're low." (Kaylin, twelve)
- "I am about ready to blow I am so stressed out. I'm a kid. I hope I'm not the only one feeling this." (Gretchen, eleven)
- "I want to get into the best college possible, like Harvard." (Jennifer, twelve)
- "If I don't get As, everybody makes fun of me for being dumb." (Penny, fourteen)
- "If I don't do well, I get upset and depressed. I have to decide my future pretty quickly. Once you get to high school, time moves really fast." (Rachel, thirteen)

You can choose to protect your daughter from both a hectic pace and adultlike stress. You can also decide to keep her from experiences that are more appropriate for older adolescents. Instead of simply accepting that "Girls grow up so much faster today," you set the standards. Determine what you think is acceptable for her in fashion, activities, and privileges, based on her age and level of maturity. You will shape your daughter's lifestyle according to these values. Of course, expect that she will not always agree with your standards.

Both mothers and daughters report that the primary arena for conflict is usually clothing. Typically, girls want to wear outfits their mothers consider too tight, revealing, or mature. Not too long ago, I saw a petite but striking young woman standing in the corner of a store, talking on her cell phone. With her leather pants, high-heeled boots, and designer pocketbook slung over one shoulder of her jean jacket, she looked like quite the fashion plate. When she turned around, however, I was dumbfounded; this sophisticate couldn't have been more than eleven or twelve!

If you have attended an evening party recently, you may have seen thirteen-year-old girls wearing strapless gowns and three-inch heels, looking much like miniature women at cocktail parties. If it is permissible to sport such overly sophisticated and sexualized outfits, what message does this give girls about what other behaviors are allowed? And what do they convey to their peers, especially testosterone-driven middle school boys? It is not surprising that the media have reported drinking and sexual activity among early teenagers attending relatively unsupervised formal parties. When young people are dressed up like adults, they are often tempted to imitate adult behavior. Moreover, other people may expect such behavior from them.

Some years ago, for example, I saw a sixteen-year-old in therapy who desperately needed to become aware of what she was communicating to others through her clothing choices. A sweet, somewhat naïve girl, Casey lived with her father and rather troubled stepmother after being abandoned by her birth mother. She usually appeared at my office door dolled up like a forties screen star. One spring day she arrived straight from school in a floor-length sundress, with a lace-up bodice that didn't quite lace up, thick makeup, and bright red lipstick. When she informed me that boys were hitting on her, it became clear that as her therapist, I would be the first adult to help her to see the connection between her appearance and how she was treated. About six months later, I was pleased to hear from her school guidance counselor that Casey had been spotted while shopping in town wearing a jean skirt, sneakers, and a ponytail. Although she still had much work to do, she had learned to dress in a manner more appropriate for both her age and social situation.

No matter her age, when your daughter wants to buy clothing you think is too revealing or sophisticated for her, don't be afraid to say so. Yes, she will probably declare you ridiculous and old-fashioned, but you can live with that. Because you know that pseudomaturity is detrimental to her, you are willing to endure her irritation with you.

To further decrease her pressure, while she is in middle school you might refrain from well-meaning motivational speeches about the difficulty of getting accepted to a good college. You probably will not permit her to attend unsupervised clubs and concerts that are frequented by older adolescents—until she reaches that age herself. By the same token, you will also expect your daughter to make the sorts of errors that are common in girls her age because she does not yet have the emotional maturity of an adult.

4. Provide Adequate Supervision

There is no doubt that your daughter's generation is being raised by a different set of mothers than your generation. Mothers today spend an average of 40 percent less time with their children for several reasons. Since 1950 the divorce rate has nearly doubled. Consequently, approximately one-third of children now live in a family headed by one parent, usually the mother. Also, from 1960 to 1997, the number of married women who work outside the home increased two and a half times. Currently, about 70 percent of wives with children under eighteen are in the workforce. This means that mothers are simply less available, a fact that does not go unnoticed by teenagers. A *Newsweek* magazine poll conducted in 2000 found that one-quarter of teenagers think their parents spend too little time with them.

This translates into fewer opportunities to chat casually, discuss important issues, convey values, and teach good decision making. Girls often struggle to handle unfamiliar or difficult social situations, armed only with myths and misinformation gleaned from well-meaning friends. Clearly, they need more adult guidance and supervision, especially in the afternoon hours. While it is often an enormous relief to mothers when girls are finally old enough to be at home without a baby-sitter or caregiver, during the middle school years it is wise to consider the potential pitfalls. As one middle school principal confided to me, "Many parents think when their kids graduate from elementary school their jobs are essentially over."

In fact, the hours from three to seven P.M. are a high-risk time period because middle school and high school girls get home earlier in the afternoon and often remain unsupervised. Acts of vandalism, as well as violent and self-destructive behaviors, occur frequently during these hours. At the most extreme, teenagers' suicidal acts most often take place in their own homes within this same time period. If you ask adolescent girls what they do every afternoon when they know they have the house to themselves, some would reply, "homework." Others would admit, "I get high and have sex." As reported in the news, some communities have experienced an increase in sexual activities among groups of young teens, resulting in the spread of STDs.

If you must be away from home during the after-school hours while your daughter is in the early teenage years, you might consider alternative arrangements. If an adult caregiver is unavailable or makes your daughter feel too babied, a buddy-sitter slightly older than herself (e.g., a high school student) might be more tolerable to her as well as cost-effective for you. Or, you can trade days with a neighbor. Enrolling your daughter in selected after-school activities also might offer additional structure. When girls accept baby-sitting or mother's helper jobs in the afternoon, their supervision of younger children essentially provides a structured situation for them too. If your young daughter must be alone after school, establish a procedure by which she checks in regularly with you or another responsible adult. Although she may protest, such a routine is ultimately reassuring and comforting. Plus, you are providing her with a model of respect and reciprocity that she can use later in healthy adult relationships.

Even if you are able to be present during these hours, it would be a mistake to expect that you and your daughter will have wonderful conversations on a daily basis. It is unlikely she will invite you to hang out with her. It is even less likely she will express her gratitude that you are there for her. In a typical scenario, you might dash home only to find your daughter in a funk. When you try to talk to her and she explodes, you can only wonder, "Why did I bother coming home?"

But take comfort that your daughter recognizes on some level you're there because you choose to be, that you love her and care about her. Sometimes, perhaps when you least expect it, she might plop on the couch while you are doing a chore or even lend a hand. She might surprise you by disclosing something important or by starting a constructive discussion. You never know.

And, speaking of supervision, it would be a mistake to assume that just because you are home your teenage daughter is fine. It pays to check in periodically to see what she and her friends are up to when they are just hanging out. You will want to know, for example, what her gang is doing for hours in her bedroom, the basement, or out in the yard.

5. Establish and Maintain Reasonable Rules

As she matures, your daughter will increasingly face situations you can neither anticipate nor prepare her for. Because she will have to make decisions on her own, without your supervision, you are helping her to develop her own inner compass. Your daughter learns this by gradually taking in and following for herself the guidelines you have provided for her. While a few teenagers are able to establish limits for themselves, the majority need their parents to establish guidelines.

However, a recent nationwide survey conducted by the *New York Times* suggests that today's families are establishing few rules for their teenagers. Among those age thirteen to seventeen, 70 percent report their parents don't limit the amount of TV they can watch, 76 percent don't regulate the time they spend on the computer, and 55 percent don't set rules about what movies they are allowed to see. Limit setting is, however, one of the most vital roles of mothering. If you don't convey what is and is not appropriate for your daughter, she will look to others for that information.

Although establishing rules is generally wise and highly recommended, *how* you do this is just as important. Based on your approach, you can either add to the reserves of goodwill between you and your daughter or, conversely, provoke her to lie and sneak around spitefully behind your back. You might use these criteria as a guide:

ARE MY RULES:

1. *Consistent with my priorities?*
2. *Simple and clear?*
3. *Positive?*
4. *Attuned to my daughter's needs?*
5. *Appropriate for her age?*
6. *Respectful?*

To illustrate this point, let's contrast (using the "Goofus and Gallant" format of *Highlights* magazine) the rule-making styles of two mothers, each of whom has a fourteen-year-old daughter:

Mother #1: Diana

Diana's approach is "to keep things simple, so we aren't always dealing with whether rules apply in one particular situation or another." She makes as few rules as she possibly can for Melissa: "That way, I'm not a policewoman. And besides, it's easier that way. There are fewer misunderstandings." Since safety and responsibility are most important to her family, her rules are established mainly around these priorities.

First and foremost, Diana is determined to know where Melissa is at all times. "Obviously, she has to call me if her plans change. And she knows her life will be hell if she ever lies to me." For Diana, teaching Melissa about responsibility translates into expecting that her schoolwork and household chores are completed well and on time. She says, "I ask just that she finishes her homework and does a good job on it, too. She has to feed and walk the dog and help with the dinner dishes before she can use the phone or computer in the evening."

These rules are positive in that they encourage Melissa to do what her parents desire in order to get privileges. There are no threats or punishments hanging over her head. As long as Melissa's grades are good, family peace is maintained, and chores are current, everyone wins.

Diana's attunement and flexibility to Melissa's changing needs prompt her to make frequent adjustments in rules, reining her in or giving her more slack, as the situation requires. For example, when Melissa enters high school, she asks for permission to accept her new friend's offer to drive her home after stopping for a snack. Understanding Melissa's desire to feel more independent, Diana is still wary about the safety issues. When they sit down together to discuss these new circumstances, Diana demonstrates respect for her daughter by asking for her input in negotiating new rules. While she reserves the right to make the final decision after consulting with Melissa's father, she considers her daughter's ideas and requests. She continues to make safety the top priority, giving Melissa clear guidelines for the minimum driving experience her friends must have before she is permitted to ride with them (see sidebar, p. 50).

Similarly, when Melissa begins dating a boy who works evenings, Diana permits her to get together with him some afternoons, thereby delaying her homework, so long as she keeps up her grades. On the other hand, when Melissa starts spending more time online every evening to continue chatting with her boyfriend, Diana also steps in. Because she thinks it is important for Melissa to read for pleasure and practice the piano, she renegotiates guidelines for computer use.

Although she says she does not always love these rules and often

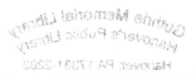

complains about them, Melissa admits they are reasonable and fair. She never questions her mother's love and genuine concern.

Mother #2: Ella

Ella has heard "so many awful teenage stories" that she is frightened her daughter, Karina, is "going to run amuck." Desperate to prevent that, she is "determined to keep her on a tight leash." Ella believes that if she does not let up for an instant and Karina is not exposed to potentially bad influences, she will remain "the lovely, sweet girl she has always been" and have no opportunities to misbehave. Ella limits her daughter to watching a few approved TV shows, and only on weekends. Despite her good school performance, she also forbids the phone or e-mail during the week so Karina is not distracted from her homework. Karina may have only healthy snacks, rather than those loaded with sugar and fat. Ella strictly bans Karina from using makeup other than lipstick and wearing jeans to school. Concerned about what she reads about today's music, Ella says, "I won't allow her to listen to the groups kids like today. Their songs are trash!"

Since Ella refuses to allow Karina to "get away with murder," she is quick to call her on any broken rules, as well as to enforce punishments. At the market one day, for example, Ella bumps into the mother of one of her daughter's friends, who remarks, "How does your daughter stay so slim? When she was over the other day, she had quite the sweet tooth!" Ella is furious that her daughter disobeyed her rule, and racks her brain to think of how she can enforce her restriction on sugar.

One weekday afternoon, she arrives home to find the girls watching *Oprah,* a clear violation of the no TV rule. Ella immediately tells Karina that her friend must leave and that she is grounded. As a result, Karina is convinced not only that her mother "treats me like an infant," but also that she will be "too humiliated" to face her girlfriend, much less to invite anyone else to her home. Frustrated and angry about this and similar incidents, Karina's attitude toward her mother deteriorates. She becomes nasty, resistant, and sarcastic; soon there are frequent blowups.

As a result of this heightened conflict, Ella's fears of Karina "turning into a typical, out-of-control teenager" escalate and she redoubles her efforts to get her daughter back in line. When Karina's eighth-grade class takes a weeklong field trip, Ella will not give permission for her to attend because she expects the supervision will be inadequate. When Karina becomes hysterical and protests, Ella says firmly, "There will be no discussion."

Ella sincerely loves her daughter and is very much committed to "doing the right thing" for her. Yet her complex and rather rigid system of rules does not take into account Karina's age or developmental needs. Moreover, because her mother's controlling approach excludes her from decisions about rules, Karina is convinced that her mother is "completely insane" and "out to get me." Even worse, she is becoming increasingly manipulative and resorts to sneaking around to ensure that she can do what she wishes. She says, "I'm not going to let my mother ruin my life."

Especially during the younger teenage years, when it is necessary and realistic to have more control over what your daughter does, it is wise to have rules that regulate both the amount of time she spends with television, video games, computer, movies, and music, as well as their content. Girls in middle school often beg to see R-rated movies, such as teen horror flicks, only to become ill with fear and fatigued by nightmares. From their point of view, they have no choice but to suffer through these movies to save face with their peers. From your point of view, there may be no reason for a twelve- or thirteen-year-old to be exposed to disturbing violent or sexual themes that she cannot yet fully understand.

By midadolescence, however, your determined daughter will find a way to see a forbidden movie on cable TV or rent it while at a friend's house. She can easily sign onto inappropriate Web sites or listen to undesirable music at the homes of peers who have more permissive parents. You would be fooling yourself to think otherwise. Suppose your daughter is at a friend's house, settled in on the sofa with popcorn and soda, ready to watch a video or DVD with a group of girls. She sees the title on the screen and realizes with dismay that it is on your banned list. Can you imagine her popping up and saying, "Sorry, I'm not allowed to see that. I'd better go home now"?

Be assured that if you have made known your values, your daughter carries them with her, wherever she is. Your best bet at this point is not to forbid with excessive rules that are unenforceable, but to monitor and sort out her experiences. When you make it your business to know what your daughter is seeing, hearing, and concerned about, you have a basis for discussion. What is her opinion of a controversial movie, its actors, its message? Does she think a character made the right decisions? What is her interpretation of the lyrics of her favorite group's latest song? Such conversations provide invaluable opportunities to counteract undesirable messages your daughter gets from the entertainment industry.

Most especially, you are able to address the roles of women in the media. Are the girls she sees obsessed with their appearance? Are they passive and pleasing to men? Valued for their intelligence? Are young girls portrayed as too sexualized? This is your chance not only to point out how these images of young women are destructive, but to underscore how differently you hope your daughter will view and portray herself. She will probably continue to be intrigued by what interests her peers. But your open-minded curiosity about, and respect for, her ideas, as well as your willingness to discuss these matters, make it less likely that your daughter will reject your values.

No matter how judicious your rules, however, there will surely be times that your daughter feels overly restricted, singled out, and babied relative to friends with more permissive parents. She will claim, "Nobody else's parents make them come home so early!" or "I'm the only one in the school not allowed to go this concert!" Constance's daughter, Leslie, for example, complains of excessive limits: "My parents are sooo overprotective. I am thirteen and I'm not allowed to see PG-13 movies. I feel like such a nerd. My parents have this ridiculous idea that modern movies are bad for you, like they'll turn me into a serial killer. They want me to watch those dumb old movies, instead. Yeah, right."

Much—if not most—of the time, you are hearing the classic cry of a teenager chafing against unwanted but necessary limits. However, if your daughter is particularly upset, adamant, or persuasive in her arguments, you might wonder, "Can this be true?" or more to the point, "Am I being overly restrictive?" Enforcing too many or too rigid rules is often a mother's way of managing her own anxiety. Ostensibly minimizing your daughter's risks, you also may be protecting yourself from intolerable apprehension. If this is a possibility, you might consider these guidelines:

ARE MY RESTRICTIONS:

1. *Based on sufficient exploration and discussion?*
2. *For legitimate reasons?*
3. *Reasonable for her age and culture?*
4. *Not out of anger or spite?*

If you decide you need objective feedback, ask mothers whose parenting approaches you most respect. If they concur with your daughter that you are too extreme, you can always make adjustments. Your daughter will be delighted to hear, "I've rethought this rule, and I've decided to change it because you're older now and can handle more freedom. From now on, . . ." You can also add, "With this privilege comes more responsibility. I expect . . ." Sometimes, however, you may decide you simply cannot budge on a particular decision. This is when you have to model standing up for your beliefs, courageously risking your daughter's wrath to maintain limits that you think are appropriate.

Even when you establish the most reasonable rules for your daughter, know that she will challenge them, probably over and again. More important, she will test her own limits, and she needs you to support that process. Your daughter has to learn what it feels like when she gives in to friends' pressure, when she feels uncomfortable in situations, and when she begins to lose control. These are invaluable opportunities for self-awareness and self-correction, which result in your daughter making gradual improvements in how she conducts herself when she is on her own.

6. Expect—and Model—Accountability

Instead of your daughter denying problems, blaming others, or covering up, you want her to take responsibility for her actions and learn from her mistakes. This means you have to take an honest look at what your teenager is doing. Recently a mother brought her eighth-grader in to see me for a consultation. She said her daughter was being picked on by teachers at her middle school. Belinda was alienating her teachers by getting out of her seat, talking loudly, not doing her work, asking to be excused, and laughing disruptively. She was also failing several classes. Rather than focusing on what was causing Belinda's academic decline and misbehavior, however, this mother directed most of her energy toward complaining about what school officials had failed to do for her daughter.

When you make excuses for your daughter, you prevent her from experiencing the natural consequences of her actions. Unfortunately, this is not uncommon among parents today. For example, several families in one suburban community protested the public high school's decision to bar students from a prom who had broken the "no substance" rule on an athletic field trip abroad. The parents' defense was, "Everybody drinks in high school. You're spoiling their memories." At issue, however, was not whether the school's zero-tolerance policy was or was not reasonable; this was certainly debatable. The point was, all the students and their parents had signed contracts indicating their agreement with this policy before anyone was allowed to attend the tournament. After the fact, when the school enforced the consequence, parents were outraged, as if they thought their children should have been exempt. But what does this "let them off the hook" position communicate to teenagers?

It is tempting to bail out daughters because we don't want them to fail or suffer. It is hard to hang back and let them experience rough spots because we prefer that life be easy and pleasant for them. To avoid embarrassment for their children or the family, some parents put tremendous effort into maintaining appearances. For them, the end justifies the means. Thus, they might choose to ignore that a daughter's desired goal (team win, good grade) was earned by misconduct (plagiarism, cheating, drug abuse). Conversely, other parents require daughters to be accountable for their behavior because they believe this is a crucial step in becoming responsible adults.

As always, if you want your daughter to be accountable, you must be too. If you want to be apprised of her whereabouts, she has to know how to contact you as well. If you are chronically late in coming home or picking her up without calling to explain, your daughter will learn that this is acceptable behavior. You might be thinking that adults and teenagers should not be subject to the same expectations; this is often true. But no one in the family should be excused from being courteous. When you apologize for your lapses, you are conveying respect and modeling how to acknowledge errors. When you share difficult experiences and quandaries you had as a teenager and even now as an adult, you are building further credibility and demonstrating that you are human.

7. Let Go Gradually

At some point, possibly when your daughter gets her driver's license or even before, you recognize with something of a start that you can no longer be absolutely sure where she is, what she is doing, or with whom she is socializing. More horrifying, you realize that you cannot *really* prevent her from attending parties or taking drugs or even having sex. It is both frightening and painful—but realistic—to acknowledge that it is no longer in your power to keep your daughter completely safe.

Mothers cope with this realization in various ways. A few joke, "I'd like to lock her in her room for the next few years." Even those who don't voice this philosophy, at least out loud, may use it to guide their parenting. Michaela, sixteen, who is prohibited from going out with friends, attending parties, or dating, says, "My mother doesn't have a clue what it's like to be a teenager. She thinks something's wrong with me just because I want to have a normal social life." According to Michaela, her mother's attitude is: "When you're in college in two years, you'll be able to do as you please."

If you want your daughter to know how to handle herself when she leaves home, she has to learn these skills now. She has to face age-appropriate choices so she will be prepared later on to make bigger decisions, to read others' behavior, perceive danger, and take steps to protect herself. As scary as it may be to let her go, you do so in part because you want her to learn as much as she possibly can while you are still around to guide and support her.

When you begin to give your daughter more privileges and autonomy, you are recognizing her growth and newfound skills. Your daughter thereby gets the empowering message, "I see how much you've learned, and I am confident that you're ready to handle more." You are also demonstrating respect for her individuality and right to be separate from you. This allows your daughter to take responsibility for her own choices—and, just as important, it frees you from the overwhelming (and essentially impossible) task of preventing her every poor decision or mistake. Truth be told, several mothers have confided that they felt palpable relief when their daughters left home because they were no longer aware of their every activity—or risk.

However, the process of letting go should not be abrupt. Your daughter should not decide one day, "I'm ready to be on my own," nor should you suddenly relinquish your mothering responsibilities in anger or frustration. One indicator of your daughter's readiness for autonomy can be how much and what kind of help she asks of you. Let her set the pace. For example, in the wardrobe arena, many mothers allow girls progressively more freedom and responsibility for their clothing choices. You may begin by letting your daughter pick out a T-shirt or belt while shopping with a friend. If she uses good judgment, you might then give her your blessing for a solo trip to buy an outfit for school or a special occasion.

As your daughter becomes sufficiently secure in her independence, she will eventually seek out you and your opinions once again. When you then join her on a shopping expedition, it will be as two women who enjoy each other's company. This is, as I have recently discovered, an experience worth anticipating. I am convinced that letting go gradually permits this process to unfold. Demonstrating great respect for your daughter's evolving needs, you are also making an invaluable investment in her developing sense of self, which is the subject of the next chapter.

The Driver's License

In preparation for the infamous Year of the Driver's License, you will undoubtedly buckle your own seat belt—literally and figuratively—as a whole new world of potential dangers emerges. The girl who acted somewhat rashly as a preteen may, as a sixteen-year-old burning for independence, eagerly and unthinkingly accept a ride with virtually anyone other than a parent: a boy she likes, a classmate known to be reckless, or someone who is too tired or intoxicated to drive. The seemingly endless list of possible hazards gets harder to ignore.

You will now be faced with a slew of decisions. For example, at what age will you allow your daughter to accept rides with older friends? How long after they are licensed? At what age will you allow your daughter to get her learner's permit? Each state determines the *minimum* age at which your daughter may drive; it is up to you to decide, based on her maturity and abilities, what age is actually best. (One note of caution: Although some parents permit teenagers to get driving experience before they obtain learners' permits, consider what precedent this is setting. This may not be the message about accountability and respect for the law you want to be giving your daughter.) After she gets her license, what parameters do you want to set for your daughter's driving? Does her school have any policies about student driving, or about giving and getting rides from each other?

Permitting your daughter to earn her driver's license is one of last carrots you can dangle; appreciate its power and use it wisely. You can specify what your daughter needs to do, including what skills she needs to demonstrate, before you will feel comfortable allowing her to learn to drive. Many parents think first of academic achievement. The standard of a B average is often used because that entitles parents to a discount on expensive automobile insurance for youthful drivers. Why not expect that your daughter display certain behaviors as well?

At a minimum, teenage girls should demonstrate trust, responsibility, and self-control. That means your daughter abides by your rules, is responsible for some family-related chores, and exhibits some degree of overall maturity in terms of how she conducts herself. For example, if she is characteristically hot-tempered, you may require her to express her anger more constructively to prove that she can keep a cool head if conflicts with other drivers arise. If she is routinely late and disorganized in the morning, you may delay her driving to school until she can be more alert and on time.

Many girls treat their new driver's licenses as green lights to go wherever and whenever they please. It is better to have an understanding beforehand that the license doesn't signal the end of the learning process. You may want your daughter to gain additional experience for various driving conditions (e.g., highway, nighttime, inclement weather). Make clear all other rules, for example, about the maximum number of passengers permitted, the wearing of seat belts, and whether smoking, eating, or drinking is allowed in the car. Also, address the use of CD players, tape decks, and cell phones. Lastly, don't hesitate to state the obvious: that driving privileges are immediately and automatically revoked if you become aware of her using alcohol or drugs.

Chapter 3

Shaping Her Sense of Self
ADOLESCENT DEVELOPMENT

"My daughter is very into pop culture. She's up on every song that comes out and watches MTV all the time. She reads all the teen magazines, some of which I don't think are appropriate for her. Caroline also wants to be eighteen, but she's only twelve. I know that girls in general are growing up fast these days, but it can't be healthy. I think Caroline wants to be seen as cool. Since she's up on all the latest styles, she's become a kind of trendsetter in her grade. On the one hand, this helps her confidence. But on the other hand, I'm not sure if being exposed to all this teen culture will do her any good in the long run. Some girls her age are still playing with Barbies. I let her go to concerts and dances because I've never had reason not to trust her. But how could I stop her even if I wanted to? Her older brother makes a lot of comments about her being spoiled and getting her own way. But she is so happy that I'd hate to interfere."
—Clara, thirty-eight

"I feel like my daughter has left, and this bizarre girl has taken her place. Melanie wears these awful clothes—big and baggy and black— that don't fit her well and aren't at all flattering. I used to bug her about wearing them, but she just got angry and stormed off, so it didn't do any good. What can she be thinking? I guess she can't be feeling good about herself. She's never done as well in school as she hoped because she has a learning disability, and since she's been in high school she seems to have given up. The rest of the family is pretty conservative. Her sister and brothers never gave me any trouble. But Melanie is different. She's even gotten in with a group of friends who I'd consider on the fringe, if you know what I mean. I don't know what I can do about all this. It's scary, but maybe I just have to accept that this is who Melanie is."
—Amie, forty-four

"I tell my daughter how terrific she is all the time. I once read that this was important for her self-esteem. But her self-confidence is awful. Sofia is always putting herself down, despite the fact that she's pretty, a good student, and has nice friends. She's very critical of her appearance. She and her friends get together and have modeling sessions, and they critique each other's bodies. I guess this is normal. It's just that she's in a miserable mood afterward. I don't know how I can get her to feel better about herself. Sofia seems to need a lot of attention and compliments. She's constantly trying to please people. Should I keep telling her how wonderful she is, or will this go in one ear and out the other? How can I get her to believe in herself?"
— Trudy, forty-eight

*E*very time your daughter leaves home, she has to make a vast number of decisions—for example, whether to turn in a classmate who cheated, uncover her skimpy camisole when she gets to school, intervene if she sees bullying, accept a ride with a friend who had a beer, go to third base with her boyfriend, try the popular drug ecstasy, or accompany her best friend when she sneaks out of the house on a Saturday night. The list of potential teenage dilemmas goes on and on.

How your daughter makes these complex choices and conducts herself when you are not around is largely determined by her sense of self—her perception of who she is in relation to her family, peers, community, and culture. In fact, developing a positive and stable image of who she is and who she wants to become is one of the main tasks of adolescence.

The pages that follow discuss how girls typically manage this developmental challenge. However, if you have more pressing or specific worries about your daughter, you may want to skip ahead. You can gain more insight into her friendships in Chapter 8, her romantic relationships in Chapter 9, and the ways she socializes in Chapter 10. This chapter will give you a more general perspective, as well as a multitude of tactics, for shaping the sense of self that influences virtually every aspect of your daughter's life.

Who She Is

Your daughter's sense of self affects how accurately she perceives the world; how logically and realistically she thinks; the use of her inner voice or conscience; and how well she manages her feelings, relates to others in relationships, and controls her behavior. A strong sense of self enables your daughter to acknowledge and understand her emotions, as well as to choose how and when to express them. The more she knows and trusts herself, the better she is able to use her ideals to balance her impulses and behave appropriately. The stronger her sense of self, the better she can solve problems and protect herself when she goes out into the world. In turn, how successfully your daughter accomplishes all this governs her self-esteem.

As your daughter grows, you will see her developing self reflected in her attitude, behavior, and the myriad choices she makes daily. For example, how does she dress and wear her hair? Who are her friends, and what sort of relationships does she have? What are her interests? Which music does she listen to? What are her long-term goals? What kind of student is she? How does she handle problems?

To illustrate, consider these two fifteen-year-old girls, one of whom is reaping the benefits of a far stronger and more stable sense of identity. Alix believes she is important to both her family and her group of friends. She prefers to have a few close pals rather than a large number of acquaintances. Her girlfriends share her twin loves: in-line skating and writing fiction. Alix says she is not ready to date. Although she attends some parties, she likes to leave early, "before people make total fools of themselves." Alix thinks of herself not as an academic superstar, but as a hard worker with some creative talent. She is proud of the fact that her classmates enjoy her stories. When she faces problems, Alix thinks long and hard about what to do, often asking her parents, older sister, or friends for advice. When she makes mistakes, she says, "Next time, I'll listen to my conscience; I knew that wasn't right."

Margot, on the other hand, is a sweet girl who likes to have many friends, but tends to be disappointed by others because she is somewhat needy and overly sensitive to being slighted. She seeks considerable attention and praise, especially from boys, to feel good about herself—and sometimes not in self-enhancing ways. When hurt or angry, Margot either fights with her friends or withdraws.

Then, when she feels lonely, she is apt to act impulsively on invitations to join her peers, giving little thought to the merits of their activities. Margot thinks rather simply and concretely about conflicts, often denying her contribution, lying to get out of jams, or manipulating others. She follows rules, but only to avoid getting caught. Margot is often anxious and confused about the kind of person she would like to be.

As your own daughter makes her way through adolescence, she will gradually develop a stable sense of self. The good news is that as her mother you have considerable influence on this process. Although you cannot make her every decision or solve all of her problems, you can support your daughter in the developmental tasks that will enable her to see herself—indeed, to be—a strong, capable young woman. Here are some guidelines and suggestions for doing so most effectively.

Key Tasks of Adolescents

1. Valuing Her Own Attributes and Appearance

As your daughter develops a firm identity, she is looking everywhere for clues about who she is. What kind of person is she? What is she capable of accomplishing? How do others see her? Is she attractive? It is wise to be aware of the sources of your daughter's information and the messages she is getting that influence her view of her own attributes and appearance. That way you will be in a better position to contribute your own opinions, correct her misperceptions, and adjust her assumptions.

• *Help Your Daughter to Discover Herself.* When you take an interest in her self-expressions, such as poetry, artwork, music, and stories, not only do you learn about your daughter, but also you encourage her to learn more about herself. When you look at old photographs or watch videotapes from her babyhood, she gets a glimpse of who she has been along the way. Even an act as simple as displaying your daughter's research report or teacher's comment on the refrigerator is a powerful affirmation of her. You may be surprised that the same teenager who insists that she "could care less what you think" will light up when she spots this small but tangible appreciation of her and her efforts in the kitchen, where others can see it too.

Thirty Ways to Value Your Daughter

1. Listen attentively when she speaks.
2. Surprise her with the hair clip she wanted.
3. Solicit her ideas and opinions.
4. Need her help.
5. Buy her favorite cereal.
6. Seek her company.
7. Keep your promises.
8. Take her out to lunch.
9. Get to know her friends.
10. Notice and celebrate her accomplishments.
11. Forgive her mistakes.
12. Knock before entering her room.
13. Pamper her when she's sick.
14. Appreciate her efforts.
15. Take her for physicals and appointments.
16. Welcome her friends into your home.
17. Display her schoolwork.
18. Don't use a nickname she's outgrown.
19. Laugh at her jokes.
20. Validate her feelings.
21. Call to tell her you'll be late.
22. Read her poetry and stories.
23. Give her a valentine.
24. Sign her up for lessons.
25. Return her library books.
26. Attend her school's Open House.
27. Cheer for her at games.
28. Make her favorite meal.
29. Celebrate her birthday.
30. Offer to give her a back rub.

• *Correct the Media's Distorted View of Appearance.* Adolescent girls, who are voracious consumers of television shows and teen magazines, are eager for clues about how to look and how to act. Yet the media portray young women as idealized—that is, as ultrathin, beautiful, and appealing to the opposite sex. According to Kaz Cooke, author of *Real Gorgeous,* the typical model is five feet nine inches tall, wears a size six or eight dress and a size A or B bra, has a narrow waist, and is built with unusually wide shoulders. Although this body type is found in only about 5 percent of the population, models are the paragons of beauty and success to which the other 95 percent of young women compare themselves.

The beauty myths perpetuated by the fashion and cosmetics industries can contribute to your daughter's growing up dissatisfied with herself. You can do your part to counteract this by making her aware of how average women really look. Educate your daughter about the variety of female shapes. At her annual physical, look on her physician's weight chart to see what normal women should actually weigh. Find interviews or autobiographies of supermodels that describe the less glamorous aspects of their lifestyle, such as the deprivation and self-torture they often experience.

• *Model a Healthy Attitude About Body Image.* You present a powerful example to your daughter in how you handle your own self-image. Many mothers progressing through middle age make disparaging comments about their deteriorating shape, flabby thighs, or discouraging weight gain. It is easy to slip into this self-denigrating pattern. Are you calorie conscious? Do you diet constantly or skip meals? Your demonstration of healthy eating, sensible exercise, and positive self-statements go a long way toward your daughter developing a strong, positive sense of self that is conducive to making smart decisions.

Such an approach can also alleviate the potentially harmful effects of teen magazines. Contrary to previous laboratory studies, Dr. Eric Stice of the University of Texas at Austin and his colleagues found that 60 percent of adolescent girls ages thirteen to seventeen are not adversely affected by ultrathin magazine models. Only girls who already have concerns about their body image, who feel pressured by parents or peers to be thin, or who lack support from their family and friends are vulnerable to excessive dieting, body dissatisfaction, and symptoms of anorexia and bulimia. These researchers concluded that if you provide your daughter a supportive, nurturing environment, you will buffer the negative messages of magazines.

When speaking of other women's appearance, emphasize their manner and demeanor instead of traditional beauty. Some girls already think this way. When researchers at the University of Arizona's Teen Lifestyle project asked three hundred teenage girls to describe the ideal girl, Caucasian teens had a nearly uniform response: a thin, tall, usually blond girl. But African-American girls deemphasized a physical ideal and focused more on how a girl projected herself than on her looks. Moreover, when asked for examples of beautiful women, they spoke of their mothers and grandmothers. No matter their race, all girls should value the manner in which women conduct themselves far more than whatever physical attributes are currently in vogue. When you are people watching with your daughter, point out women who seem comfortable in their own skin, who move in a self-assured and easy manner, instead of those who are just gorgeous.

Tattooing and Piercing Her Self

When your daughter wants to tattoo or pierce, she may be trying to forge her unique identity by identifying with a particular subculture, just as she adopts a distinct style of dress or music. At the same time, she may be flexing her independence by viewing a tattoo or body piercing as a testament to her ability to make decisions about her own body. In effect, she may be saying to you, "This is *my* body!" along with its corollary, "Not yours, Mom."

In your mind, tattoos may conjure up images of motorcycle-riding, leather-jacketed hoodlums whom well-brought-up, decent daughters did not bring home to their mothers. This stigma probably stems from ancient times, when tattoos were used to brand criminals and slaves. Today, however, prisoners and other groups, such as seamen, have adopted tattoos as signs of pride. Although you may still regard them as shameful, body piercing and tattoos have become more widely accepted in many social groups. As a result, it is the rare mother who escapes confrontations about them with her teenage daughter.

If you are especially fortunate, your daughter will consult you *before* the fact. If so, be sure to tell her how much you appreciate the opportunity to discuss this with her. How you respond will depend on your level of tolerance for these choices, the prevailing norms among your friends and family and, of course, your daughter's age. Whatever her age, discussion and negotiation are your best initial approaches. Find out why your daughter wants to tattoo. What does it mean to her? Encourage her to learn more about the history of piercing or tattoos. She could read *Written on the Body; The Tattoo in European and American History*, a scholarly anthology edited by Jane Caplan, who is a professor at Bryn Mawr College.

When it comes to a permanent tattoo, a reasonable position is that until your daughter is an adult she cannot expect to make decisions that will affect her forever. Permanent tattoos are a prime example. Laser removal of tattoos is both painful and extremely expensive. There also may be religious considerations. For example, those who have tattoos are prohibited from being buried in a Jewish cemetery. The best argument, some mothers report, is that temporary tattoos are better than real ones because "getting tattooed is like deciding to wear the same necklace for the rest of your life. You'll probably get tired of it." Better to have the option of changing body decor in the future.

Whereas a mother's biggest dilemma used to be at what age to allow her daughter to pierce her ears, now it is whether to permit her to double-, triple-, or multiple-pierce her ears, or to pierce her cartilage, eyebrow, nose, tongue, navel, or even more private parts of her body. Your daughter should do her research about piercing. Learning that some facial areas are highly prone to infection and that navel pierces can be highly painful and take up to a year to heal is enough to dissuade many girls—or at least prompt them to postpone. There is no down side to your daughter delaying her decision. The urge to join her friends in a mad dash to the piercing shop may be virtually forgotten six months from now when the clamor dies down. So you might ask your daughter to wait for a certain time period, promising to reevaluate the decision in a few months. She may lose interest in the craze before then.

If at some point you see your daughter's desire to pierce her body as a tolerable declaration of independence—especially, say, as a better alternative than a permanent tattoo—your willingness to negotiate can be helpful. First, you might put your heads together to find the safest, most hygienic setting, learn about follow-up care, and plan the best time to do it. Then, pick your poison. Discuss with your daughter the pros and cons of various sites. Your daughter should consider what piercing may convey about who she is. Although hardly definitive, there is some agreement that while navel pierces are considered cute and sexy, those on the eyebrow, lip, or nose are often a statement of rebellion, "I dare to look different." Tongue piercings are a badge of courage, and genital piercing, paradoxically, is thought to claim girls' privacy. Considering the visibility factor, you may opt for a navel stud over more obvious nose or eyebrow rings.

What if your teenager makes such decisions without your knowledge or permission? Your response is probably age-determined. When your fourteen-year-old daughter, for example, comes home with a belly-button ring, you can insist that she take it out. When she is older and about to leave home, that tactic is probably both unrealistic and less prudent. You may have to accept that your young adult daughter has pierced without your consent. But regardless of whether she had your blessing, don't be surprised if you feel sad and even queasy at the sight of your daughter's new piercing. After all, she has practically maimed the very body you have protected since she was born. Perhaps you can console yourself with the thought that she may soon grow tired of her rings or studs—and at least they are temporary. The tiny hole that remains will remind both of you of this phase of her adolescence.

• *Focus on Attributes More Than Appearance.* If your daughter is obsessed with her appearance, harmful effects could ripple throughout her self-image, confidence, and ability to use her intellect. One study illustrated how women's shame about their body size and shape is detrimental to their academic performance. Along with her colleagues, Dr. Barbara Fredrickson of the University of Michigan asked male and female college students to put on either a sweater or a swimsuit, complete tests about objectification and body shame, and eat a Twix candy bar while alone in a changing room. Whereas men who wore the swimsuit felt silly, women were filled with shame and disgust. All the women scored lower than the men on math tests, but the gap was wider for the women who wore swimsuits than for those who put on sweaters.

You want your daughter's view of herself to be based on who she is and what she does rather than on how she looks. In her book, *Smart Girls*, psychologist Barbara Kerr, Ph.D., examined biographies of thirty-three eminent women who created new directions in art, science, literature, politics, and music. These women shared a similar background. As adolescents, they did not conform to the look that was popular in their day. Because they were large, plain, or not traditionally pretty, they valued and concentrated on their talents far more than their appearance.

You set the standards by focusing on your daughter's behavior and character, rather than on qualities that are superficial or outside her control. For example, try not to be overly concerned with her appearance, number of boyfriends, or other measures of social success. Consider instead her intellect, gifts, and inner qualities along with her actions. Is your daughter a kind and caring friend? A voracious reader? Does she write creative and personalized messages in cards? Is she self-disciplined? Is she a good listener? Does she take initiative and responsibility? Does she have a knack for imitating voices and accents? Can you count on her quick wit or sense of humor?

Having said all this, however, it would be naïve to overlook the fact that girls crave compliments on how they look. Your daughter will beam when you and her father admire her. But give some thought to what precisely you want to reinforce. There are subtle but important differences in what you emphasize. For example, "You look so pretty today" and "You have such beautiful skin" address something that is not in your daughter's control—and, therefore, may change at any time. On the other hand, "I love the way you put together that outfit," and "That's a really flattering new hairstyle" take notice of what she has done herself to feel good about her appearance.

• *Challenge the Media's Portrayal of Young Women.* According to a study conducted by an advocacy group called Children Now, your daughter is more likely to see women in the media preoccupied with personal appearance and romance than with going to school or working at their jobs. In fact, in magazines such as *YM, Sassy, Teen,* and *Seventeen*, there were three times as many articles discussing dating as school or careers. These are the perceptions of women your daughter may try to emulate, unless you present and discuss alternatives. If she is exposed only to women who are overly romantic, obsessed with looks, passive, and determined to please men, this is what she will think she must do.

In another national study, boys and girls ages ten to seventeen were asked who they most admired on television. Not surprisingly, boys' top ten selections were all men. But eight of the girls' top ten selections were also men! This research suggests that teenage girls need powerful female role models who personify the values and achieve the goals they hold most dear. You might identify women your daughter can admire. Make her aware of those who have made a difference in politics, literature, business, journalism, medicine, sports, and other arenas.

• *Recognize the Range and Flux of Your Daughter's Assets.* No matter how wonderful your daughter's talents, it is important not to pigeonhole her. It is unfortunate when girls are constrained by narrow reputations within their families, such as "She's our athlete" or "She's the jolly one." Girls then feel pressured to live up to these labels. For example, she may fear losing her identity if she quits her sport or feels depressed. It is therefore better to convey the sense that your daughter's assets are not fixed; they may well change markedly over time. Areas of weakness may improve as she matures. She may deliberately shift her attention to different pursuits. But at any given moment, there is a spectrum of character traits and behaviors that she can take pride in.

• *Elicit Her Self-Pride.* It is crucial that you convey to your daughter that her main reason for putting forth effort and working hard is to feel good about her achievements. You want your daughter to grow up knowing that she is not obligated to please others, especially if it means compromising her own values and goals. While you are certainly proud of your daughter, it is more important that she feel proud of herself. So when she shows you a stellar report card or an improved grade, instead of saying, "I'm so proud of you," consider commenting, "You must feel so good about what you accomplished." When she is in social situations as a teenager or young adult, you want her to look inward rather than to her peers for cues about desirable behavior and good decisions.

• *Praise Selectively.* Rather than giving your daughter global endorsements, be specific in your praise. Of course you are her biggest fan. But that doesn't mean you think she excels at everything. And it does not help your daughter to say that she does. If she specifically solicits your opinion, aim for being as positive as you can while maintaining your honesty. For example, if she is not a fabulous basketball player, don't tell her that she is the star of her team. Instead, note that she is a good team player because she passes the ball so well to her teammates. Praise the way she enthusiastically congratulates the winning team as evidence of her fine sportsmanship. Saying that your daughter isn't tops in everything prepares her, without denigrating her, for the reality that there will always be girls who are smarter, more athletic, or friendlier. There will always be classmates who get better grades or SAT scores.

• *Criticize Carefully.* Compliments can become meaningless unless they are balanced by equally honest constructive criticism. But because teenage girls are often ultrasensitive, especially to their mothers' judgments, it may be challenging to be honest without being hurtful. For example, your daughter may be crushed if you detest an outfit she spent hours in her room perfecting, or if you are offended by a remark she thought was clever. *How* you give her feedback can make a difference. For example, instead of saying, "I'm ashamed by how you ignored that girl at dinner just because you thought she wasn't cool," try "In the future, I'd like you to make all of our guests feel welcome in our home, just as you always feel more comfortable when other teenagers include you in conversation." Similarly, rather than telling your daughter she is behaving like a brat when she stubbornly refuses to apologize for hurting a friend, try correcting her empathically: "It can be hard to say you're sorry, but it's often a great relief when you can move past a fight and feel close to each other again."

2. Differentiating Herself from Others

Another way your daughter builds a sense of self is by figuring out how she is different from other people, including her peers, her siblings, and, yes, even you. Understanding how this works, you can be instrumental in helping her with this key developmental task.

• *Recognize Why She Forms Certain Alliances.* During adolescence, your daughter is likely to revisit issues that she previously may have taken for granted, such as her family, race, or religion. Girls who feel different in any way, perhaps because they are adopted, come from an unusual background, or have a disability, may try to work through identity concerns during adolescence by allying themselves with certain peers. Your daughter may suddenly seek out friends and boyfriends who share her unique characteristics or, conversely, are completely different. This may explain her shifting alliances and efforts to fit in with a new or particular peer group.

• *Resist Comparisons to Her Peers.* One, girls understandably resent such comparisons. When you tell your daughter that so-and-so is always polite, well dressed or cheerful, for example, she is not likely to think, "Gee, then I guess I'd better try to be more like her." Instead, your daughter probably thinks something on the order of "Well, then I guess you'd rather have her as your daughter than me!" In other words, your daughter probably is offended and will become defensive or indignant.

Two, it is unwise to suggest that your daughter model herself after girls you think exemplify desired characteristics when you may, in fact, be dead wrong. Your impressions may be biased or inaccurate simply because you lack facts. What you see is perhaps not at all what is really going on. In fact, several mothers who were initially impressed with their daughters' friends—their respectful manners, style of dress, and cheerful disposition—were later flabbergasted and felt a bit foolish when they learned more. Here is what these mothers have to say:

"My daughter's best friend was always exceedingly polite when she came over. She never failed to say thank you and to be gracious about everything she was offered. These fine manners were exactly what I wanted my daughter to learn. Later on, though, this same girl tried to kill herself. I found out how hard she had been working at being perfect, how she couldn't tolerate even one small flaw in herself." (Maria, forty-six)

"When my daughter was in high school, she went through an awful stage of dressing in fashionable but rather odd styles that were truly ugly. One of her good friends continued to dress to the nines. Every time I saw her I said how beautiful she looked and how she obviously valued her appearance. Imagine how ridiculous I felt when my daughter finally told me that she had a habit of shoplifting clothes from the mall." (Graciella, thirty-nine)

"My daughter is quite moody, laughing one minute and nasty the next. One of her closest friends was always so happy, so consistently upbeat, that she was always a pleasure to be around. Well, I learned recently that her parents sent her to drug rehab. I had no idea!" (Helene, fifty)

As these examples illustrate, it may be unfair or even unwise to compare your daughter to her friends. If you knew more, you might be horrified to learn what you are suggesting your daughter emulate.

• *Don't Compare Her to Siblings.* It is even more difficult to resist comparing your daughter (usually unfavorably) to her brother or sister. However, developmental research offers sound reasons for parenting children differently, even if they are both girls. Children are born with genetically based variations in their reactions to the world and their ability to regulate themselves. Thus, even if you could mother two daughters precisely the same way, your experiences would not be the same because they would respond differently to you. Mothers of twin girls have provided evidence that substantiates these realities. Also, research demonstrates that because each of your children is constitutionally different, she elicits different parenting from you. For example, if one of your daughters has an irritable, difficult-to-soothe temperament, she is more likely to provoke hostility, criticism, and coercive discipline. Compared to a child who entered the world with a sunny, easygoing disposition, the difficult girl's interactions are more apt to create a troubled mother-daughter relationship.

Still, in many families the oldest child seems to establish an implicit norm that later siblings are expected to follow. Yvette, sixteen, says, "All my older sister did was stay home and read. She hated to go out and had no social life whatsoever. So my mom is always saying to me, 'Your sister never went to parties, why should you?' It's totally unfair!" On the other hand, Kendra, fifteen, is paying the price of an older sister who got into drugs and had a teenage pregnancy. She complains, "My parents are trying to get it right this time, and they won't even let me out of their sight. I feel like I'm in jail, and I didn't even do anything. I just want to be normal."

Nori, fourteen, puts it bluntly, "My brother was really messed up, and so now my mom thinks I'm going to become a drug-addicted slut." She asks, "How can I get her to realize I won't follow in his footsteps?"

No matter how hard you try, you cannot mother each of your children exactly the same way. Since it is impossible to parent completely equally, you might as well make decisions based on your daughter's unique abilities and needs. Depending upon each child's respective strengths and weaknesses, you might need different strategies or degrees of parental authority to bring about the same result. When you find time to be with each of your children separately, you are respecting their individuality and conveying how special every relationship is to you.

In addition, you might avoid falling into the trap of trying to be absolutely fair to your children and distributing goodies perfectly equally. Although your daughter may wave the flag of sibling unfairness whenever she feels slighted, disappointed, or angry, it is wise not to buy into proving her wrong—simply because it would be impossible. There will always be one child who needs and therefore receives more of your attention, help, or family resources. It is better to assure your daughter that you will always do your best to give her whatever she needs.

• *Accept That Her Tastes May Be Different from Yours.* In order to figure out who she is, your daughter also needs to differentiate herself from you in looks, behavior, and even thoughts. This process, however, can be highly anxiety-provoking and even hurtful to mothers. It can feel awful when your daughter denigrates your style, your beliefs, and your choices. Recently, as a well-known television anchorwoman interviewed me about selecting clothes with teenagers, she suddenly exclaimed, "I just want to say to my daughter, 'Do you really *like* that?' I'm forty-five and she's thirteen, and I have good taste!"

Again, picking out clothes and accessories may be the first method by which teenagers discover and assert their individuality. Amy Lynch, editor of *Daughters* magazine, describes teenage girls as "shopping for an identity." In the search for who they are and who they want to become, they try out new looks they can portray to others. Consequently, according to Ms. Lynch, a must-have purchase is more than just a shirt or fashion accessory. It is a need "to express what may be a new part of her."

So what do you do when your daughter picks out an outfit that you think is awful? This all-too-common, even classic, mother-daughter situation calls for using your BRAIN.

To Be flexible, ask yourself what about her clothing, if anything, you can tolerate. After all, you understand that her getup may just be a reflection of the current fad that is going to peter out in a week or two. Ask yourself how you can compromise to support this new expression of her self. Such an approach communicates that you acknowledge and accept her changing needs and tastes as a teenager.

NOT

> MOTHER: That is simply hideous! What are you thinking?
> DAUGHTER: You always hate everything I wear!

TRY

> MOTHER: That skirt is really unique, and it looks sort of cute on you. How would you feel about changing just the top so it complements the skirt more?

It is vital to be Respectful of your daughter's feelings, as well as her right to have different preferences from yours, despite the fact that the outfit makes you cringe. This conveys to her that you support her being her own person, separate from you.

NOT

> MOTHER: Did you really think I'd let you out of the house looking like that?
> DAUGHTER: You're such a witch; leave me alone!

TRY

> MOTHER: What do you love about that skirt?
> DAUGHTER: Well, the look now is to have these layers. I like how it flows.

OR

> MOTHER: It's definitely not my taste, but if it makes you feel good, wear it well.
>
> DAUGHTER: But does it look okay on me? Tell me the truth.

When you remain <u>A</u>ttuned to your daughter's feelings and needs, you try to understand what she is seeking by wearing that outfit. Does she think it makes her look older, cooler, more appealing to boys? Your discussion enables her to learn these things for herself, contributing to the way she sees herself.

NOT

> MOTHER: Why do you always have to look exactly like everyone else?
>
> DAUGHTER: You don't know what you're talking about!

TRY

> MOTHER: How do you think that outfit flatters you?

OR

> MOTHER: How does it make you feel to wear it?
>
> DAUGHTER: I don't know, but it's better than those dorky jeans I wore yesterday.

When you stay appropriately <u>I</u>nvolved, you avoid the temptation to stick your head in the morning paper to avoid seeing that she left for school in the morning barely clad. You care and see it as your responsibility to help her with the image she projects—both to herself and others. Thus, at times you might have to tell your daughter clearly but tactfully that her outfit is too something (e.g., short, tight, revealing, etc.) to meet your standards for decency.

NOT

> MOTHER: You can wear that, but don't complain to me when you ruin your reputation.

TRY

> MOTHER: I wonder what that see-through T-shirt tells people about you?
> DAUGHTER: Nothing! But it has a little spot; maybe I'll go change.

Above all, when you are Noncontrolling, you refrain from issuing arbitrary demands, and allow your daughter to take a more active role in choosing her own outfits and assessing whether they fit her emerging identity.

NOT

> MOTHER: Get upstairs and take off that disgusting halter right now!
> DAUGHTER: You can't tell me what to do!

TRY

> MOTHER: Gee, I think we need to discuss that teeny top you're wearing.
> DAUGHTER: Why? Does it make me look fat?
> MOTHER: No, it's not that. But I think it's the wrong look for a youth group trip. Let's figure out what you might add that would make that outfit okay.

At various times, you might suggest she wear a cardigan or outer shirt over skimpy, revealing tank tops, or ask that she wear skirts of a minimum length to school. Although there is no guarantee your daughter will still be wearing what you recommended when she arrives at school, at least you know that she heard your point of view and understands the underlying values. Lastly, peruse magazines with her and people watch to assess what looks she admires. It may be easier for your daughter to see what is attractive on others rather than on herself, especially within the confines and poor lighting of a typical fitting room.

• *Promote Her Unique Interests and Activities.* Adolescence is a time of liberating experimentation and self-discovery. In finding her self, your daughter may try out different activities and test her talents and abilities in novel ways. Mothers often struggle when their daughters are extreme in this area, either floundering to find anything that interests them or frantically trying to do everything at once. Your daughter may need more time or gentle encouragement to pursue what piques her curiosity and gives her pleasure. Exposing her to different group and individual activities, especially noncompetitive ones, may help. Consult *The Girl Pages: A Handbook of the Best Resources for Strong, Confident, Creative Girls* by Charlotte Milholland for thousands of ways to help your daughter discover what excites her. Be aware of giving her the message, however, that she has to excel at *something*. Or, even worse, that she has to excel at *everything*. Your daughter's genuine passions will arise from within, in due time.

Many times, mothers become intensely invested in their daughters' long-term activities. That is why it can be especially hard when your teenager wants to give up her sports or hobbies. After all, you have been hauling her to practices, supporting her at games and meets, paying fees, and buying equipment. You also may have enjoyed this same sport when you were younger. But your daughter may suddenly compare herself to her peers and conclude, "I really stink." For example, since preschool my daughter participated in dance recitals, relishing the costumes and performing on stage, even though she was always cast as a flower rather than a prima ballerina. But at twelve she insisted, "I'm horrible at this and I'm never going to be a dancer, so I might as well quit."

When your daughter considers quitting her sport, her participation on the math team, or her seat on student council, your reaction is key. Although you might wish to encourage or even force her to continue, you may be neglecting her other valid emotional and social needs. Your daughter may need a break to avoid burnout or simply want to pursue another interest. If she stays involved just to please you or her father, there is empty satisfaction in her success. She is not being true to herself.

Instead, try to get to the root of her dissatisfaction. If necessary, modify your daughter's schedule to ease the pressure. Her coach may be amenable to her missing one practice per week. Or allow her to take an emotional vacation from a season. Perhaps if she takes a break from competition she will reexperience her initial pleasure in the sport. In the end, you may need to support her exploration of other activities that currently intrigue her. Today, this could be kick boxing or writing haikus; in a few months, it might be the guitar or yoga. Whatever you decide, your daughter will benefit from your acknowledging her evolving needs. Validating her right to have a say in how she spends her time contributes to her strong sense of self.

3. Thinking and Solving Problems Effectively

Your daughter's thinking skills are what enable her to size up social situations, define problems, gather essential information, brainstorm possible alternatives, decide on solutions, and put them into effect. If her first idea does not succeed, she has to make contingency plans. Planning ahead and evaluating the possible consequences of her actions also prevent her from behaving impulsively. As your daughter assesses the success of her actions, she decides whether her behavior is worth repeating, or if she should avoid making the same mistake next time.

• *Demonstrate Good Problem Solving.* Treat everyday situations as opportunities to teach your daughter these essential skills. A sibling fight over the TV, conflicting schedules, a forgotten homework assignment, a social gaffe—all are possible learning experiences. When you are respectful of her, collaborate with her, and elicit her participation in discussions, you are making invaluable strides. You hope that when your daughter is not in your presence she will apply these skills. It is when teenagers fail to think of alternative solutions or to appreciate the likely consequences of their actions that trouble often ensues.

For example, Andra is a fifteen-year-old ninth grader whom I saw in consultation. For years, she struggled both academically and socially. Viewing her peers as more popular and talented than herself, she desperately wanted them to accept her. During lunch one day, Andra reportedly approached a senior she barely knew and bought a small amount of marijuana from him that she then gave to a friend. She was caught, taken to the principal's office, and formally charged by police. Although she had no criminal or disciplinary history, the school gave Andra a two-month mandatory suspension. Despite daily home tutoring, she fell behind in her studies and felt even more isolated from her peers. As the weeks passed, she became increasingly bored, depressed, and anxious about returning to school.

Andra's parents, teachers, and professional consultants were all mystified about what prompted her to engage in this flagrantly illegal act—and in school, of all places! When I asked about her motivation, Andra replied, "I just wanted to do a favor for a friend." Focused on trying to impress and win over a potential ally, she either failed to consider or chose to ignore the larger issues: the fact that she was breaking the law, the possibility of getting caught and suffering severe consequences, the unlikeliness of earning this girl's friendship.

• *Use This Decision-Making Framework.* A mother who attended a parenting lecture I gave at a large girls' school shared with me a sensible technique she and her husband developed to empower their two daughters to think through important decisions effectively. Miriam Cronin and her husband encourage their girls to ask themselves these four questions as a first step before approaching their parents:

1. Is it safe?
2. Is it legal?
3. Is it moral?
4. Does it make sense?

If the girls answer no to any of the four questions, they know the action is a poor one. If there is any confusion or disagreement, they can talk about the dilemma together. This simple but by no means simplistic technique accomplishes several things. One, girls are given the chance to practice making responsible choices for themselves. Two, this format encourages girls to develop astute thinking skills by prompting them to address specific criteria. Three, because these questions are complex, disagreements and controversies are bound to occur. Thus, this technique also encourages parent-child discussions about using values to guide one's choices. If Andra, the girl who was suspended from school, had stopped to ask herself these questions before she bought drugs, she might well have avoided months of heartache.

4. Taking Appropriate Action

Your daughter's belief that she is in charge of herself enables her to act on her own behalf. All along, you have been encouraging her to take charge appropriately in social situations. Whenever there is a problem, you hope that she will use whatever resources are available to her to find workable solutions. In this way, she is developing an active approach to problems, rather than allowing others to make decisions for her or expecting others to take care of her.

• *Give Your Daughter Credit for Her Successes.* If she believes she has the power to affect her own life, she will be that much more inclined to take action. In an effort to be modest and avoid the stigma of being conceited or full of herself, however, some girls are reluctant to take credit for their accomplishments. Instead, they attribute their successes to factors outside of themselves. For example, a teenager will often say she was lucky to win her singles championship in tennis because her biggest rival didn't compete. Or your daughter might credit her A- on a chemistry experiment to the genius of her lab partner—in other words, to anyone or anything but herself. Emphasize to her that while everyone benefits from support, teamwork, and even chance, she could not have earned her good grades, accolades, sports victories, or other successes without her own talent, hard work, creativity, and commitment.

• *Grant Her Privileges Based on Her Abilities.* When your daughter shows good judgment, respond by praising how she handled the situation. Perhaps you might give her additional privileges as well. She will come to appreciate that freedom is earned, not granted arbitrarily. In this way you are giving her incentives for behaving appropriately. Your daughter experiences firsthand that positive consequences follow her desirable choices. This is highly empowering, encouraging her to take appropriate actions in the future.

• *Support Your Daughter's Active Solutions.* Although this sounds obvious, sometimes it will be difficult. After all, your daughter may propose a plan that you are too tired or busy to enact. This is when you have to be accountable, resisting the temptation to ignore or dismiss her valid motivations for your own purposes. Your daughter is never too young to experience your genuine support of her problem solving.

I still recall vividly an incident that happened when my daughter was only three. She had been invited to a nursery school classmate's birthday party. When we arrived at the family's enormous gym, where the party was to be held, Mason's mother greeted us at the door and asked me to fill out a name tag with my daughter's name and telephone number. I soon understood the reason for this request. The gym was already filled with thirty-five or so energetic three- and four-year-olds, several roving clowns, and various game stations and amusements. Leaving my daughter to enjoy the festivities, I made my way home. Perhaps forty-five minutes later, I had just sat down to relax with a book when the phone rang and I heard Mason's mother say, "Your daughter says she's ready to go home now."

Although the last thing I wanted to do was trek up that mountain road again, I was compelled by my daughter's request; this was truly a first. She was usually so enthusiastic about adventures and new experiences, and I couldn't remember her ever being clingy or eager to return home. But after forty-five minutes, the noise, commotion, and number of bouncing small children were apparently too much for her. She wanted out. Fortunately, my daughter was able to remove herself in a rather straightforward and positive way. Instead of acting up or throwing a tantrum, she simply told her friend's mother, "I'm ready to leave now." On the way back, I assured her that calling me was exactly the right thing to do.

5. Developing an Inner Voice

When you make distinctions between thoughts and deeds, as well as between good and bad behavior, which are two of the parenting principles discussed in the last chapter, you contribute to your daughter's emerging inner voice, or the spokesperson of her conscience. When you are not around, it is this inner voice that reminds her when the behavior she is considering would clash with her values and those of her family. Using her conscience indicates that your daughter has taken to heart all your wisdom, internalized all your admonitions, and not forgotten your occasional threats.

• *Take Her Reactions Seriously.* If you want your daughter to have a powerful inner voice that won't be quieted, respond to her reactions respectfully. Teach her to pay careful attention to gnawing discomfort and the voice of her conscience; they are powerful signals alerting her to internal conflict or potential harm in relationships. Your daughter's uneasiness can thereby become a valuable resource, a beacon to guide her as she learns to handle the complexities of life on her own.

Miranda, the thirty-eight-year-old mother of Mia, thirteen, says, "I kept thinking my daughter's refusal to stay after school for band practice was simply to get on my nerves. Much later, I found out that the teacher was meeting individually with students, and Mia wasn't comfortable around him. She was apparently afraid that if she told me, I would talk to him or call the school and embarrass her. I wish I had discussed this more with her at the time." Discovering the source of your daughter's uneasiness can help you to validate and amplify the whispering of her inner voice. This helps her to learn to trust her gut feelings and act accordingly.

• *Don't Ignore Her Lapses of Conscience.* If you want your daughter to develop a clear sense of what is right and wrong, you have to be willing to acknowledge how she really behaves. Yet mothers usually prefer to see their daughters in the best possible light. It is hard to confront their selfishness, meanness, spite, jealousy, and other offensive characteristics. These qualities suggest that daughters are not what their mothers would like them to be. Occasionally, this realization triggers negative reactions in women, evoking memories of their own past behavior as teenagers, or even flickers of what they currently dislike in themselves.

Although it is tempting to overlook your daughter's minor lapses of goodness, when they are repeated or especially despicable you are obliged to act on them. For example, if you think your sixteen-year-old daughter manipulated a much-wanted, last-minute invitation to the senior prom from the boy she likes by starting unkind rumors about the girl who was supposed to go with him, you might choose not to ignore your suspicions. If the way she conducts herself is more important to you than whether or not she attends a particular dance, communicate your strong support of a healthy conscience that asserts itself when you are not around.

• *Teach Her That the End Does Not Justify the Means.* In the same way, emphasize that the way she goes about reaching her goals must sit right with her, regardless of whether she ultimately succeeds or fails. For example, if your daughter's good grade on a history term paper was earned by copying a classmate's work, her inner voice should holler. Similarly, the momentary glory of winning a game can be exhilarating, but girls cannot feel gratified if their victory was earned by means other than honest effort and talent. They cannot feel genuinely good about themselves when deep down their conscience objects. Thus, if a teenager knows her behavior is wrong and her inner voice objects, her self-image suffers in the long run.

5. Handling Her Mistakes

It is imperative that girls learn to handle their failures along with their successes. This need, however, is often neglected, with unfortunate results. If your daughter is to develop a strong sense of self, she must accept and come to terms with her mistakes, benefiting from them by not repeating them in the future. This is the learning process you wish to support.

• *Tolerate—No, Expect—Failure.* Girls who aspire to perfection suffer in many ways. Much has been written about the association between perfectionism and eating disorders such as anorexia and bulimia. In my practice, I have also seen an inordinate number of girls whose desire for perfection creates overwhelming anxiety. It is unnerving to teenagers when they can imagine only two possibilities: unattainable perfection or failure. Whether they strive for an ideal in academics, sports, or social areas, these girls have great difficulty focusing on the tiny but real steps they need to take along the way. They essentially become immobilized, accomplishing very little.

It is healthy to have the mind-set that no matter how well-adjusted your daughter is, she will sometimes have problems. In the social realm, she will quarrel with her friends. Not everyone will like her. Occasionally she might be excluded from a party or not invited to a dance. She herself might do something insensitive or cruel. Although you and other adults learn to take these experiences in stride and move on, many mothers seem to expect their teenagers to be perfect social beings.

• *Play Monday Morning Quarterback.* Your daughter's failures will teach her just as much as, if not more than, her successes. Yet she may be unwilling to look at her contribution to a problem (in fact, she might be irate that you would even imply such a possibility). So when she comes to you distraught, it is wise to suggest in a curious rather than accusatory manner, "Let's figure out together what happened." You are encouraging her to be accountable, as well as communicating the reality that she has not yet learned how to handle many dilemmas. When you say, "I know you are upset, but let's see what you can learn from this. Maybe there's a way you can do this differently in the future," you are conveying empathy and re-spect. You are also helping her to separate her own role in the situa-tion from factors over which she had no control.

For example, suppose your daughter agreed to help a good friend with a project, but then decided to accept another pal's more attrac-tive invitation to join her in an activity. When your daughter com-plains that the friend she was supposed to help is now angry, it is wise not to jump to her aid with assurances that "it's not your fault; you didn't know that you would be away" or "She'll get over it, and it's better for her to do the project herself, anyway." Equally unhelp-ful would be "Well, you didn't expect her to be happy, did you?" or "That was pretty mean of you!"

Instead, ask your daughter how she sees the situation. To encour-age her empathy, ask her to consider her friend's perspective: "If you were Suze, how would you feel?" What does she think is her respon-sibility to her friends? What are its limits? How would your daugh-ter handle things differently next time, and what has she learned from this incident? Even when your daughter bristles with your im-plied criticism—after all, you are suggesting the possibility that she might have been less than a perfect friend—she is hearing questions that she may ask herself later in private. You are therefore stimulat-ing the development of her internal problem solving, which is an es-sential part of a strong sense of self.

6. Protecting Herself in the World

When your daughter has a strong sense of self, including a forceful inner voice, she feels capable of taking action and handling herself in all sorts of situations, including those that make her uncomfort-able. Above all, as she experiences increasingly challenging social dilemmas, you want her to be able to protect herself.

• *Explore Her Discomfort.* When your daughter tells you her lab partner is weird or her coach is creepy, you may want to look be-yond your knee-jerk reaction to the pejorative label. Your daughter may be communicating discomfort that she feels but cannot yet articulate well. At those moments, if you hear yourself begin to lecture her on judging people, giving others a chance, or being nice, take a moment to reconsider. Instead, try asking, "Something must be making you feel uncomfortable. What do you think it could be?" Even if she cannot answer you, asking the question validates her uneasy feeling and encourages her to take it seriously. You are raising the volume of her inner voice so it drowns out distractions from taking care of herself.

• *Give Her the Chance to Work Out Conflicts.* Considering the factor of your daughter's age, you want to give her as many opportunities as possible to navigate relationships and resolve problem situations. Even a young daughter might be given the chance to settle squabbles typical of her maturity level. For example, Shirley, forty-three, recalls a time when her fifteen-year-old daughter, Stephanie, was in first grade and called her to be picked up early from a play date:

> She and another girl had been invited to her friend's house one Saturday morning. I was a little concerned because the other girl who was going to be there had a reputation of being rather forceful, and I wasn't sure that Steph could hold her own. I suppose I was also worried about the whole two-against-one thing. Anyway, she called me not long after to ask if she could come home. The girls had gotten in a fight about what to play. I ran out the door to pick her up. Now that she's a teenager, though, I see that Steph is still doing that. Whenever she has a little disagreement with a friend, she runs away rather than deal with it. She stays in her room, won't take the friend's phone call, and waits for things to blow over. Looking back, I should have let her stay. Not just that time, but lots of times. Steph still needs to learn how to cool off and figure out how to work out disagreements.

To respond most effectively for your daughter, you must be cognizant of what these social situations evoke in you. If you are socially ambitious for her, you may focus too much on her opportunities to be included and too little on her learning to be selective. If you have a need to feel in control, you may react to your daughter's requests for help by feeling manipulated. In awkward social situations, mothers who are self-conscious themselves may be more eager to avoid the embarrassment of a scene than to understand what their daughters are experiencing. But the more you can sit with your anxiety and give your daughter the chance to work things out for herself, the better she can manage and protect herself in difficult circumstances.

As you begin to address and fine-tune your parenting style to match your daughter's needs, as well as to shape her developing sense of self, you will undoubtedly have many chances to try out and apply all that you are learning. That is because mothering a teenage daughter will, if nothing else, provide you a never-ending succession of daily issues and choices. The next chapter will prepare you for these challenges by giving you some tools for basic, but productive, discussions with your daughter.

Chapter 4

Daily Issues, Daily Choices
DISCUSSIONS

"Since my daughter has been in middle school, she's gotten quieter and quieter. We rarely talk about anything of substance, and when we do it's usually a one-way conversation. I wonder if she speaks more openly to her friends. Sometimes I've overheard her on the phone, and she seems to hang up abruptly. When I ask what's going on, she usually goes silent or tells me that I can't possibly understand. Once in a while she says that someone was mean to her. I think it's hard for my daughter to speak up about what's bothering her. Is this normal for a teenage girl, or should I be worried that she has a problem? She has a nice group of friends, and I want her to be able to work out whatever differences they have so she can enjoy her teenage years."
                                                    — Belinda, thirty-nine

"My conversations with my daughter have deteriorated to the point that I dread having to talk to her about anything significant. When she was younger, she was such an easy, agreeable child. But she doesn't accept everything I say anymore. As soon as I say no, she starts arguing with me. She questions me in this arrogant manner about why I said this or did that, as if she thinks I'm a fool. She gets really fresh and says, 'You don't know what you're talking about.' I never would have dared to speak to my mother like that; she wouldn't have stood for it. In fact, my mother is appalled by the way my daughter treats me and wants to know why I let her get away with this. All I want is to be close to my daughter, and yet Sarah seems to have little respect for me. I don't think I'm being unreasonable. Why is this happening?"
                                                    —Arabella, forty-three

"I don't know how to deal with my daughter these days. All she cares about is hanging out with her friends and going to parties. Even though

I give her the same curfew every night, she keeps coming home late. I can't understand why she keeps doing that because it only gets her grounded. The more I try to talk to her about this, the more defensive she gets. Lately, she's been giving me one-word answers. When I try asking her to explain, she acts as if I'm being ridiculous. I know this isn't right; it isn't the way I want us to be. Can't we sit down together and get these things straight, like two civilized people? Maybe I am being unreasonable giving her a midnight curfew. Should I extend it, as she wants? Will that help—or will it make things worse? I'm so confused about all this that I haven't been able to think straight!" —Bettie, fifty

On Monday your daughter may implore you for her own telephone line so she can receive calls at any hour; on Wednesday she may warn you that her very life will end if you forbid her from attending the hot party that everyone is going to this weekend; and by Friday, she may beg you to waive her usual curfew so she can enjoy every last moment of that magnificent occasion. Just when you think you've got these situations under control, she may ask you for a separate online account, tickets to go by herself to visit a friend who moved, the age at which she can begin to date, or permission to go to a club with her friend's older brother. You have scarcely taken another breath before the issues become whether she can attend unsupervised events, drink wine or beer at family holidays, and serve alcohol to her friends at her after-homecoming party.

These are just a sample of the issues that emerge in the daily life of a teenage girl, all of which require you to become a perpetual referee in the game of adolescence.

Besides replying to these direct requests, you make other choices in response to your own concerns for your daughter. You have to decide how to react when she devotes herself to rescuing troubled classmates, wants to skip school after a best friend's rejection, or pursues a boy who obviously does not reciprocate her interest. You have to decide whether to call the parents of a friend who is hosting a party to find out if they will be home, whether to share that information with other parents, and, if you do, whether to tell your daughter that you have done so. Not to mention the more general but vital decisions about how you run your household, how you live your life, and what values you emphasize.

If you sometimes think that mothering has become an endless series of impossible decisions, you are not alone. The good news is this chapter will give you a framework you can use to work out whatever issues and problems arise. In addition to becoming better prepared to tackle the everyday dilemmas, you will also gain tools that you can use later on to address the hard topics—for example, your daughter's determination to maintain friendships with girls who clearly use or snub her (Chapter 8); a boyfriend whose posses-siveness scares you; oral sex (Chapter 9); and the risks of binge drinking (Chapter 10).

If, however, you have been jolted by discovering a new problem or are currently in the midst of a bad patch with your daughter, you might prefer to jump ahead right now. Chapter 6 provides more ur-gent help when your daughter gets in trouble, and Chapter 7 offers sound strategies for discipline. But when things calm down a bit, you may want to refer back to this chapter, perhaps over and again, since you can apply this basic blueprint to every conversation you have with your daughter during her teenage years.

The Merits of Discussion

Many of the daily issues and problem situations that emerge in the course of parenting your daughter are best handled by the two of you sitting down together and discussing them. In addition to your spouse, friends, or other advisers, your daughter is actually a great resource. When you are both truly invested and engaged in conver-sations, there are many mutual benefits.

One, discussions provide a means for the two of you to remain attuned to each other and closely connected. Though you may not always agree, at least you can find out what the other is thinking and feeling. Grace, seventeen, who attends an academically demanding girls' school at which I spoke, expressed the sentiments of many girls who grow up with little discussion with their parents:

"I'm a college-bound senior. I have a brother who's a sophomore in college but he's never left home and a nine-year-old brother as well. I am the middle child. Recently, my parents have become extremely overprotective of me. I went from having no curfew to a ten P.M. curfew, for no reason. Now, in order to go out I have to be accompanied by my brother. When I asked them why, my parents' explanation was 'because we said so.' How am I expected to respect their wishes if they don't even give me a reason for their actions? I'm leaving next year; shouldn't I be allowed to live as an adult and make my own decisions as long as it's within the parameters of the law?"

Two, a sensible approach to these discussions will enable both of you to get enough relevant information to clarify the issues. That way, your choices will be clearer. You need to understand the situation from your daughter's adolescent perspective, including her feelings and desires. She needs to realize the larger issues from your parental viewpoint. That way, neither of you is operating in a vacuum.

Three, these conversations are often your most valuable method of trying to influence your daughter. This is your opportunity to communicate your fears, wishes, principles, and expectations. This is your chance to share your most teachable lessons through powerful stories. That is why this chapter is devoted to helping you to do all this most effectively.

Four, such discussions offer invaluable long-term benefits. Essentially, this process enables you to convey values and model skills that your daughter will use for the rest of her life—for example, listening, getting information, deliberating, negotiating, compromising and, especially, problem solving. If you would like your daughter to be able to handle problems effectively outside the family, the best place for her to practice is within your own relationship, in the daily interactions and discussions you have with her.

In teaching her these vital life skills, you are addressing the concerns of many schools across the country that have introduced emotional literacy into the curriculum. Programs for younger children have used storytelling and role-playing techniques to improve impulse control, empathy, and cooperation. In the higher grades, literature is often used to teach about friendship, caring, and decision making. These efforts have helped countless children to exercise better emotional self-control and to resolve conflicts more effectively.

Just recently I read that Arizona State University's psychology department will be reaching out to parents of its freshmen by offering an online, for-credit class, "Student passages: a decision-making course for parents." According to *Monitor on Psychology*, a publication of the American Psychological Association (APA), this course "teaches parents problem-solving and decision-making skills to inform them about the challenges their children face at college and to help them develop skills they can apply in their jobs and in other relationships."

Your discussions with your daughter can accomplish these same goals. You can help her to sort through the issues involved, think of alternatives, anticipate potential consequences, weigh benefits versus risks, and, guided by personal and family values as well as her own inner voice, make the most prudent choices. Whereas some problems lend themselves to easy solutions, others are complex, life-altering decisions. Over time, you are helping your daughter to reduce impulsive, poorly thought through behavior and unfortunate repercussions. As you teach her to assess people and relationships, she will learn about trust, respect, and reciprocity. As you encourage her to express disappointment and disagreement adaptively, to avoid provocative or inflammatory behavior, and to defuse others' inappropriate anger, you are helping her to take good care of herself in relationships.

Relearning How to Talk with Your Teen

If your daughter has not yet hit the teenage years, you might be wondering, "What is the big deal about having a discussion with my daughter?" You are recalling the rather simple and straightforward dialogues you are used to having, probably on a daily basis, around her dilemmas and requests:

> DAUGHTER: Mom, can I sleep over at Carly's house?
> MOM: No, honey, not tonight.
> DAUGHTER: Why not?
> MOM: Because we're leaving very early tomorrow morning.
> DAUGHTER: But I want to and you never let me.
> MOM: I'm sorry, but you can't tonight.
> DAUGHTER: Fine, but can I sleep over next week?

MOM: Maybe. We'll have to see.
DAUGHTER: Okay.

These days, this same chat may be anything but simple. Despite your love for each other and the closeness of your relationship, talking with your teenage daughter about her life may get decidedly complicated. Between the urgency of the issues you discuss and the heated emotions that are often provoked, you and your daughter may dance around each other like two novice jousters, tentatively trying out each and every word to find comfortable ground and avoid misplaced steps. Perhaps you'll be wary of using certain buzzwords that inevitably cause sparks to fly and abruptly shut down dialogue. It is very likely, in fact, that you may find yourself mired in convoluted discussions with your daughter—you know, the kind that are layered with subtle subtexts, challenges, and hidden agendas, the kind that instantly make your head throb and seem to divert you from the very issues you need to address:

DAUGHTER: Mom, I'm gonna stay at Jasmine's house tonight, okay?
MOM: Well, just a second, I'm not sure. What are your plans? (Thinking: Didn't I hear that her parents are hardly ever at home?)
DAUGHTER: How would I know? You keep asking me that, but you know we never know what we're doing 'til the last minute! (Thinking: Why doesn't she get it?)
MOM: Well, I'll need some information before I can give you permission. (Thinking: What isn't she telling me? And what can I ask without starting a fight?)
DAUGHTER: (Silence)
MOM: Are Jasmine's parents going to be home? (Thinking: Should I call them?)
DAUGHTER: I don't know, and besides, they trust Jasmine to stay by herself. They don't treat *her* like a two-year-old.
MOM: Uh huh. Well, are you planning to go out tonight?
DAUGHTER: Do you expect us to sit at home baking cookies and watching the Family Channel like a couple of complete dorks?
MOM: No, but I'd like to have some idea of what you *will* be

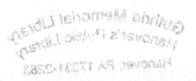

doing. (Thinking: This is going nowhere fast and I don't have energy for a fight, but I'm definitely not comfortable with this situation.)

DAUGHTER: Maybe we'll go to Serena's for a while. You're not going to say I can't leave the house, are you? You said if I got better grades you'll let me have more freedom, and I got an A- on my science test.

MOM: Yes, I did. Um, is Serena having a party?

DAUGHTER: Not at all, Mom! You always assume Serena's going to have a huge party, like with kegs and drugs and stuff! I know you don't like her.

MOM: I didn't say I didn't like Serena. (Thinking: How did I get into this?)

DAUGHTER: Yeah, but you don't. I can tell. What's wrong with her having some friends over? It's just a get-together!"

MOM: (Thinking: Is there a difference between a party and a get-together?) Are her parents going to be home?

Does this sound familiar? Like many mothers, you may secretly try to avoid these conversations with your teenager. This is next to impossible, however, as you are probably the parent who gets the brunt of daily questions and requests. No matter how loving and involved fathers are, they usually lack patience for back-and-forth phone calls, complicated arrangements, and last-minute changes. Therefore it may be left up to you to tackle these dialogues, despite the fact that you are unsure about how to approach them, expect that they will be pointless, or fear they will turn unpleasant.

From the start, you may struggle to understand exactly what your daughter is saying. In fact, you may believe you need training in cryptography to decode your daughter's communications. That is because the typical teenage girl employs numerous strategies—some deliberate, others unconscious—to avoid directly answering your questions. You just need to decipher her teenage communication. For example, when you ask your daughter directly whether Jasmine's parents will be home the evening of her party, here are some of her possible replies, the strategies she is employing, and the translations of what she is really saying:

Your daughter's reply	Strategy	What she really means
"Her mom'll definitely be there!"	Half-truth	Her mother will be there when she arrives, but is going to the movies later.
"Of course!"	Out-and-out lie	They're out of town.
"I'm going over to Fiona's house first. Don't worry, we'll figure it out from there."	Evasion	I'll make arrangements that will sidestep direct confrontation.
"Jasmine said they would."	Omission	But she's probably lying.
"We're responsible, Mom!"	Rationalization	We're not, but I don't think that should matter.
"If my stupid sister hadn't gotten drunk, you wouldn't be asking me . . ."	Blaming others	I don't want to take responsibility for this.
"I'm sure she wouldn't be allowed to have a party unless they're home."	Denial	What I don't know won't hurt my plans.
"We're just having a few friends over, Mom!"	Minimization/ Equivocation	If I don't call it a party, it'll be okay with Mom.

Sometimes when you hear these answers you can remain calm and patient enough to rephrase a question and try to sort out what you have learned. You may even be able to step back and think, "What is going on here? What are we *really* talking about?" But like many mothers, at other times you will struggle valiantly to stifle the exasperation (e.g., "Just tell me what's going on already!") and outrage (e.g., "I know you're lying to me; I insist you tell me the truth right now!") that threatens to burst from your lips. On a bad day, you will doubt that even the most sophisticated technology could help you navigate these treacherous conversations.

But knowing how important it is for you and your teenage daughter to be able to sit down together and talk about these daily issues, you know you must hang in there and keep trying. It becomes all too clear why a new collaborative method is necessary (but not always sufficient) to have meaningful discussions.

This approach encourages you to envision discussion a little differently. Conversation is not merely an opportunity to pass on certain messages to your daughter (i.e., lecture her), but a joint venture in which you two work together to explore a dilemma, address the important issues, and, when appropriate, find a mutually agreeable solution. You are essentially using your BRAIN to guide you in Being flexible, Respectful, Attuned, Involved, and Noncontrolling in discussions. Otherwise, your daughter will shut down, there will be no communication, and your influence will be nil.

As you will see, this framework can help you to avoid some of the pitfalls the mother and teenage daughter above encountered in their dialogue about the upcoming party (a classic conversation that may occur weekly in your own home throughout the next several years). Remember, however, that a collaborative approach to discussion does not mean giving your daughter equal say. When it comes to granting permission and other matters, you get to make the final decision. Here is a general formula for making the most of discussions:

Acknowledge Your Part in the Partnership

One of the most powerful ways you demonstrate integrity and convey good faith is to acknowledge to your daughter that your discussion—indeed your entire relationship—is not only about her. You too are an integral part of that partnership. Therefore, you are willing to look at the role you play and the contributions you make to all your interactions and conversations, especially when they do not go smoothly.

This is not merely an exercise. You *are* profoundly affected by your daughter's issues—and you respond accordingly. In fact, it would be absurd to believe that your daughter's life would *not* have an enormous impact on you. For example, when your little girl tearfully admits to you that her best friend excluded her from the lunch table or betrayed the very secret she'd sworn she'd keep forever, your heart breaks for her. You are flooded with emotion, including empathy for your hurt daughter and the painful knowledge that you could neither protect her nor ease her suffering.

In the middle of a conversation with your daughter, you may also become aware of a parallel between your experience as a teenager and hers. Many mothers have described being hit by feelings, some several decades old, that washed over them like an unexpected ocean wave, leaving them momentarily breathless and shaken. If you discover that she is suffering from the stigma of going too far with a boy, for example, you may be caught off guard by the powerful emotions that rush in—awareness of her shame, fury at her poor judgment, and indignation that the boy's reputation remains unscathed. Or, as she speaks of friends who are competitive or unreliable or needy or disappointing, you might react according to your own similar struggles in relationships, past or present. How can these reactions not affect how you speak with your daughter?

There are also more subtle ways that you influence conversations. For example, when she points out a crush, introduces a friend, or speaks to you about her social life, she watches carefully to see how you will react. As girls in this culture learn so well, she reads your facial expression and tone of voice along with your message. She perceives when you wait two beats in order to measure your words. She senses when you bite your tongue, perhaps even guessing at what you hold back. Your daughter takes in and responds to all that information, which, in turn, shapes her own responses to you.

> MOTHER: So, I forget, what classes and activities is Jasmine in?
> DAUGHTER: What do you mean?
> MOTHER: Well, you know, does she get good grades? Is she in any sports?
> DAUGHTER: Why don't you just admit you don't like Jasmine?!
> MOTHER: What? Why are you saying that?
> DAUGHTER: You're doing that thing again. Whenever you hate one of my friends you ask me all these weird questions in a weird voice and you make that sighing noise. You're so obvious!

If there is one thing I learned in raising my own daughter, it is that even when I try my hardest to contain my feelings, rearranging my features and keeping a tight rein on my tongue, she is able to see right through me, always detecting far more than I intend to convey. There never seems to be a way to remain truly neutral! That is why, as you will see below, it is usually better to state your concerns more directly. With thought and practice, you can also become more aware of when your automatic responses to your daughter are shaped more by your own personal sensitivities than by what she is actually saying. Doing so, you will avoid inadvertently derailing discussion.

2. Separate Sass from Substance

The developing teenage mind is capable of probing and analyzing issues differently, profoundly altering your discussions with your daughter. She also has a vested interest in your approving her requests, and truly remarkable determination to convince you to see situations her way. Thus, she is resourceful in using her sharper thinking skills to her advantage. Because she can dig deeper into the underlying meaning of situations, the motives of people, and the nuances of interactions, she may question and challenge almost everything you say. She may interrogate you, grill you, and cross-examine you without pause in an effort to get to the root of your thinking, especially when the conversation doesn't sit right with her. To exploit holes in your arguments, she may use your own past decisions to plead her case. For example, she may retort, "But why can't I go to Jasmine's house tonight? You always let me take a break and relax on Friday nights after a hard week of tests."

In her efforts to convey her pressing needs, along with her outrage about your failure to recognize them, your daughter may patiently rephrase and repeat herself as if speaking to a simpleton. Or, she may use her growing vocabulary and reasoning skills to express all of her viewpoints in various ways until you finally understand—and hopefully even appreciate them. At times you may be shaken by the scathing remarks and biting accusations made possible by your daughter's newfound verbal abilities.

From the perspective of her developing mind and social skills, your daughter's arguments and counterpoints should not be auto-matically interpreted as back talk or sassiness, but rather as efforts to address substantive issues important to either or both of you. Her questioning of you, though admittedly more exhausting than a five-mile run, is not necessarily the same as disparaging you or con-testing your authority. Though her inquisitiveness is most often prompted by your making a decision other than the one she desper-ately wants (i.e., no), your teenage daughter is truly curious about your reasoning.

As you learned in the last chapter, your daughter's sense of self also influences how she approaches conversations. The stronger and more capable she feels, and the more deeply ingrained her beliefs and inclinations, the more vociferously she may challenge you. The clearer her view of justice, the harder it may be for her to let go of perceived unfairness. Although this may intensify or prolong your debates, comfort yourself with the notion that these are the very qualities you want your daughter to have once she leaves home. Be-cause you are giving her the chance to practice being assertive with you, she will be that much better able to voice her opinions and stand up for herself with others.

3. Create a Respectful Tone

Having said all those positive things about discussing important is-sues with your daughter, you may be reassured to know that I am not suggesting you should do so *endlessly* or at all costs. Unless you are careful, this is a real possibility. As you know, your daughter has a great investment in the outcome of your discussions (i.e., your de-cisions), she probably enjoys demonstrating her impressive verbal arguments, and she undoubtedly has far more energy than you to continue discussions. Thus you may find yourself embroiled in de-bates that have taken on a life of their own or become the focal point of family dinners. It is therefore important to set some para-meters for your conversations, according to one of the main princi-ples of parenting: stating clearly what is and isn't acceptable to you.

Judging when conversations are no longer constructive is an art. One, decide when all pertinent questions have been asked and an-swered. After your daughter has given her oral arguments, so to speak, you might summarize what you heard so she knows you really listened and got her perspective. Your decision may not be the one your daughter wanted, but it was based on correctly hearing her position. If your dialogue continues for what seems like forever or goes around in circles, recognize that discussing has probably become badgering.

Two, prevent your discussion from escalating into accusations, yelling, or foul language. Depending upon your own personality and tolerance, your daughter might be given clear limits to refrain from screaming, swearing, name calling, insults, or other actions, which quickly transform constructive conversations into hurtful fighting. When she has an occasional lapse of self-control, you can clearly but firmly reiterate your policy. Though you welcome her thoughts and ideas, and wish to understand her feelings, she must express them respectfully: "I'd like to hear your views, but I won't listen when you yell or speak rudely" or "We're finished discussing this right now."

What if your daughter refuses to listen to you and keeps arguing after you tell her to stop? Not surprisingly, this is one of the questions I hear most frequently from mothers attending my parenting lectures. Since you are the adult, it is up to you to decide when a conversation is getting out of hand and take responsibility for ending it. Some mothers describe persisting in arguments simply because they refuse to give their daughters the satisfaction of having the last word. However, giving in to this wish and granting a teenager's minor victory has always seemed to me a more than acceptable price to pay for terminating a pointless or even destructive discussion.

To ensure that talking stops, it is perfectly reasonable to leave a room, issuing a reminder, "This discussion is over. Come get me when you can talk about this constructively." Close the door of your bedroom or bathroom, play music loudly if you must, and take a deep breath. You are not withdrawing from the relationship, merely ending the conversation. You are not withholding your love, just your immediate attention. This sets the tone for the kind of discussions you want your daughter to have with you and others in the future.

4. Clarify Your Respective Concerns and Goals

Your discussions will have a sharper focus when you and your daughter are clear about what is important to each of you. You both

might be trying to resolve a dilemma, get more information, understand each other's reasoning, or express what is on your mind. During her adolescence, however, you and your daughter may often
have different goals and worries. Yes, you both want her to be happy
and to enjoy a full social life that includes satisfying friendships. But
what your daughter considers in the realm of acceptable or normal
socializing may be completely different from what you consider reasonable or desirable. She will most likely make far more provocative
requests (or demands) during the teenage years because of her far
more pressing social needs.

Your daughter is less interested in pleasing her parents than in
making friends and assuring herself that she fits in with her peers.
You knew that friends would be important at this stage, but perhaps
you underestimated to what degree her social life would become
the be-all and end-all, the primary reason she drags herself out of
her warm bed in the morning to endure boring classes, rushes home
from school in the afternoon to read her e-mail, and dreams
throughout the day of telephone conversations she plans to have
that evening. As such, your daughter's twin goals are to ensure that
(a) she is included in any and all peer group plans, and (b) you do
not stand in the way of her participation.

As the guardian of her health and safety, however, your concerns
about her well-being—and even her survival—may at times over-
shadow these other valid desires.

Using the same discussion of the upcoming party, let's examine
your respective concerns and goals. In this case your daughter's
problem is how to get your permission to go to the party. More immediately she has to decide how best to talk to you so that you will
allow her to attend. While your daughter may truly believe that her
life will be ruined if she isn't at that party, especially if a boy she likes
is supposedly going to show up, your adult perspective may say
otherwise. Your problem, therefore, is whether to grant that permission. Being clear about this helps both of you to get to the point:

NOT

> DAUGHTER: Why are you always interrogating me about
> everything?

> MOTHER: Why are you always bugging me to be with your friends every minute?

OR

> MOTHER: Why can't you stay home once in awhile?

TRY

> MOTHER: Look, I know you really want to go to this party, but we need to talk about the particulars so I know whether that's going to be okay.

Focusing on what each of you want from the conversation prevents you from digressing into general accusations and nastiness and helps you to ignore any sidetracking attempts. Gently nudging the conversation back to your respective goals helps your discussion to be more constructive. For example, you might avoid semantic arguments, such as whether your daughter wants to attend a gathering, a get-together, or a party. Instead, state your concerns clearly, especially emphasizing what is and isn't acceptable to you.

NOT

> MOTHER: Is Serena having a party?
> DAUGHTER: Not at all, Mom! You always assume Serena's going to have a huge party, like with kegs and drugs and stuff! I know you don't like her.

TRY

> MOTHER: We're not comfortable with you socializing at someone's house unless a parent is there. How can we resolve this?

5. Welcome the Process

When you are truly collaborative, not only do you remain involved in your daughter's life, but you also invite her to participate actively in your discussions. It is often the process you go through—rather than the end result—that is most beneficial in the long run. In fact, your discussion has an ultimate goal beyond its immediate outcome (in this case, whether or not she goes to the party). You are teaching your daughter about the vital skills of attentive listening, negotiation, and compromise.

A collaborative approach is key. When she was younger, your daughter may have been satisfied—or even comforted—by statements such as "Because I said so" or "I'm not going to change my mind." However, these tactics rarely work during adolescence. In fact, use them only if you wish to ignite a teenage tantrum! Just when she is bound and determined to feel grown-up and independent, your unilateral decisions rub your daughter's nose in her detested dependency and therefore make her feel infantile. Obeying Mom's rules is now repulsive because this reminds her of the babyish compliance of her earlier years. Instead, she wants to assert her new, liberated self.

Respecting these developmental needs, you will undoubtedly avoid categorical responses that essentially exclude your daughter from the decision-making process. Instead, you want to hear her goals and to understand her point of view. When you voice your own concerns, your daughter learns more about your reasoning, even if she doesn't agree. For example, if you say you are worried that there may be underage drinking at this unsupervised party, your daughter knows what issues she must address in her discussions with you. She realizes your reluctance to let her go is not about her poor quiz grade in French, taking her sister's CD, or even your fight with her father; it is about safety.

Your daughter will come to realize that going to the party is contingent upon her successfully allaying your fears. As long as she is truthful, her persuasive arguments will convince you that she has thought through the issues, anticipated possible consequences, and come up with sensible solutions. In this way you are facilitating your daughter taking on more responsibility for protecting herself.

NOT

> MOTHER: I said you can't go, and that's that!
> DAUGHTER: But why not? This is so unfair!

OR

> MOTHER: I'll talk to your dad about it, and we'll tell you our decision.
> DAUGHTER: You don't understand anything!

TRY

> MOTHER: I can't give you an answer yet. Let's talk about this.
> DAUGHTER: Why do we always have to talk about these things? It's no big deal. Everybody else is going!
> MOTHER: Your father and I don't want you to go to unsupervised parties where there may be drugs and alcohol.
> DAUGHTER: Mom, there are always kids who do that stuff, even when the parents are home.
> MOTHER: Then how can we know if you'll be safe?
> DAUGHTER: I'm not going to drink, Mom. I've had plenty of chances already.
> MOTHER: Why have you decided not to?

When you and your daughter can discuss such important issues collaboratively, with honesty and mutual respect, you are abiding by the values that you may otherwise merely speak of abstractly. Believe me, these efforts will go a long way toward avoiding future problems. Above all, as you explore more specific aspects of adolescent socializing, you will observe over and again that the teenager who repeatedly bumps against the wall of her mother's unremitting restraint often feels compelled to prove her independence through pointedly rebellious, sometimes self-defeating behavior.

6. Don't Expect Immediate Results

Developmentally, you know that your daughter is loathe to agree too readily with you or to be especially appreciative of your input because she wants to feel independent. Therefore, you are unlikely to have this sort of conversation with her:

> MOTHER: I'm uncomfortable with this party because Jasmine's been in trouble a lot at school and hasn't shown

the best judgment in the past. Unless her parents are supervising you, things could easily get out of hand.

DAUGHTER: You're right, Mom. Thank you so much for telling me. I won't go.

In fact, as discussed in the last chapter, in order to forge her own identity she may differentiate herself from you by contesting everything you say and do. Even when she asks for your opinions, it seems to be for the sole purpose of refuting them. Thus, whereas your daughter used to come to you for all the answers, she may now behave as if you don't have *any* answers. At times in fact, she may even seem to pity you for your unfortunate deficiencies!

With this in mind, how can you best approach these conversations?

Realize that your daughter is essentially using you as a sounding board. By challenging you, she is gaining key information about your beliefs, as well as discriminating them from her own. This is how she learns new ideas and sorts through multiple viewpoints, deciding which to take as her own. When she says something especially provocative or even outrageous, don't assume that is what she actually thinks or feels. Then you will be less likely to overreact.

NOT

DAUGHTER: Mom, the whole school gets drunk every weekend. So what?

MOTHER: Is that so? Well, if that's how you feel, I guess you're not going out anymore.

TRY

MOTHER: I don't want you to drink because it's harmful at your age, and I expect that you will always stay in control of yourself.

DAUGHTER: You're so uptight. What's wrong with letting loose once in awhile?

MOTHER: You can relax and have fun without putting yourself at risk. What do you suppose happens to girls who get drunk at parties and can't think clearly?

Her growing appreciation for complexity and nuance may result in her asking probing questions, some of which may make you uncomfortable. In fact, she may suddenly demonstrate a keen interest in breaking through your espoused principles to expose any hint of inconsistency or hypocrisy. Naturally, if your daughter senses any ambivalence or confusion in your thinking, not to mention pretenses in your behavior, she will happily and helpfully point this out to you.

NOT

> DAUGHTER: You're not exactly a teetotaler, Mom. Are you telling me that you never went to parties when you were my age? You never got drunk?
>
> MOTHER: Don't you dare get fresh with me, young lady. You'll find yourself grounded for a month!

TRY

> MOTHER: This discussion is about you and whether this party is a good idea. I don't think at your age you should be with people who are using substances. It's not okay to socialize where there aren't adults around.

Using a collaborative approach to discussion, you also do not expect your daughter to agree instantly to do whatever you suggest. Being noncontrolling means that whenever possible you try to offer suggestions rather than issue demands.

NOT

> MOTHER: If you want to go to the party, call Jasmine right now and say I have to speak to her mother to find out if they will really be home tonight.

TRY

> MOTHER: I can't let you go unless there will be a parent there. How are you going to find out if Jasmine's mother will be home?

OR

> MOTHER: There are a couple of ways you can find out. You might want to speak to her mother directly, or you can ask Jasmine to have her mother call me.

Again, your daughter is unlikely to agree with you or take your position. But know that as long as you are having such discussions, she is listening to your words and digesting them. Learning about your principles, values, and expectations will be helpful when she has to make her own decisions in social situations. Though she might rebut your arguments to your face, an hour later she may use your very words to bolster her own position with her peers. This will be made clear to you the first time you overhear your daughter wisely echo your exact line of reasoning in a conversation with another adult, friend, or sibling.

Being realistic, you know that even your most judicious strategies will not guarantee fruitful discussions with your daughter. Though you may sometimes learn more about what she is thinking and feeling, often you may find yourself trying to converse with a resistant or unresponsive daughter—the quintessential brick wall. What do you do then about getting more information? The next chapter gives you the whole scoop on your alternatives, including the merits and risks of snooping. Read on.

Curfews—A True Collaborative Effort

Here is how you might use curfews—admittedly a prime battle starter in many households—as a wonderful model for constructive, collaborative discussions. After all, when you sit down with your daughter you are discussing far more than a time on the clock that will determine whether she arrives home punctually. I believe the traditional way most parents establish curfews (i.e., a certain time when you're fifteen, half an hour later when you're sixteen) misses the mark in several ways.

One, parents should not decide curfews on their own. To help your daughter learn the most about safety, responsibility, and problem solving, curfew discussions should involve her. Also, the more she actively participates in the negotiation process, the more likely she is to consider her curfew a reasonable, perhaps even tolerable, compromise—and therefore respect it. Two, curfews should not be arbitrary, but rather tailored to every situation. The essential question needs to be: What is the most reasonable hour for your teenage daughter to return home after a particular activity on a particular occasion? Three, curfews should be flexible. Because of changing variables, a curfew established on Friday night may be entirely inappropriate a mere twenty-four hours later, on Saturday night; therefore, curfews must be revisited, if only briefly, on every occasion they are applied.

Arbitrary curfews don't work well, and here's why: Let's say you give your daughter a blanket midnight curfew. If she is going to an eight o'clock movie, what might she do afterward? If she is thirteen, say, and her friends do not yet drive, she might hang out at the theater or elsewhere unsupervised. But if she is sixteen and has her license, she might drive around for an hour or two looking for a party. Thus, unless your daughter has specific plans after the movie, you might prefer that she come right home. However, even if your daughter is only fifteen, given different circumstances you might prefer that she stay out until five A.M. For example, if she is going to the junior prom, that may be the hour when she could be guaranteed a safe ride home.

The first goal of any curfew discussion is probably to establish basic information, such as: what your daughter is planning to do, who she is doing it with, where she is going, and what time *she* thinks it is reasonable to return home. What is her rationale for wanting to stay out until a certain hour? By involving her and inviting her to respond to your challenges, you are eliciting her reasoning. You are thereby giving her partial responsibility for thinking through the situation and coming up with solutions. In this conversation, you will undoubtedly consider such safety issues as the nature and location of her activity, the norms of your community, and your daughter's age and skills.

This is how you might discuss and negotiate these issues with your daughter:

NOT

> DAUGHTER: I'll be home at one.
> MOM: In the morning?
> DAUGHTER: Of course!
> MOM: No way. You'll be home at eleven.
> DAUGHTER: Mom, that's ridiculous! Nobody else has to be home until one. I can't!
> MOM: You can and you will. Be home by eleven or don't go out.

TRY

> DAUGHTER: I'll be home at one.
> MOM: Wait a minute, let's discuss this. What's your plan?
> DAUGHTER: I'm not sure yet. But I think Tina's mom is driving us to the movie and then Audrey's father is picking us up.
> MOM: Who is "us," and what time is the movie you're seeing?
> DAUGHTER: The nine forty-five. And I'm going

with Tina, Audrey, Greg, Dana, and maybe
Tyler.

MOM: So what are you going to do from eleven
forty-five until one?

DAUGHTER: Audrey's father is taking us all to
the diner.

MOM: I'll be comfortable with this plan if you
definitely have rides both ways. And you have
to call me when you get to the diner.

DAUGHTER: Fine.

If you give your daughter a curfew, you need to enforce it by staying awake or asking her to wake you
when she gets home. Otherwise, what is the point?
Prudent vigilance suggests checking in with your
daughter whenever she arrives after an evening out.
Always acknowledge and appreciate her punctuality, as
this is not only courteous but increases the chance of
her being on time in the future.

Flagrant or repeated violations of curfews demand
immediate discussion of what is going wrong and what
your daughter can do in the future to rectify the situation. Although some mothers—and even parenting
experts—advocate strict adherence to curfews (i.e.,
consequences for even one minute past the designated
time), as long as your daughter is making a concerted
effort to honor her curfew, it may be foolhardy to
make an issue out of only a few minutes' lateness, especially if it is infrequent. When you give her the
benefit of the doubt, you are making deposits of goodwill in the mother-daughter relationship.

Chapter 5

To Snoop or Not to Snoop
INFORMATION GATHERING

"Since my daughter's become a teenager, she's been so secretive about everything in her life that I'm afraid I have no idea what's going on. It's especially scary because I don't know how I'd be able to tell if anything is wrong. What if she is having a problem I don't know about? The other day I decided that I really had to find out what's going on, so I went into her room and looked around. I went through her desk drawers, where she keeps a lot of papers. I found notes she had written to friends and little scraps of papers with poems she had started. I couldn't believe some of those things! There were a lot of references to sex—things she obviously knows about and thinks, things she said she wanted to do with boys. I can't believe it was my daughter who actually wrote those words! Now I'm even more scared. Were those just wishes, or is she actually going to do some of those things? What should I be doing about this?"

—Penelope, thirty-nine

"While I was doing the laundry I found something in the back pocket of my daughter's jeans. It was a note that one of her closest friends had written to her, a girl I've known since they were in preschool together. Maybe I shouldn't have done this, but I read the note. It was quite shocking. My daughter's friend used vulgar language, she made reference to 'getting trashed,' and she mentioned what several girls in my daughter's group supposedly did last weekend. I have no idea what I'm supposed to do now. Should I tell my daughter I found the note? Should I assume it's true? Should I tell her friends' parents? I've never dealt with a situation like this before. There's no manual I can check to see what is recommended."

—Sasha, forty-five

"A few days ago when I was in the pharmacy, I bumped into two women who are the mothers of my daughter's friends. What they told me

made my blood run cold. They found out that last Friday night our girls actually left the youth group meeting where we had dropped them off and went to a party. An older boy apparently picked them up and drove them over to another boy's house whose parents weren't home. I'm planning to confront my daughter, but I'm not sure just how to do it. If she tries to deny it, I certainly have proof. But if she asks me how I found out, should I tell her the truth? It could start a big problem between my daughter, her friends, and their parents. It's a horrible feeling to find this out from someone else!" —Arianna, forty-nine

*T*he minute you walk into your daughter's room, you are amazed to spot her tiny, red-striped diary sitting right at the edge of her bed, in plain sight where you and anyone else could see it. When you realize that it is unlocked, its little silver key on her night stand, you are absolutely riveted. At once several different thoughts begin to swirl through your head. Your first impulse is to rush over, grab it, and pore through those pages. Once and for all you would know what is really going on in your daughter's life. You would get all the specifics you're dying for, but that she doesn't seem to tell you anymore. More than that, you could finally understand what is going on in her mind—what she *really* thinks, and how she *really* feels about all the important matters. It is particularly tempting because lately you have been wondering if she has been completely honest with you.

It is only right, you tell yourself, that you remain in touch with your daughter's life throughout her teenage years. As her mother, it is your parental responsibility to be informed. After all, how are you supposed to help her, guide her, and protect her if you don't know what she is thinking and doing? Yet you can't completely ignore your own inner voice, which is at this moment questioning whether it is right to peek into your daughter's most private possession, her personal diary. Is it ever okay to snoop?

"Wait a minute," you remind yourself, "the girls were talking about something the other day that got me worried." Overhearing their whispered giggles from the next room, you thought you thought you heard the words "staying in the grass," "high," and "all summer." You couldn't help but become a bit suspicious. Surely reading your daughter's diary is the only way to reassure yourself that she is neither in trouble nor heading in that direction. As her mother, isn't it your right—indeed, even your obligation—to act on such concerns? Of course, you have to ensure your daughter's safety.

Now all you have to do is figure out the best way to do that.

This chapter will help you evaluate what you need to know and your best bets for finding out that information. As you progress through these pages, you will feel more confident in assessing whether or not you should snoop into your daughter's life.

Your Need to Know

Unless your ever-more-private teenage daughter chooses to tell you information about her world—her friends, her desires, her romances, her worries, her school life—how are you supposed to remain aware and involved? Even with the wisest approach to discussions, as described in the last chapter, you don't always get all the information you want or need. You would like to know—and, I believe, it is prudent to find out—who your daughter mingles with on a Saturday night, where she is hanging out after school, and what she actually does when she is out of your sight. If you are to remain involved in her life, these are not unreasonable questions.

Will you know everything? Absolutely not. But learning at least something of what is going on helps you to better appreciate and empathize with her experiences. Knowing about her everyday life keeps you more closely connected with her. Also, you need as much information as possible to make good judgments. Despite these legitimate needs, however, many mothers complain that it is difficult to obtain even the most basic facts about their daughters' whereabouts and activities.

In addition, there are circumstances that make your desire for information feel more urgent. One, as your daughter progresses through adolescence and becomes more reticent about her life, you may feel left out. After X number of years of hearing her confidences, the realization that you are no longer privy to her social world can be disappointing and even disturbing. Consequently some mothers become bound and determined to wangle their way back into their daughter's inner circle, any way they can.

Two, your daughter's lack of communication with you can make you uneasy. The less she talks, the more you may worry that there is something she is withholding from you. The more you perceive her as vague or evasive or nonforthcoming, the more wary you may feel. Your mounting apprehension may reach a point when it is intolerable; you may think, "I have to know what's really going on, and I have to know it now."

Three, your desire for information may be intensified by the sense that your daughter is being less than truthful. In fact, you may become concerned about what she could be trying to cover up. Even worse, you may learn for a fact that your daughter has lied to you. An actual breach of trust is like a crack in the cement that binds you and your daughter together. Your recognition that "Maybe I am not as in tune with her as I thought" can intensify your desperation and determination to find out the absolute truth.

Four, getting more information about your daughter and her life seems an absolute necessity if she messes up—or appears to. In a crisis you need to know everything, you need to know it fast, and you need it to be true. For example, you may get a call from her school principal that she broke a rule, fought with a classmate, or was disrespectful to a teacher. Your daughter may be arrested. You may find a pill on the floor of her room or a condom wrapper in her garbage. Obviously, the more potentially serious the problem, the more intense your efforts to find out specifics.

It is not that the truth will always allay or even eliminate your worries. While your daughter's clarifications will sometimes put your mind to rest, at other times your anxiety will climb further. Knowing this, some mothers are tempted not to probe for fear of what they may unearth. However, in my experience an "ignorance is bliss" approach to child rearing is not only unwise but often regretted. When mothers eventually do find out upsetting information about their daughters, they often confide, "I should have known about this sooner." When a problem left unchecked has grown bigger, mothers are sorry they haven't "already done something to deal with it."

For many reasons, therefore, it is wise to have as much accurate information as you can to parent your teenager effectively. Yet at the same time, how you go about getting facts is just as critical. The strategies you use to gather information enormously affect the kind of relationship you will have with your daughter during these adolescent years.

Information: Aim for Getting Just Enough

When you suspect your daughter may be in trouble, or in times of actual crisis, it will be clearer that you need to get the whole story— no matter how she feels about it. At such times risking her displeasure is the least of your problems. But when it comes to everyday matters, the issue becomes, "How much information do I really need?" In fact, you will probably need to grapple with this question over and again, perhaps each time you are confused, worried, or feel excluded from your daughter's life. As a general guide, though, using your BRAIN will not steer you wrong.

Being flexible, for example, you anticipate that the amount and nature of information you get directly from your daughter will vary according to her personality, prevailing mood, and the stress she is experiencing at any given time. You will thereby adjust your expectations. Beatrice, forty-seven, says, "My daughter Elise is the most exasperating child I know. I'm very open about things and willing to talk, but she couldn't be more opposite. She never tells me anything! Her best friend, Janelle, tells her mother everything, even which boys she kisses. I'm so jealous." In fact, during Beatrice's frequent conversations with Janelle's mother, she often hears tidbits she otherwise would never have known. "Just yesterday," she says, "I found out the new boy in school asked Elise out several times, but she kept turning him down. This was news to me!"

When you are Respectful of your daughter's privacy, you refrain from prying unnecessarily. Although Beatrice used to wonder what she was doing to discourage Elise's confidences and would take her daughter's reticence more personally, she now accepts that, "This is just my daughter's way." She is more willing to wait for her daughter to speak up, or to be satisfied with whatever she learns from her conversations with others. Choosing not to share what she learns from Janelle's mother, for example, she respects her daughter's right to decide if and when she wants to discuss these matters. In this way, Beatrice also tries to be Attuned to her daughter's cues.

Aiming to get just enough information helps you to be appropriately Involved in your daughter's life. Like many mothers, you may struggle to strike that ideal balance between too hands-off and too intrusive. On the one hand, paying close attention to whatever information is available helps you to stay involved. For example, Cornelia, forty-eight, received a phone call from the mother of one of her daughter's closest friends, alerting her to the possibility that the girls may have been involved in an incident of vandalism in their community. However, she discounted the woman's concerns before following up and investigating them. If she had been absolutely honest with herself, Cordelia would have admitted that she was choosing not to know this information. Being less involved in her daughter's day-to-day activities was more comfortable for her.

On the other hand, no matter how interested and involved you want to be, do not expect to pry out of your daughter the details of who was involved in the latest high school substance scandal or what emergency prompted her friend's frantic phone call. Recognizing that she wants and needs more privacy, make a concerted effort not to intrude. Not only is it unwise to interrogate her about the specifics of her life, but when she and her gang are around, honor the in-jokes and the conspiratorial looks that cloak them in secrecy. Seek the most appropriate degree of involvement.

It is worth noting that a few mothers report feeling *too* involved in their daughters' lives—and not by choice. These mothers hear each exquisite detail of their daughters' daily life: the blow-by-blow of every argument, the precise manner in which a friend made a fool of herself, exactly how a boy got sick when he drank too much at a party . . . you get the idea. If you are one who needs a crowbar to extract information from your daughter, you might wish to trade places with these mothers. However, there is a downside to being too involved. As Robin, forty-five, says, "There are times when my daughter gives me *way* too much information. She's too old to tell me every little thing. And besides, I get sucked onto her emotional roller coaster. One day she's on cloud nine because the boy she likes smiles and says hi when she's at her locker, and the next day she comes home in a terrible mood because he walks right by her. I wouldn't be a teenager again for anything. It's upsetting and exhausting just hearing about it."

Finally, you are Noncontrolling when you give your daughter the degree of privacy that is appropriate for her age. Obviously, it is easier to accept her having her own life when she is finishing high school than when she is still in middle school. Still, to refrain from trying to control her, don't order her to fess up about her latest crush. Try not to insist that she tell you what is on her mind (as if you could). With the usual pang, you may realize that part of letting your daughter go gradually is admitting that you cannot control completely what she shares with you. Be sure to make clear, however, what is and is not acceptable to you in terms of her privacy.

Privacy: Rethinking Your Past

As always, before you can convey your values to your daughter, you need to be clear in your own mind. You might first reflect on where your ideas and biases about privacy come from. Of course your own upbringing is undoubtedly a key source. As a teenager how did you and your parents handle this issue? Did your mother grant you privacy to make phone calls, keep personal papers safe from prying eyes, and visit with your friends? Or did she think it was her right to go through your belongings? Did you ever think she overstepped her bounds and, if so, how did you feel about that? Just as important, how did your mother's approach to privacy affect your relationship?

How much did you choose to tell your mother about your life? Do you remember deliberately deciding not to disclose certain information? Looking back, many mothers realize sheepishly that although they related to their mothers only a fraction of what actually happened, somehow they expect their own teenage daughters to tell them the minutiae of their lives. If you didn't tell your mother who you were dying to date, why you were avoiding your former best friend, and whether you sampled beer at someone's cookout, why should you expect your daughter to tell you? Once again, you may have thought that because you are so much savvier than your own mother, your daughter would surely keep you in her loop. Unfortunately, it probably isn't working that way.

If you lied to your mother and snuck around behind her back, ask yourself why you did so. Were you afraid of her disapproval or punishment? Were you ashamed to tell her the truth? Did keeping part of your life to yourself make you feel more grown-up—or guilty? These insights may help you to be more attuned to your daughter's feelings about privacy. Keep in mind, however, that your daughter might not feel the same way you did about these issues. She may not be inclined to share every last detail of her life with you, even if that is what you did with your mother. If this is your expectation, you may be disappointed, angry, or worried about what could be wrong with her. You might need to accept that the norm for your relationship with your daughter will be different.

Clarify Your Parameters About Privacy

Once you sort out your past influences, you might examine how they shape your beliefs about raising a teenage daughter today. How does privacy fit in with your goals of teaching her to make smart choices, accept responsiblility, and take good care of herself in relationships? It is wise to convey these ideas straightforwardly with your daughter. Early on, have a discussion about your family's values. You might explain that as she grows up, both of you will have a number of difficult choices to make about what to share with each other and what to keep to yourselves.

Spell out how much privacy you think is appropriate—and, of course, the conditions under which her rights will be revoked. For example, you might clarify whether or not you believe your daughter's room and its contents are off-limits to you. Or conversely, do you consider her bedroom part of your home and, therefore, anything within its walls within your domain? Some mothers find it acceptable to search their daughters' rooms and to read anything they can find. I believe that although you may certainly gain additional information this way, you stand to lose far more—specifically, your daughter's respect, her trust in you, and immeasurable goodwill in your relationship. If you must use this approach, at least warn your daughter so that she is prepared.

Other mothers believe it is inappropriate to search through pockets, drawers, and backpacks, but consider fair game whatever their daughters leave lying around on dressers, beds, or bathroom counters. Their thinking goes, "If my daughter left it out, I'm entitled to look at it." If you happen to find her e-mail screen on the computer or trip over the journal she left on the den floor, do you believe you have the right to read them? This issue is less clear. In fact, you might wonder if she left these items out so that you would see them. You may not know for sure, but consider the possibility that something is troubling her that she would like you to know but cannot tell you directly. Wherever you draw the line in these situations, be sure that your daughter knows what to expect.

Most especially, your daughter might be told how far you would go to get information about her without her knowledge or permission. What circumstances, if any, do you believe would warrant your snooping? For the reasons that will be explored later in this chapter, I believe you should assure her that you see this as a last resort, to be attempted only after all other sources of information have been exhausted, and only if you have genuine, significant concerns about her health or safety. Although your daughter will not act happy about the prospect of your delving into her life, on some level she will be relieved to know that you are committed to doing anything and everything in your power to protect her. You can also point out to her the obvious: The more she tells you, the less you will feel in the dark, anxious, and compelled to snoop for information.

Why She Doesn't Disclose Everything

You would think that your daughter would be so eager to dissuade you from getting information by talking about her with other people or, heaven forbid, snooping around, that she would attempt to be forthcoming. Yet as you well know, trying to get basic facts can be as maddening as squeezing out the last drop in a tube of toothpaste. In response to a question as straightforward as "What did you guys do all afternoon?" your daughter may dole out monosyllables that do little to clarify your understanding (e.g., "I dunno," "What?", or "Not much").

Candice, forty-three, describes a common dynamic: "My fourteen-year-old daughter has practically become a clam. I'm kind of worried about what I don't know. Maybe everything is fine, but I can't be sure. What if there's something wrong, and she won't tell me?" The more closed your daughter is, the more frantic you can become to extract information. When she feels that you are virtually prying her open she redoubles her resistance to self-disclosure. Thus your efforts not only fail miserably but backfire. In turn, you become increasingly frantic to reach her. This vicious cycle has inspired many a frustrated mother to declare, "I'm at my wit's end. I give up!"

Appreciating why your daughter may not be as forthcoming as you would like can be helpful. Here are a few reasons:

"I Don't Know!"

When you ask your daughter what she thinks or how she feels about a situation and she says she doesn't have a clue, don't assume she's purposely being evasive. The truth is, she may *not* have a clue. During the adolescent years, girls are often overwhelmed by confusing, conflicting, and mercurial emotions. At any given time, she may be unable to verbalize her thoughts or describe her feelings. Thus your daughter can be completely flummoxed by your perfectly reasonable inquiry about how she feels. In fact, she may think, "How am I supposed to know?" Moreover, you may get caustic responses to your questions simply because they highlight your daughter's confusion or heighten her discomfort.

"It's Too Embarrassing!"

What you may consider mundane or even trivial your daughter may find too humiliating to express. If she and her friend have a fight about something your daughter said or did, she may be too self-conscious to share it with you or anyone else. You may understand her reluctance to divulge her foibles to others, but would hope and even expect her to feel comfortable telling you. After all, you are her mother! But for this very reason you may be the last to know. Your daughter may want to present herself as mature, sophisticated, and capable in order to gain your approval or permission. However, don't assume that the details your daughter considers too embarrassing would be alarming; you might well think the issue rather unimportant.

"It's Too Hard to Explain!"

Whether or not it is truly difficult for your daughter to explain, when she says this what she usually means is "I don't want to explain." She may not want to bother articulating something just because you are interested in it. Moreover, she might consider an incident that occurred a half hour ago to be ancient history not worthy of recounting. Maybe she wonders why you would even care. Or perhaps what she means is that your question addressed the very tip of the proverbial iceberg; explaining would require tremendous background material that she has neither the desire nor the inclination to share with you. Take this comment to mean "Never mind, Mom" and don't push her unless you have a good reason to do so.

"It's No Big Deal!"

When your daughter minimizes the importance of your question, she is indicating her uneasiness in giving you a response. Maybe she is withholding facts from you because she knows you would disapprove. By not telling you, she is avoiding the internal discomfort (and probable consequences) of your objection. Even when she says the matter is no big deal, however, your daughter's behavior conveys something different. She is telling you that she can anticipate your reaction because she knows your values. And that, to you, is the big deal. In this particular case, she may have chosen to take a path different from the one you would have recommended. But at least you know that she knows where you stand. If her safety is not at risk, let the matter go.

"Why Should I Tell You?"

When your daughter counters your inquiry with this loaded question, she surely has something on her mind. She may be implying that she is uncomfortable divulging information to you because of any number of complaints: You don't listen carefully enough, you will be judgmental, you will punish her, etc. In addition to these problems, however, your daughter also may be worried that sharing information with you about her friends would be tattling on them. Above all, teenage girls have an inviolable code of ethics that dictates: Never, under any circumstances, rat on a peer to an adult. That means she will avoid disclosing names of other teenagers or discussing specifics of rumors making the rounds: which classmate was arrested for possession of marijuana, who reportedly has sex with multiple partners, or who was caught cheating. It is important, however, not to interpret her protectiveness of her peers as an endorsement of their behavior. Her refusal to provide or even confirm incriminating information simply honors this unspoken understanding among teenagers. Whether or not you agree with this policy, you probably have to respect it.

"It's My Business!"

This exclamation is essentially a declaration of your daughter's independence. Because she wishes desperately to escape any situation redolent of her earlier childhood, she is protesting your continued maternal watchfulness. What she really means is that she loathes your need to "know every little thing about me!" Again, the information your daughter chooses to withhold is not necessarily worrisome; it is just hers. One of the questions I hear most often from teenagers is "How can I get my mother to stop being so nosy? She reads my mail, and listens to phone conversations, and won't give me any space."

These protests, which are legitimate signs of your daughter's maturation, are worth considering. In many cases, particularly when matters are not serious or scary, it will be reasonable for you to back off, giving her the privacy she craves and ought to have. At the same time, you can teach your daughter what she can do to make this easier for you. She can remember this simple formula: The more she keeps open the lines of communication, the more she enables you to relax. Rather than clamming up and frustrating you with non-answers to your questions, your daughter can learn to say:

> DAUGHTER: Sorry, Mom, but this is private between my friend and me.

OR

> DAUGHTER: I don't want to talk about that, but it's definitely nothing bad.

OR

> DAUGHTER: I promised my friend I would keep her secret. It's nothing dangerous.

When you give your daughter appropriate privacy, you are powerfully declaring your respect and confidence in her. Perhaps not at that particular moment, and maybe not even when you would most desire it, but in time that trust will pay dividends. I can't guarantee this, of course, but if you have laid the groundwork, sometime in the future your daughter will suddenly and spontaneously confide in you. Meanwhile, on occasion you may be faced with the need to get more information than she seems inclined to share. Before you decide to snoop, you might ask yourself this series of questions:

Have I Gotten the Most Out of My Observations?

It is possible to get terrific information about your daughter without asking, probing, interrogating, or snooping—just by using your powers of observation. Consider my top four recommendations:

• *Adopt the Wallpaper Solution*

An excellent source of information about your daughter's social life is observing her and her friends in all sorts of places: when you volunteer at school, when they are invited to your home, when you take them somewhere, or when you see them leaving an activity. Yet you may underestimate the value of observation because you know that teenagers tend to get self-conscious and turn silent when adults are in the vicinity. Strategically then, your best bet is to adopt the demeanor of tasteful wallpaper. By that I mean you should be everywhere—but fade into the background. You don't want to be so visible or loud that you call attention to yourself or become unbearable. Your goal is to create a cozy and soothing presence that will make your daughter and her friends forget you are there, get comfortable enough to be themselves, and speak freely.

• *Take Note of Her Interests*

You can also learn more about your daughter by being attentive to her interests. Make it a point to listen to some of her favorite music. What is the emotional tone? The message? Take a look at the magazines she reads. Ask your daughter to explain the meaning of any unfamiliar slang expressions. Staying current with both the ever-evolving lingo and fleeting fads helps you to interpret what you hear. With your daughter, watch television programs that portray teenagers. Asking her how she would have handled the story's predicaments not only tells you what topics your daughter is familiar with, but also gives you insights into her thinking. When you discuss fictional characters rather than her or her friends, you are apt to learn more about your daughter's real views.

Similarly, you get valuable information about your daughter's social views when you see her criticizing her friends and, especially, her siblings. You may hear her, for example, berate her sister for being mean to a younger girl, for lying to a friend, or for failing to keep a promise. Instead of asking her to be quiet or telling her to mind her own business, you might use these situations to learn more about your daughter.

For example, according to Lin, forty-six, her seventeen-year-old daughter, Amy, "went ballistic when her fifteen-year-old sister, Lacey, started a rumor at their school about a new girl who was getting to know Lacey's best friend. She came home furious about her sister's behavior and was determined to berate her until Lacey apologized and made amends. I asked both the girls what they thought was a reasonable thing to do when you feel threatened by someone. I ended up finding out that each of them had had the experience of someone's encroaching upon her special friendship. It was great to learn how they thought they should handle jealous feelings and still feel good about themselves."

• *Look Out for Auto Communication*

Just as you can learn more about your daughter while driving alone with her in the car, chauffeuring groups of teens offers invaluable opportunities to get a keener view of their social life. Before they learn to drive, volunteer to take your daughter and her friends shopping, to athletic practices or games, and to the movies. This strategy offers several advantages. When you are the parent picking them up from parties, you get a firsthand impression of what may have happened there and whether there were any problems. Also, you know for sure that your daughter's ride home has not been drinking!

Let the girls choose their own radio station, tape, or CD so they feel comfortable in the car. Once they relax and are immersed in conversation, their voices will often block out the music. When you act like wallpaper in the car, your teenage passengers will perceive you as concentrating intently on driving. Remarkably, they will virtually forget you are there. As if a plastic partition has sealed off their compartment in the car, they will speak as if they don't think you can hear them. Don't comment or ask any questions! If you are lucky, you will hear many interesting facts and get a vivid picture of the dynamics and goings-on among your daughter and her friends.

• *Be Watchful at Home*

As far-fetched as this may sound, a commonly overlooked source of information is actually what goes on in your own home—not only if you are away, but while you are present, either busy doing something or fast asleep. Many mothers have been devastated to discover that they missed signs that daughters had been engaging in inappropriate or risky activities. Belinda, forty-nine, for example, had difficulty awakening her fifteen-year-old daughter and a friend after a sleepover. "I had been suspicious that her crowd was drinking at parties, and was trying to find what was going on. The answer was right under my nose! The girls apparently went into my liquor cabinet and helped themselves to vodka. They could have gotten alcohol poisoning, they could have died while I was asleep in my bed." Other mothers have learned that preteens explored pornographic Web sites on their family computers.

Even more worrisome, I hear many stories in therapy about teenage girls whose mothers are unaware of sexual activities in their own homes. For example, some girls sneak in friends during the wee hours of the night. Jamee, sixteen, says, "My friend Delia told these guys she knows to come over, so we went down to her basement and she let them in through the garage so her parents wouldn't hear. She went in the next room with this guy she likes, while me and this other girl sat and watched TV with his two friends. When they all left, we went back upstairs to go to sleep."

You would be amazed how often I hear of girls who routinely sneak out of their homes while their parents are sleeping. In the suburban area in which I practice, those who are too young to drive call older friends or taxis to take them to surrounding towns, where they go to parties, meet boys, and sometimes drink or take drugs—scenes their parents know absolutely nothing about. Then toward dawn, they sneak back into their homes. These are not girls who would be considered severely troubled, nor do they come from terribly dysfunctional families. Many are fairly good students. However, for a variety of reasons they crave the stimulation of risk-taking adventures, and prove resourceful in carrying them out without their parents catching on.

Hearing these stories over and again in the therapy office has convinced me that mothers need to be more watchful at home. Not only can observation potentially keep your daughter from dangerous activities, it can also clue you in to what is really going on in her social life.

2. Have I Approached My Daughter Most Effectively?

Being more alert and observant, perhaps you spot an item in your daughter's room that has made you uneasy. Or maybe you hear a potentially incriminating story about her and her friends. It may be unclear whether the issue is minor or serious. You need to get further information from her so you know whether there is indeed cause for alarm. However, you would like to avoid starting World War III in the process. So how can you best confront your daughter with your concerns? Here are some strategies to ease the way:

• *Be Aboveboard*

Although you may walk on eggshells for fear of provoking your daughter's fury or indignation, avoid beating around the bush with her. When girls have to guess the reason their mothers want to speak with them, they quickly become frustrated and find ways to end the conversation. Plus, some teenagers may worry that you are upset about something far worse than what they are presently imagining. So take a deep breath and say what you have to say—tactfully and nonprovocatively.

NOT

> MOTHER: You know what I'm talking about, don't you? I'll bet you can guess.

TRY

> MOTHER: We need to talk about what happened last night after you were dropped off at school for the dance.

• *Gauge Her Approachability*

Although your heart may be in your throat when you are anxious to find out something from your daughter, be attuned to when she is most receptive to talking. This may require you to be patient just when you feel least able to do so. For example, since she might be prickly in the morning but less guarded when sleepy, you may have to wait until bedtime. Or your daughter may let down her guard when she is coming down with a cold or otherwise in need of comfort. It often takes self-control not to blurt out your most rampant worries!

NOT

> MOTHER: Come on, you'll be late for school. But while you're getting your coat, tell me who called so late last night and what was such an emergency?

TRY

> DAUGHTER: I'm freezing, Mom. Can you make me some hot chocolate?
> MOTHER: Sure. Do you have any plans for tonight?
> DAUGHTER: Not really. Nothing special, anyway.
> MOTHER: No? Oh, by the way, I was wondering . . .

Similarly, even though you may have obsessed about a particular issue all day while your daughter was at school and are now most eager to get to the bottom of it, try not to pounce on her the moment she gets off the bus in the afternoon. Occasionally a girl may be eager to spill or more accurately, to dump the stresses of her school day on her mother. But if you are trying to get your daughter to talk, this may in fact be one of the worst possible times.

NOT

> MOTHER: Before you start your homework, there's something I have to ask you about.
> DAUGHTER: Oh, no! Please, go away! I had the worst day! My science teacher gave me a C+ on my lab report just because I forgot to put in one little section. And now you're bugging me!
> MOTHER: We'll get to your science grade in a minute. First off, let's talk about who called you so late last night. Was there a problem?

Teenagers often flee to their rooms precisely to escape interrogations. Your daughter may need her solitude to review her day, its high and low points, to analyze conversations, and to assess her status with various friends and potential romances. When you knock on her door to find her lying on her bed, don't assume she is doing nothing. Your daughter may be engrossed in riveting reflection or reexamination. If so, she is apt to see your attempted friendliness as an interference—if not an outright intrusion—into her reverie. As Violet, fifteen, describes, "I just like to lie in my room and chill for a while, you know, to think about my day and stuff. But my mom keeps knocking, like every five minutes. First she has to give me something, then she needs to get something, then she has to ask me something. Why can't she just leave me alone?"

TRY

> MOTHER: You look tired. Why don't you rest before dinner?
> DAUGHTER: Yeah, that sounds good.
> MOTHER: Do you think you can finish your homework at a decent hour? I'd love to spend some time together.
> DAUGHTER: I think so.

• *Portray Curiosity*

When you approach your daughter to get important information, your heart may be pounding and you may be sweating more profusely than when you work out. After all, you want to know and at the same time, you may be afraid of what you may hear. But this is when you might work hard to keep your emotions in check. Your daughter is less apt to go on the defensive or clam up when you approach her with matter-of-fact curiosity. For example, avoid being accusatory. Also, be careful you don't inadvertently *tell* your daughter how she is feeling, for that will surely put an end to any inquiry. Above all, to encourage your daughter to talk, you should not assume you already know the answers to your questions.

NOT

> MOTHER: What the heck is this baggie in your garbage? Are you on drugs? You'd better come clean right now, or I'll haul you over to rehab.
> DAUGHTER: Are you crazy?

TRY

> MOTHER: You know, I found this in your garbage and I'm wondering what it is.
> DAUGHTER: What do you mean?
> MOTHER: I mean, what was it for and why is it in your garbage?

• *Respond to Her Cues*

To make the right decision about when to back off a topic and when to press on, you might be responsive to your daughter's cues. When she claims she doesn't have answers to your questions, avoid pressuring her or berating her (e.g., "You *must* know!"). Instead, wonder aloud (e.g., "Maybe it seems confusing right now" or "It might be hard to talk about your friends"). This puts a powerful suggestion in your daughter's mind that she may be inclined to think about in private. Similarly, you might relate a story about a past situation that is similar to hers (e.g., "When I was your age, I accidentally did something that made your grandmother nuts with worry. . . ."). If you see that she is not inclined to divulge information, suggest that she reflect a bit and agree to check in with her later.

3. Have I Exhausted Alternate Sources of Information?

Like some mothers, you might try coaxing, cajoling, or even bribing your daughter to divulge information, all to no avail. You simply cannot force her to talk. When it comes to the really big or important issues, you won't be able to stop there. So what is your best response when your daughter is obviously distressed or displaying signs of potential problems and yet stonewalls even your gentlest inquiries? You might want to explore these other avenues:

• *Maintain Community Contacts*

To stay informed and up-to-date, get involved in your community. You may volunteer in the school, which gives you marvelous opportunities to monitor your daughter and her classmates. Just recently I made a few interesting observations during my son's eighth-grade lunch period while I collected permission slips for a skating party sponsored by a community drug awareness organization.

Similarly, when you serve on a committee in your synagogue or church, participate in neighborhood or charitable organizations, or attend parent-teacher association meetings, lectures, or workshops, you may get unexpected information. These events often give you the chance to chat informally with the mothers of your daughter's friends. During these conversations, you may glean interesting snippets that complete the picture you have been forming about what is going on in your daughter's life. When you read the local paper and school newsletter, you get the lowdown on what is going on among youth in your community. All this intelligence supplements what your daughter tells you, enabling you to make more informed and sensible decisions.

• *Call the School*

If you need more information about your daughter's overall adjustment or details of what may be going on socially, you might consider calling her school. School personnel can be a terrific source of information beyond your daughter's academics. For example, guidance counselors are often in the know about girls' general contentment, specific difficulties, and shifting social patterns. Teachers, library staff, and cafeteria aides are in a good position to observe your daughter's daily demeanor and interactions with classmates. In my experience, principals and vice principals are a wealth of information about their students. If you are concerned about your daughter, don't hesitate to call. You don't have to say that you suspect a problem or specify the exact nature of your worries. Simply ask for a progress report on your daughter. How is she doing? Have her teachers noted any changes in her behavior or performance? Do they have any concerns?

• *Speak to Other Moms*

There are times when you might want to consider speaking with other mothers to get more information. I don't mean that you should ask pointed questions about their own children's whereabouts and activities, for obvious reasons. I also would not recommend that you pass on rumors you have heard or make known your own worst fears about teenagers in your community. Although you may have close friends with whom you can share such confidences and ask delicate questions, you probably want to avoid putting the mothers of your teenager's friends on the spot by asking them specifics about your daughter.

A preferable route is to ask general, gentle questions. For example, you might wonder, "How did your daughter's party go the other night?" or "What have you heard about the new teen center?" Based on the mother's replies, you can follow up with "What happened?" or "What is your sense of that?" or "Is there anything we should be concerned about?" In this way you are welcoming further details, but not interrogating the other mother or pressuring her to talk about topics that may make her uncomfortable. Even in a casual conversation, you never know when someone will off-handedly mention a fact that to you is a major news bulletin. That is one reason why keeping in touch with other mothers potentially benefits all of you by allowing you to pool your information.

4. Am I Aware of the Pitfalls of Snooping?

According to *Merriam-Webster's Collegiate Dictionary*, to snoop is "to prowl or pry; to go about in a sneaking, prying way." But your daughter's probable definition of snooping is this: any behavior that results in your knowing things about her or her life that she didn't choose to tell you herself. Although some parents are hiring detectives, relatives, or siblings to tail their teenagers and report on their activities, this is hardly an approach I would suggest.

Similarly, whereas some women believe reading diaries is a perfectly acceptable way of keeping in touch with their daughters' thinking and activities, others are appalled by the notion. Since this controversy is one of the most frequent issues I am asked to comment on by both parents and journalists, I will discuss the diary in some detail. First, it is important to consider how the typical teenage girl views her journal or diary.

• *What Your Daughter's Diary Means to Her*

Because she believes her diary is totally private, this is the one place your daughter can comfortably express her innermost feelings, thoughts, dreams, fears, fantasies, hopes, and frustrations. She assumes her words will be completely confidential, read by no one but herself. Therefore, she does not bother to make distinctions between fact and fantasy. She documents freely her every emotion, no matter how transient or insincere or melodramatic. Any complaints about others are cheerfully detailed, without concerns about whether they are deserved or exaggerated. It does not matter if, upon rereading yesterday's entry, your daughter says to herself, "I said I hated Mom? I wonder why?" or "I can't believe I thought *that;* how stupid!" The things she believes with all her heart on Monday morning are often viewed as totally ridiculous by Tuesday—or even, possibly, by Monday night. So how can you know how she *really* feels?

Your daughter's diary assists her in building her sense of self specifically because it enables her to sort through her thoughts and feelings without reserve. In her writing, she can safely adopt different attitudes, beliefs, and personas without fear of being judged or having to defend herself. She can critique people closest to her without anxiety about inciting their anger or retribution. That is, unless you snoop.

- *Interpreting the Information*

Whether the information you get from snooping comes from her diary, e-mail, letters, notes, or creative writing, it is difficult—if not impossible—to determine whether what your daughter expresses happens to be true. For example, suppose you read in her short story about a gym teacher who is a "scary psycho pervert." Alarmed about what this could mean, you may read and reread that story looking for clues. Could your daughter have alluded to a horrifying incident or was her provocative, sensational label merely prompted by an unappreciated or misinterpreted comment in the locker room (e.g., "Girls, stop staring at each other and get changed quickly!")? These tidbits of information that you glean from snooping usually prompt more questions than answers. You are then burdened with sorting through and assessing the validity and seriousness of anything you learn.

Similarly, suppose you come across literature from Planned Parenthood in your daughter's room. Unless you speak to her directly, you will not know if she has obtained birth control, merely is considering getting birth control, thought about doing it but changed her mind, got the literature for a friend who needs it, or obtained the brochures as part of a school research report. Obviously you will need to follow up.

- *Violation of Trust*

Of course the biggest problem with snooping is that you are violating the basic foundation of mutual respect and trust in your relationship with your daughter. Each of you expects the other to abide by standards of decent behavior. This includes honoring your respective rights to privacy. When you snoop, even if it ultimately turns out to be warranted, your daughter will get the message that you think it is okay for you to sneak around, but not for her. She is unlikely to appreciate this double standard.

For example, thirteen-year-old Clara was devastated when her mother alluded to her romance with a boy who had recently moved into a nearby apartment. "The only way my mother could've known how I felt about Paul was if she read my journal. That was private and she knows it!" Clara said. "She'd flip out if I ever did anything like that to her. I'll never trust her again."

If you decide for whatever reason that you must snoop and break your daughter's trust, don't count on restoring it instantly just because you're The Mother. Trust works both ways. While you can demand that your daughter obey and respect you, you will have to regain her trust the hard way, just as your daughter would have to do if she broke your trust.

5. Do I Believe Snooping Is Warranted?

Given these potential consequences of snooping, there seems to be only one well-founded reason for using this strategy: as a last-ditch effort to ensure your daughter's health and safety, and only after you have exhausted all other channels. You don't dig for dirt unless the matter is serious and you have no other choice. In fact, it is with your heart in your mouth that you take a peek into your daughter's private world.

In other words, I do not recommend snooping whenever you are curious about her life, frustrated by her protectiveness of her friends, concerned about her apparent unhappiness, or unsure how to help. As your worries increase in seriousness, the possibility of snooping becomes more justified (but again, only after you have pursued all other possible sources of information). For example, you might be worried about her involvement in questionable activities, have clear evidence of outright lies or broken rules, and fear imminent risk to her health or safety.

• *Consider Signs of Risk*

You might use these warning signs for potentially serious problems as a gauge for whether you should delve relentlessly into your daughter's private life. The more of these criteria she displays, the more you may be compelled to snoop:

- dramatic change in mood
- prolonged discouragement or sadness
- marked change in personality
- shift in her friendship circles
- declining academic performance
- increased secretiveness
- possession of substances or drug paraphernalia
- chronic lying
- behavioral problems in school
- evidence of self-injury
- a suicide note
- sudden conflict with peers or adults

• *Trust Your Gut Feelings*

Just as you are helping your daughter to respect and pay close attention to her inner voice, you too have to trust your gut feelings. Even if your daughter has exhibited few of the signs above, if your intuition is telling you there is a problem, take it seriously. Perhaps it is nothing you can put your finger on, but merely a fleeting or recurring feeling that something is wrong. In my experience, a mother's intuition is usually right. So, if you sense something is amiss with your daughter, trust your instincts and follow up. Darcy, the forty-eight-year-old mother of a twenty-four-year-old, tells this story about her experience when her daughter was a junior in high school:

My daughter went through a rough time. First, there was a subtle change in her mood. When I asked her what was wrong, she would only say, "Nothing" or tell me to leave her alone. She didn't talk about her friends anymore, and I noticed the phone was pretty quiet. Then she was getting a lot of stomachaches and headaches, like she used to when she was younger and felt nervous about going to school. I called her school psychologist, who told me her teachers had noticed a change; she rarely participated in class anymore. They were also concerned about her. I guess I got desperate and looked around her room. I found a lot of really macabre poetry, along with two six-packs of beer hidden in the back of her closet. When I confronted her with all this, she just got angry. But I took her to a therapist, who eventually helped her with her depression. She had been drinking to make herself feel better. Thank goodness that episode is well past us now. After my daughter graduated from college, she told me more about what caused her problems back then. Apparently, she was upset one weekend because her boyfriend dumped her. She went to a party, drank too much, and ended up having sex with her best friend's boyfriend. Her whole group was disgusted with her, and after that made it clear they wanted nothing to do with her. She felt really alone."

Darcy tried to address her initial concerns directly with her daughter, but found herself stonewalled by silence. She then acted on her gut feeling that something was terribly wrong. When she called the school and they too were concerned, she felt she had no choice but to investigate the possibility that her daughter was in some sort of trouble. Indeed, the poetry and beer only fueled her fears. Her daughter's reaction upon being confronted further convinced Darcy that she needed professional help. Had she not taken her daughter for treatment, it is possible her downward spiral of depression, substance abuse, and self-defeating behavior would have continued unchecked.

6. Am I Prepared to Come Across Information I Would Rather Not Have?

If you are to snoop, you must consider the very real possibility that you will find out information not only about your daughter, but about other teenagers. Because of your questions about the validity of this information, you may face the especially difficult dilemma of not knowing what to do. In fact, this is a rather complex issue that can have enormous repercussions for your relationship with your daughter.

• *Know Your Obligations*

If you find out or suspect something harmful may be going on with your daughter's friend, for example, you will need to figure out how to react. For example, when Myra, fifty-six, read her fifteen-year-old daughter's e-mail, "I got the impression that one of her best friends may have been sexually abused by someone in her family. It was ambiguous, but I felt really in a bind about what to do." Another mother surmised from what she read in a note found in her daughter's room that her boyfriend could have been using cocaine. Whether or not such information is true—and you may never know—you may be compelled legally or morally to act on it to protect another child. If in doubt about what to do, you may need to seek guidance from an attorney, the police, your local school, or the state child protection agency.

• *Tell Other Parents?*

When you find out something about another teenager, you will face two rather unattractive choices: to tell the parents or to keep quiet. This is a highly complex dilemma that requires much deliberation, soul-searching, and reference to personal values. Unfortunately, potential risks abound from either course of action.

Suppose you sense your daughter and her friend are acting strange when they return from a shopping trip. You comment on their behavior, but neither girl offers any reasonable explanation. Still suspicious, you sneak into your daughter's room later in the evening when the girls are out and discover that they have probably shoplifted merchandise from a local store. What do you do? Your options are to do nothing, to call the friend's parents and inform them, or to insist that the girl report the incident to her parents herself, rather than forcing you to be the messenger.

It seems to me that you would be more likely to make sure the information was communicated to the other parents if (a) the accuracy of your information was confirmed, and (b) their daughter had engaged in an illegal or potentially dangerous activity. Also, the closer the relationship between your daughter and her friend and the better you know and care about the girl, the more you may take action to protect her. When you already have a rapport with the parents, it is easier to approach them with this sort of potentially disturbing information. You may already feel assured that they will welcome or even appreciate your honesty, especially if your families have a tacit agreement to help each other keep your daughters safe.

• *Be a Role Model*

Many mothers I speak to are reluctant to inform other parents of what they learn about their children for two main reasons. One, they are afraid (sometimes accurately) the parents will not be pleased to hear the information and therefore will be inclined to kill the messenger. Second, they fear that if their daughter finds out, they will have damaged their relationship. However, you may need to model for your daughter that sometimes you have to do what you believe in your heart of hearts is right, even if people initially get upset with you. If the situation were reversed, would you want the other parent to inform you? If so, you might decide that you have to risk your daughter's possible negative reaction and her resultant wrath.

I believe that if your daughter asks you outright whether or not you have shared information about her friend, you should not deceive her. You are not, however, obligated to apprise her of your action. How her friend's parents gained their knowledge is beside the point. There are some parental decisions that can remain between you and other adults. Yet even when you choose not to disclose this matter to your daughter, consider the possibility that the other parents will tell their own child. If that girl subsequently informs your daughter what you did, brace yourself for an even more irate teenager. Your daughter may well feel doubly betrayed. This still does not mean, however, that what you did was wrong.

In fact, you are demonstrating to your daughter that it is acceptable and even obligatory to divulge secrets when there is the chance that someone is engaging in harmful activities. This gives her another perspective on the typical teenage moral code, which prohibits ratting on friends, even if they are endangering themselves, for fear of getting them in trouble. If your daughter subsequently discovers a friend's suicidal thoughts, unsafe sexual behavior, or abusive relationship, she might be more inclined to break confidentiality in order to seek appropriate help.

7. Should I Confess to My Daughter That I Snooped?

Once you get the information you were after, you have to decide whether or not to tell your daughter how you found out. Many mothers struggle with this dilemma.

• *Keep Focused on the Issue*

If you feel guilty about how you went about getting the goods on your daughter, you may be inclined to be overly apologetic or defensive. The discussion then becomes sidetracked—that is, focused on your action (e.g., "Mom, how dare you do this to me!") rather than on your daughter's need to take responsibility for her inappropriate or dangerous behavior, where it rightly belongs. You might want to remind your daughter that although you would have preferred not to get information about her without her knowledge and permission, you did so only because you felt there was no other alternative and you believed her safety was at risk.

• *Don't Lie*

Since it is important to be accountable for your own behavior, avoid lying to your daughter if she asks directly how you found out something about her. Instead you might say something on the order of, "It really doesn't matter. Now that I know what's going on, we can deal with it."

For sure, your next big hurdle is what in the world you should do with the distressing information you find out about her. At times, you may feel as if your whole universe has caved in. While your first impulse may be to lay down the law and punish her until the next millennium, a part of you may realize that this complex issue merits your most careful and thoughtful attention. The next chapter will prepare you for this possibility by helping you to respond effectively when your daughter experiences trouble.

Cell Phones and Pagers

This generation of daughters, coming of age during the information age, is enjoying the technological explosion of the telecommunications industry. Even girls who are all thumbs when it comes to a dishwasher or vacuum cleaner somehow prove adept at operating the most obscure features of pagers, cell phones, and television remotes. At some point your daughter may try to convince you that without these highly coveted items her life cannot possibly continue. You are likely to hear, "Everyone else has one, Mom!" In making a decision about whether your daughter will join the increasing number of teenagers who are using pagers and cell phones, consider the pros and cons.

The most obvious advantage is that by calling her cell phone or pager, you can check in with your daughter more easily and frequently when she is not at home. Barring the occasional no service zone, you can also be assured that your daughter can call you anytime, no matter where she is. This may help her to get out of sticky situations, and to save face while doing so.

The downside occurs with possible abuses. It is wise to establish guidelines and limits beforehand. Since you have less awareness of your daughter's cell phone or pager, you have less control over where and when she speaks to friends, not to mention who might be calling her. Theoretically, she could get calls in the middle of night without your knowledge. For some girls, a cell phone may therefore exacerbate existing difficulties with planning time effectively and completing homework. In addition, be clear about your expectations regarding her monthly bills. This encourages your daughter to learn self-discipline, as well as good money management.

As with all parental decisions, you will weigh the pros and cons. If your daughter makes good choices about her use of these devices, they can be priceless purveyors of your peace of mind.

Chapter 6

When She's Caught

TROUBLE

"Last year, when my daughter was fifteen, she told me she was going to her friend's house one day during their midwinter break. I thought nothing of it. But when Katya wasn't home by dinner, I called over to Meghan's house and her mother said the girls hadn't been there all day. Now both of us were upset. Much later, Katya came home pale as a ghost and very apologetic about what had happened. Although both girls knew this was forbidden, they took a bus into the city. What they didn't count on was the bus getting into an accident. Apparently, a police investigation delayed their arrival for over three hours because no one was allowed to leave the scene. The girls were frantic when they knew they would be late and we would find out what they did. Truthfully, things haven't been the same since. Now I'm frantic every time I think of what could have happened. And I'm still afraid of what she'll do next."

—Marge, forty-one

"My fourteen-year-old daughter, Francesca, is in big trouble because of what she did last weekend. She and a friend watched TV until pretty late, said goodnight and went into her room. I thought they were sleeping. Something woke me up in the middle of the night and I went in there. The first thing I noticed was that her room was freezing because the window was open. At first it looked like there were two bodies sleeping in Francesca's bed because the girls had rolled up clothes and pillows under the covers! I locked the window and taped up a note that said, 'Come see your parents.' Then I waited up the rest of the night, anxious to make sure they were okay. Part of me is still furious and disgusted with my daughter. I never thought she could be so dishonest or sneaky. If she pulled this kind of a stunt, what else could she be doing?"

—Tanisha, thirty-four

"Last night I got a distressing call from my daughter's guidance counselor. It seems she's been giving some of her teachers trouble, which is not like her. Plus, her grades are slipping. The counselor wondered if everything was all right at home. I told him I haven't been comfortable with some of my daughter's new friends. They don't seem to have much supervision. When he confirmed that these kids are suspected drug users, I got really scared. I searched her room and found rolling papers in one of her drawers. I must've warned her about getting involved with drugs a million times. I'm not going to yell because that never helps; she just gets mad and walks away. But I'm so sick about all this, I don't think I can look at her."   —Kirby, thirty-eight

As these stories attest, no matter how wise and self-aware your daughter or how effective your parenting, at some time during her adolescent years she will probably err. If you dwell on what could happen as a result of these mistakes, you will undoubtedly endure years of sleepless nights and make bulk purchases of Maalox. Yet it is wise to accept that your daughter will not be perfect. She will probably behave like a typical teenager. That is, on occasion she may disobey your rules, get herself in hot water, blurt something foolish, lie to you, sneak around behind your back, or behave regrettably. In fact, such behaviors are practically an adolescent rite of passage. This chapter will prepare you for the day when your daughter gets caught doing these things so at least you can respond as well as possible. Above all, you will be able to avoid some of the typical reactions that not only aren't helpful, but can actually exacerbate matters.

Learning About Trouble

The suspicion that your daughter has strayed into off-limits territory or is flirting with risky behavior may come slowly, prompting you to ask yourself, "Am I imagining this, or is there really a problem?" Naturally, if you have the misfortune to awaken in the middle of the night, these are the thoughts that instantly pop into your mind. Trying to quiet your fears, you may choose to wait until you have more evidence. Or, as discussed in the last chapter, you may decide to ask your daughter directly about your concerns, check out other sources of information, and, as a last resort, do whatever is necessary to find out what is really going on.

Even if your daughter does not confess to what she has done, you may discover undeniable proof, or you may hear the bad news from a school official, your daughter's sibling, a friend, the police, or another parent. One way or another, though, you have gotten the confirmation that you desperately wanted and at the same time, most dreaded. There is no turning back now; you know that your daughter used poor judgment and may, in fact, be in some sort of trouble. What should you do?

Thinking Ahead: Remedies for a Range of Problems

If you are like many mothers, getting this news will send your mind whirling into high gear. If your daughter's mistake isn't just a typical teenage thing and she has a bigger problem, what decisions might you ultimately face? To figure out how you need to respond, you might mentally assess your daughter's overall adjustment, her personality, the seriousness of her error, and whether this is an isolated incident or part of a longer history of difficulties. Based on these factors, you may then consider a myriad of possible actions, which range from minimal to monumental.

Occasionally, for example, you might decide to do nothing, at least for the moment. You may keep the information to yourself, strategically storing it away to use at some later point. Or you might simply tell your daughter that you know what she did, and leave it at that. For some girls, minor trouble requires only that. If your daughter is sensitive to criticism or eager to please you, merely passing on the news you heard may be enough to prompt her to correct her behavior. For example, Audrey, fifty-two, casually mentioned to her twelve-year-old daughter, Maura, that her friend's mother was taken aback by her language. Mortified, Maura hastily promised that she would never again swear in front of an adult. As far as Audrey knew, Maura kept her word.

The more serious your daughter's transgression, the more you may struggle to know how best to respond. For example, you might be inclined to be more stern if she fails to honor your limits, rejects your values, disregards school rules, or risks her safety. You will probably be even more reproachful if this mistake is part of a chronic pattern. In many cases, you may begin to think of what consequences your daughter should experience as a result of her behavior, a topic that will be covered in the next chapter on discipline.

At some point, you may wonder if you need professional help to make these decisions. Many psychological conditions, which you do not have the expertise to address, can impair your daughter's perceptions, reasoning ability, and problem solving, resulting in poor judgment. Therefore, if any of the following statements are true, it would be wise to consult a well-trained mental health clinician who can advise you if further evaluation is warranted:

- Your daughter is making the same mistake repeatedly.
- Her behavior is deteriorating.
- She is having difficulties in more than one area, such as in school, at home, and with her friends.
- She may have an eating disorder.
- Her thinking is confused or illogical.
- She may be suffering from depression or anxiety.
- You suspect substance use.
- She is harming herself, either deliberately or unintentionally.

In some cases, you might consider the possibility that your daughter needs more intensive care, such as participation in a structured day treatment program, medication, inpatient services, or rehab for drugs and alcohol.

If your daughter uses poor judgment at school, you may confront changes in her schedule or even her placement. Sometimes, after much discussion and consultation with the experts, you may decide that your daughter would be better off in a special therapeutic or boarding school environment. When problems are especially serious, the decisions may be taken out of your hands; the school may make recommendations or issue consequences for your daughter. These days, for example, in the fearful climate that prevails, students who break a zero-tolerance rule at school (e.g., if they bring a weapon or sell drugs) may be subject to prolonged suspension or mandatory expulsion.

As you start exploring this mind-boggling spectrum of possibilities, however, you can easily lose sight of what really ought to be your chief mission: addressing the problem with your daughter. In fact, you can't truly determine the best course of action until you learn more about the incident and her role in it, assess the seriousness of the trouble, and observe her reactions to being caught. Thus your first priority is deciding how to respond to your daughter. Especially given how devastated you feel, how can you deal with whatever she did, yet still remain flexible, respectful, attuned, involved, and noncontrolling? You want to do what is right, but not at the expense of your relationship; you want to preserve the closeness you cherish. Although reaching these goals may seem as unlikely as traveling to Neptune, with a little reflection and practice they're actually doable. The first step is to become aware of how you tend to react in crises.

Understand Your Reactions

1. Recognize and Accept Your Initial Shock

It is far easier to stay calm and consider options in a clearheaded, objective manner when you hear about some other mother's daughter who got in trouble. Imagine learning that a teenager cut school for a week, drove her parents' car without a license, engaged in undesirable sexual behavior, or was taken to an emergency room after drinking too much. You may be nonjudgmental and even empathic if it is your friend's girl who was involved in such exploits. But when it is your daughter, you may be thunderstruck that she chose to put herself in these potentially dangerous situations.

Of course during crises it is understandably difficult to keep your wits and make clearheaded decisions. In fact many mothers find themselves unable to think at all! Instead, they typically describe experiencing an onslaught of complex, sometimes utterly overwhelming emotions. Merle, forty-eight, the mother of sixteen-year-old twins, put it this way: "When one of my girls told me that her sister had gotten a sexually transmitted disease, I felt this whooshing sensation in my head and thought I would faint. I can't even describe the flood of feelings, but it was like I was suddenly underwater." Ana, forty-two, said, "Learning the truth about my daughter's behavior felt like a slap in the face."

Other mothers have reported similarly visceral sensations, such as "being kicked in the stomach," "punched in the solar plexus," or "heart-stopping panic." You too may feel distraught, overwhelmed, and virtually paralyzed. If you have such a powerful reaction, reassure yourself that it is perfectly normal. More important, it is temporary. Part of what you are experiencing is shock, which renders you momentarily paralyzed.

Give yourself time to process what you found out about your daughter. Let the information sink in gradually before you feel the need to act on it. If someone calls you to tell you what your daughter did, after listening politely to the news say that you will call back once you have given the matter some thought. By all means, don't feel pressured to comment prematurely. You are required neither to defend your daughter (e.g., "Oh, that's not possible. My Missy would never do that!") nor to publicly lambaste her (e.g., "Don't worry, she'll be sorry to be alive when I get a hold of her!"). Just dealing with your own feelings is more than enough for now.

2. Consider the Influence of Your Past Mistakes

As you may realize, your reactions to your daughter's mistakes are undoubtedly influenced by your own. In fact, as you probably know, each time you address another aspect of parenting, you will be encouraged to revisit how your own teenage experiences may be influencing you. For sure, before you can decide how best to respond to your daughter's lapses of judgment, it is only fair to reflect first on your own.

When you look back, how do you assess the damage of your teenage years? What mistakes did you make? Although it may be unpleasant, try to be thoroughly honest with yourself. What was the worst thing you did that your parents actually found out about? Do you remember how it felt to be caught? When you think of your daughter's behavior only from your parental position, it is easy to be sanctimonious. But when you remind yourself of your own teenage experiences and feelings, you can be more understanding of your daughter—and more understanding of her unfortunate behavior.

Brigette, forty-seven, remembers vividly when her parents came home unexpectedly to find her half-naked and in bed with her boyfriend. "It was definitely the worst moment of my life," she says. "I don't think I've ever completely gotten over it. Somehow, in that instant, I changed forever in my parents' eyes." Experiencing a far different sort of incident, Glenna, forty-four, recalls similarly adverse, long-lasting effects: "When I was thirteen, I got caught stealing Beatles cards from a five-and-ten-cent store in our town. I was so ashamed and afraid to face the manager that I avoided that store for the next five years. In junior high and even high school I always made up excuses not to go inside whenever my friends wanted to run in for nail polish remover or school supplies. In fact, for years the shame tortured me more than any punishment my parents could have given me."

In retrospect, some women conclude that their teenage mistakes were unnecessarily calamitous or humiliating. Your outlook on your own early crimes, tempered by maturity and experience, can influence your reactions to your daughter's adolescent foibles. Juana, now thirty-nine, tells of when she was sixteen and made the mistake of agreeing to go to a dance with a boy she didn't like to win back her ex-boyfriend:

"My friends were all going," she said, "which made me want to go even more. I knew Russell would find out, and I was trying to make him jealous. Dominic was excited that I agreed to go with him and was incredibly sweet, but as soon as we arrived I saw Russell! I wanted to be with him so much that I basically dumped Dominic and danced with Russell. It was such an awful thing to do that practically everyone I knew was mad at me. I felt so alone. Then things didn't work out with Russell after all, so I thought my life was over." When she looks back, however, Juana says, "It was a pretty typical example of a girl who thought she could handle anything letting herself get carried away and not doing the right thing. Not something I'm proud of—I certainly hurt that nice boy—but it's not like I killed someone."

When women revisit their mistakes, they recall drinking too much, taking drugs, getting involved with the wrong guys or at the wrong times, concocting elaborate tales to hide their activities, and treating people poorly. They also may recollect not thinking twice about deceiving their parents. Although the cost of teenage mistakes varies from negligible to immense, women universally conclude that

Should You Tell All?

Many parents struggle over whether to divulge their own teenage activities and times of trouble to their daughters. There are rather different ways to approach this issue. It is one thing to admit that you went through periods of self-doubt, felt isolated and lonely, and made your share of mistakes, especially when your child is in a similarly difficult position. It is quite another to describe your exploits in glorious detail. Those who advocate confessing their past argue that daughters (a) resent parents who seem holier than thou, (b) relate better to parents who aren't such old fuddy-duddies, (c) are more inclined to heed parents when their warnings are based on actual experience, and (d) are therefore less likely to repeat their parents' mistakes.

My experience with teenage girls, however, indicates a wider range of outcomes. Because they prefer to think of their parents as ideal, girls often feel not only let down but also aghast and resentful when forced to see Mom in this less desirable light. They feel burdened by this news. This is especially true when mothers discuss previous sexual activities and substance use. Not a single teenage girl in the last twenty years has ever expressed delight that her mother had a sexual partner other than her father.

Girls also are confused by information that contradicts what you are teaching them. When you say, "We smoked pot, but we realize now how bad it is, so you shouldn't do it," your daughter is apt to think, "If my parents smoked pot, why shouldn't I?" Your strategy may backfire because you lose credibility; teenage girls attend far more to your behavior than to your words. No matter how regretful you may be, when you admit that you deceived your parents you are modeling this behavior for your daughter. You are saying, in effect, "Lying and sneaking around are normal, even expected."

It is also hard for your daughter to compare your activities to hers because the times and contexts have changed. What may have been a minor risk when you were a teenager could well be treacherous today. Objectively, as described earlier, the world is now a more dangerous place. While a decade or two ago the worst consequence of unprotected sex was probably pregnancy, today it is the deadly HIV infection. As another example, although marijuana is about one hundred times more powerful than it was in the 1970s and more often laced with other drugs, try convincing your daughter that getting high is more dangerous for her than it was for you!

If you do decide to spill, make sure you are doing it for the right reasons—that is, to give your daughter information to make better choices in her life—rather than to make her see you as more with-it or youthful. Think carefully about what you disclose because once you tell her something, you can't take it back.

they learned a great deal from each of their errors. In thinking of their own indiscretions, mothers are reminded of many of the mistakes they fervently hope their own daughters will not make. But often they make exactly the same errors.

Even worse, some women raising teenage girls are pervasively haunted by their own traumatic childhoods. They cannot forget their sense of guilt, shame, and complicity in the events that hurt them or others. Thus they vow never to allow their daughters to do what they did or to suffer similar consequences. Yet in their anxiety, mothers may unwittingly fail to recognize that their daughters' mistakes are indeed repetitions of their own pasts. Through the distorted lens of their own teenage memories, they may either overlook their daughters' troubles or, conversely, read too much into them.

3. Clarify Your Beliefs About Her Errors

How you view your daughter's mistakes determines in large part how you respond to them, affects your mother-daughter relationship, and, most especially, influences whether your daughter ultimately repeats them. Therefore, it is important to consider how you tend to view errors, and to make any necessary adjustments:

• *What Does It Mean to You When Your Daughter Messes Up?* Are you inclined to brand her forever in your mind as a black sheep ("She always was my difficult child!")? Do you immediately panic about serious issues (e.g., "Maybe there's something terribly wrong with her!")? You might want to avoid rushing to such judgments. Instead first concentrate on discussing all the facts and underlying issues with your daughter.

• *Do You Reflexively Assign Blame?* Do you usually view errors as someone's fault? For example, do you tend to chalk up your daughter's unfortunate behavior to the bad influence of undesirable people in her life (e.g., "She's exactly like her father!" or "If only she wasn't friends with Sally!")? Do you immediately criticize yourself for possible failures and mistakes (e.g., "Maybe I shouldn't have been so strict with her!" or "Maybe I should get stricter!")? Or do you decide that your daughter is purposely trying to hurt you (e.g., "Is she determined to make my life a living hell?")? If so, remember that your focus should be on helping your daughter to understand where *she* went wrong. When you are respectful of this process, you step back and give her the chance to grapple with this question and come to her own conclusions.

• *Does Her Mistake Indicate Problems in Your Relationship?* Are you apt to view her error as a condemnation of your relationship? In some cases, difficulties between mothers and daughters do contribute to girls' rebellious and self-defeating behavior. If you and your daughter habitually battle, struggle with trust and respect, have a tenuous connection, or fail to work out mutually agreeable rules and expectations, her negative behavior may be designed to elicit a certain reaction from you. Either deliberately or unconsciously, your daughter may want to make you upset, angry, more attentive, or even alarmed. She may be hoping you will regret a previous decision, change your mind, or become more solicitous of her wishes. If your daughter is using self-defeating behavior as a last-ditch strategy to deal with a troubled mother-daughter relationship, seeing a therapist together even for a few sessions may help her to learn healthier and more adaptive ways to communicate, as well as assist both of you in improving your relationship.

In the majority of cases, however, teenage girls do not make mistakes for the distinct purpose of making their mothers angry. For a moment, think back to when your daughter was a toddler and made a game of throwing her spoon off the tray of her high chair. Each time you picked it up from the floor she giggled in delight and threw it again, yet she was not trying purposely to frustrate you or make you late for work. She was merely experiencing—and relishing—her newfound power to affect you. In a parallel way, your daughter's present behavior, no matter how troublesome, is best viewed not as a personal attack on you, but as a normal process of testing her burgeoning abilities.

4. Put Your Reactions in Perspective

When you are clearer about what beliefs and biases you bring to these crises with your daughter, you may be better able to understand your strong reactions and put them in proper perspective. Although you might not experience every one of the feelings listed below, and perhaps not precisely as described, it might help you to know that these are all common reactions of mothers whose teenage daughters are caught making mistakes:

• *Disbelief.* Most mothers are not neglectful or uncaring, yet what mother would want to believe her daughter could behave meanly, blatantly disregard rules, or carelessly neglect her safety? This could well be why teenagers in therapy routinely describe outrageous and rather obvious exploits that somehow their mothers never notice. With this in mind, you might want to be extra alert to

cues and take seriously whatever information others share with you. Although it is difficult, keep your mind open to the possibility that there may be more going on in your daughter's life than you know, or that the bad news imparted to you by a messenger could actually be true. Be kind to yourself about your desire to disbelieve, but keep your eyes wide open.

• *Fear.* Since she was born, one of your main maternal missions has been keeping your daughter safe. It was a whole lot easier when all that that required were baby locks on kitchen cabinets, crossing guards, bicycle helmets, and the occasional product recall. Now that she is a teenager, keeping your daughter safe has taken on a whole new meaning. Each time she experiences a first—a solo trip to the store, a coed party, getting a ride with a licensed friend, going out with a boy—you are reminded that your ability to protect her is limited. Letting go can be scary! Although you set ground rules, that only gives you peace of mind when your daughter follows them. When this serenity is shattered by her mistakes, your resulting fear can permeate everything you do and say. Recognizing and harnessing this emotion is challenging but crucial if you want to be most effective in responding to trouble.

• *Disgust.* There are times when, in all truth, you find your daughter's behavior not just worrisome but repulsive. This does not make you a bad mother. Your reaction to what happened may actually be physical. Not a few mothers have reported feeling nauseated or sickened by their daughter's behavior. When Marlene, fifty, heard that her sixteen-year-old daughter had gotten drunk and vomited all over her best friend's new car, she said, "I keep seeing that scene in my mind's eye, over and over. I can only imagine how filthy my daughter must have felt."

When the graphic or repulsive vision of your daughter's misdeed intrudes upon you relentlessly like an overplayed movie scene, it may be helpful to recognize that your daughter is probably disgusted with herself. Expressing your revulsion, particularly if she interprets this as a rejection of her, may be more than your daughter can bear. Since you want to prevent her from giving up on herself, remember that she needs to know you will not give up on her. No matter what her behavior, she can count on your love, respect for her dignity, and emotional support.

• *Disappointment.* Although you may know intellectually that

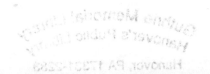

your daughter is not perfect, it is a different matter entirely to be faced with the fallout of what she's done. Moreover, realizing just *how* imperfect she is and in what *ways* she is imperfect may be more difficult than you imagined. How disappointed you may feel when your daughter's behavior is not what you think it should have been! You may be forced to revisit your hopes and expectations. Are they reasonable? If so, share your belief that your daughter is capable of doing better, especially when you can identify specific skills that she can work on in the future. On the other hand, sometimes your disappointment signals your need to come to grips with what you see as your daughter's flaws. She may not be as compassionate as you would like, able to blend in socially, the leader among her peers, or sought after by the opposite sex. But you can and should expect that she will always use the best possible judgment.

• *Anger.* Anger is a common reaction to your daughter's mistakes; your love for her and your desire for what is best for her make you furious that she made such poor choices. You may well ask, "How could you have done this to yourself?" or "How could you have put yourself at such risk?" A high school senior named Mallory was a serious, highly disciplined student who was going to be valedictorian of her class and the presumed recipient of the English award. When she was caught plagiarizing a term paper two months before graduation, Mallory's mother was livid: "How could she have jeopardized all her hard work? What if everything she's done so far goes down the drain?"

As you know, anger and fear often go hand in hand. You may be angry that your daughter chose to risk harming herself and afraid of the possible damage she has done in the process (e.g., to her reputation, her friendships, her safety). You may also fear that she will continue to behave in ways that are not in her own best interest. Be cautious, however, about expressing only anger. Not only are you likely to elicit anger in return, but it easy for your daughter to overlook the underlying fear, hurt, and deep concern you have for her.

• *Hurt.* Hurt is a close cousin to anger and fear. When your daughter makes mistakes, you may be wounded by her apparent disregard of all the advice you have lovingly offered, the wisdom you have struggled to impart, and the values you have worked so hard to convey. When your daughter goes and does something outrageous, you can even feel as if she discarded a part of you. Although these complex feelings are understandable, they are best addressed apart from your interactions with your daughter. She has enough to handle! Speak with a trusted confidante to work through your feelings so they do not fester. There is probably not a mother of a teenage girl who cannot empathize and commiserate with the hurt that often accompanies a daughter's unfortunate behavior.

• *Self-Blame.* On some level, you may interpret your daughter's transgressions as a reflection of your own deficiencies as a mother. "I must have done something wrong!" is often the initial cry of mothers hearing about their daughter's errors. This, of course, is not necessarily the case. Like all mothers, you probably have not been perfect. You may have ignored or minimized early signs of problems, or failed to enforce punishments. But that did not cause your daughter to make poor choices. She needs to take responsibility for that; if you blame yourself, you will prevent her from doing so. Allowing your daughter's crises to make you feel inadequate as a mother is also putting an unfair burden on her. She should learn to make better choices for her own well-being, not just as a testament to your mothering skills. Avoid getting mired in a rut of self-blame and guilt, which drain energy faster than an overloaded circuit, and concentrate your efforts on helping your daughter to learn from her mistakes.

• *Shame.* Your daughter's mistakes can evoke in you feelings of self-consciousness and shame. Many mothers, upon hearing that their daughters' exploits have become public, agonize, "What must people think of us now?" Of course you would like your family to be viewed as functioning well. No doubt you would prefer to avoid being embarrassed by your daughter's behavior. But beware of focusing more on damage control than on making sure her needs are met.

For example, when two sophomores experimented with a dangerous drug and had to be revived by paramedics, their mothers had far different responses. Naomi's mother was aghast that the local newspaper printed what had occurred. She quickly called the reporter and requested that they not inform the school because she wanted to prevent her daughter "from being punished further by her foolish action."

Cordelia's mother, on the other hand, immediately contacted the school and made an appointment to talk to counselors about what happened. She asked for guidance about how to deal with this episode with her daughter, referrals for therapists, and help in identifying community resources. This mother was determined to help educate other teenagers about the dangerous but little-known drug that nearly took her daughter's life. Cordelia's mother may have felt some shame or embarrassment, but she did not allow these reactions to get in the way of taking positive action. Moreover, she found that helping others along with her own daughter was healing in itself, enabling her to feel that something good came of this unfortunate incident. Cordelia too benefited from seeing her mother deal courageously, openly, and positively with her problem.

• *Resentment.* When your daughter makes a serious mistake that requires further evaluation, treatment, legal services, or community service, this often translates into the expenditure of additional time, money, or emotional resources. Sometimes this can make mothers resentful. When her daughter was involved in an escapade of stealing beer from the local grocery store, Bertha, forty-eight, complained about the increased pressure she faced as a result: "I've had to take off so much time to take Nanci to the lawyer, to court, and now to different schools to perform her community service hours. My boss is getting fed up, and my work is piling up. And now I need to work more than ever because we have to pay such huge legal fees!"

Especially if your daughter seems incognizant of your sacrifices, resentment can accumulate. Plus you may become bitter about the need to make other changes as a result of her mistake. For example, finding out about her sexual activities may require you to see her as more grown-up and less innocent than you would have liked. Her behavior may have destroyed your serenity; you fear you will always be on edge, peeking around corners. You may now see yourself as older, taking on the image of your own mother. Once again, it is helpful to be aware of these reactions. Although you have every right to such feelings, unless you come to terms with them they can wreak havoc on your efforts to be positive and effective in dealing with your daughter.

5. Manage Your Feelings

Even if you believe your reactions are excessive or unhelpful, don't berate yourself for them. How can you *not* be upset? This is your daughter who messed up! But before you can successfully address the trouble she has gotten herself into, as well as the underlying issues involved, you have to get your feelings under control. These strategies can help neutralize unproductive feelings and rein in those you believe are definitely over the top:

• *Distract Yourself.* Don't dwell on your negative feelings. More important, refrain from reviewing them in your own mind or recounting the details of your daughter's misdeed to others. This will only fire up the intensity of your emotions. Instead try a soothing activity such as yoga, meditation, or listening to music. Or focus on a task that you find engrossing, whether that is balancing your checkbook, surfing the Net, or reading a mystery.

• *Empathize with Her.* To minimize or deflate negative feelings, put yourself in your daughter's place and imagine what may have been going through her mind. Specifically, try to empathize with her adolescent mindset: desperately wanting to fit in with her friends, being eager to feel grown-up, needing a thrill, miscalculating risks. Even if you can partially understand what she was thinking, you may be better able to approach your daughter about this issue.

• *Focus on Her Good Choices.* It is unlikely that your daughter's situation was all bad. When you can find whatever may have been positive in her behavior, it can help to ease your negative reactions. Once you identify these good choices, store them away for later. They will come in handy when you speak with your daughter.

• *Remember the Learning Process.* Remind yourself that your daughter was not born with good judgment, but has to learn it. Plus it is better that she makes these mistakes now, when you are able to help her correct them and grow from them.

• *Get Perspective.* Similarly, tell yourself that telling a whopping lie at age sixteen does not translate into your daughter growing up to be a brazen sociopath. Maintain future time perspective.

• *Commiserate.* It can be comforting to speak to a friend who is currently going through similar issues or better yet, one who has already lived through such episodes. Not only are you not alone, but your daughter's situation is rarely unprecedented.

• *Be Thankful.* Since the motto "It could always be worse" often puts an incident in proper perspective, repeating it to yourself can be comforting.

Approach Trouble Effectively

When your own feelings are manageable, it is time to get ready to address the problem with your daughter. Before you say word one to her, however, you must think through the situation in your own head.

Part One: Focus on Behavior

The most helpful prerequisite is adjusting your mind-set. That is, the best preparation for discussing your daughter's mistake with her is coming around to seeing her action as the result of a poor decision—rather than as an indication of perverse or incorrigible behavior, a purposeful attempt to provoke you, or evil doings.

Because she is young and has yet to fully develop skills, she either forgot to think before she acted or used bad judgment. If she overlooked essential cues, she couldn't evaluate the situation properly. Or swept away by more immediate needs—to satisfy her curiosity, to be included, or to escape from uncomfortable feelings—it didn't dawn on her to consider the consequences. Perhaps she was naïve, impulsive, unassertive, or overly concerned with pleasing others. Your daughter probably has much to learn about reading and trusting people. Also, she probably has much to learn about herself. One thing is for sure: As she matures she must pay more attention to her inner voice.

Sixteen-year-old Nadia's story is a striking example of bad judgment. At a party one evening, she decided to try ecstasy. "I wanted to see what E was like because everybody told me it was great and I'd have the best time. It was New Year's Eve, which made it really special. I took the little pill my sister's friend gave me, but then I thought it was strange that I didn't feel happy or anything. I just got kind of sleepy. Then I got together with this guy I've liked forever. But I'm not sure exactly what happened because I don't remember. I think maybe we had sex, but I haven't seen him since that night." Some months later, Nadia discovered that the drug she tried on New Year's Eve was not ecstasy; she had in fact given herself GHB, the date-rape drug!

When you focus on behavior, even ghastly mistakes are viewed more easily as correctable. Nadia's initial bad decision to experiment with drugs prevented her from protecting herself later in the evening. Under the influence, she chose to be in a most vulnerable situation with a boy. One bad decision led to another, much like a stack of dominoes toppling over. These are the horrific situations you desperately want your daughter to avoid. But, if she doesn't, you are terribly anxious for her to learn from them and not repeat them.

When your daughter is in trouble, then, the best approach is to address the question: Where did she go wrong? What have you learned about how your daughter handles dilemmas that arise in social situations? At what point did her thinking or problem solving break down? More important, what has she discovered about herself? And, of course, what does she need to do differently in the future?

When Ellen, a seventeen-year-old high school junior, reported in therapy that she had been date-raped the previous weekend, she hesitantly reported that this was the second time this had happened to her. As she herself admitted, the first time should have been the last time. A sweet, friendly girl, Ellen came from a family divided by divorce and troubled by substance problems among her older siblings. In therapy she was sorting through her feelings about her father's recently moving to another city and her mother's romance with a much younger man.

As Ellen explored these two date-rape experiences, she understood how her desire for a boyfriend and need to see herself as attractive interfered with her judgment. She was also determined not to emulate her father's notorious condemnation of people who were different or nonconforming. For these reasons, she ignored rumors about these boys, missed cues that might have alerted her to their ill intent, and placed undeserved trust in them.

When Ellen began to understand how these situations were recreations of traumatic incidents in her past, she was all the more determined to protect herself better. Frightened about the chance of pregnancy or contracting an HIV infection, she followed through on suggested testing over a six-month period. In addition, more alert to her own vulnerabilities, she began to change the way she formed relationships, developing a healthy cautiousness about getting intimately involved until she was confident in knowing young men better. Ellen was determined to be more careful with her safety in the future.

Like Ellen, your daughter may make mistakes as she is learning to become a better judge of character. She may need more experience in sizing up people, learning to read the subtleties of their feelings and motives. Teenage girls, in their idealism and romanticism, have to learn the unfortunate lesson that people are not always what they appear. Ellen's friend, who initially seemed so solicitous and caring, took full advantage of her vulnerability.

By the same token, your daughter probably has to learn that she herself cannot always be trusted. As she finds herself in novel situations, her beliefs, values, and sometimes even her courage have yet to be tested. With her evolving desires, mercurial emotions, and frequent changes of heart, her sense of self is still in flux. In truth, she is not always who she thinks she is.

For these reasons, seeing your daughter's mistakes as evidence of poor decisions gives you wonderful opportunities to discuss—and improve—her future choices. Along with focusing on her behavior, you might try this plan whenever she gets in trouble:

Part Two: Use a Ten-Step Plan

1. Take Your Time

Although you may feel as if you will literally burst if you don't confront your daughter within a second or two of learning the news, waiting is usually better. It will probably require your utmost self-control not to rush into your daughter's room and spew your frustration, disappointment, anger, or whatever emotions are most pressing. But delaying helps you to think through carefully what most concerns you, and therefore to approach your daughter most effectively. Just as in the last chapter you gave some thought to when your daughter would be most likely to disclose information, now you might consider when she would be most receptive to discussing what happened. For example, it is inadvisable to begin a serious talk when your daughter arrives home at one A.M., when both of you are exhausted, or when she is under the influence of alcohol or drugs or has just had a fight with her boyfriend.

One exception to the waiting principle is if your daughter senses that something is amiss, perceives that you are treating her differently, and asks you what is wrong. When you honestly acknowledge your distress, you reinforce her observational skills and validate her perceptions, which are crucial to her developing inner voice. Besides, she might otherwise worry about far more serious and frightening possibilities than whatever actually occurred. But it is perfectly acceptable to say, "I'm very concerned about what happened, but we're both really tired. I'd prefer to talk about this when we're more rested and can think clearly."

2. Get More Information

Another reason it is wise not to react too quickly is that you may fail to get all the pertinent information. Adrianna, thirty-nine, describes awakening one morning to find that her fourteen-year-old daughter had not come home. "I was in a panic and furious, of course, and I pictured all sorts of terrible things. When I called the friend who she was supposed to be with, no one answered. So I tried another friend, who told me she was at the first friend's house. Finally the mom answered. She said the girls were still sleeping, and apologized for not bringing her home the night before, but it seems my daughter had gotten sick with a stomach flu. They had tried calling me many times to tell me that she would be sleeping over, but the phone rang and rang. Then I remembered that I had been online until very late, so they couldn't have gotten through."

It is always a great relief when your fears turn out to be unfounded. Many situations do in fact appear worse than they really are. So first find out if your information is accurate. Consider your daughter's explanations. (But please note: Before you relax prematurely, it is wise to remember that teenage girls do tend to deny, minimize, or distort their involvement with trouble. The beer cans or pills or matches in your daughter's possession never seem to be hers, but always belong to her friends.)

After your daughter is caught and presumably contrite, you might expect her to be more responsive to your questions than when you are casually asking for information. However, this may or may not pan out. When she replies with something on the order of, "How do I know?" or "Why do you keep asking me that?" she is not necessarily being difficult or resisting your efforts to get to the root of the problem; she probably does not know herself.

Your best strategy may be not to ask *why* your daughter made the choices she did, but rather to ask her to describe *what* happened. Of course even this tactic does not guarantee success. Although this initial conversation may yield more questions than answers, try to maintain a low-key, cooperative approach to gathering information. (That is, it is best not to launch an interrogation worthy of the Inquisition.) Just as you do with everyday matters, you can fit together whatever your daughter discloses with the information you learn from other sources. In a crisis you may feel as if you are hastily assembling a five-hundred-piece jigsaw puzzle. But hopefully, over time, you will be rewarded with a clearer picture of where your daughter's judgment broke down.

3. Assess the Seriousness of the Problem

The information you learn from your daughter and other sources is invaluable in helping you to assess the seriousness of her mistakes. Not all episodes of experimentation are alike. Not every broken rule has the same ramifications. Just as you make distinctions between her good and bad behavior, and between her thoughts and deeds, also appreciate the nuances in your daughter's troublesome incidents. Let's use the example of learning that your daughter used alcohol. You might consider the crucial factors of where she did it, with whom, at what age, and in what circumstances. Each of the following scenarios would probably elicit significantly different concerns:

A) During a discussion, your thirteen-year-old daughter confides that she sampled a sip of vodka at her best friend's house one afternoon while the parents were at work. She explains that she was just curious about the taste.

B) You find out from her friend's mother that when your fifteen-year-old daughter told you she was going to the movies earlier that night she was actually at a party where she and her friends drank. When this woman picked up the girls, your daughter said she wasn't ready to leave the party and would get a ride home from an older boy later in the evening.

C) At seventeen, your daughter goes out one evening and returns home well before her curfew. When she dashes furtively up to her room you become suspicious, so you follow her and knock on her door. Despite your casual inquiry about possibly smelling alcohol on her breath, she vehemently denies drinking; however, later you observe that the car is parked askew.

D) You return home from a weekend away and, despite the fact that your sixteen-year-old daughter stayed with her friend's family, you find a stain on the living room chair, candy wrappers between the sofa seat cushions, and empty liquor bottles in the outdoor trash can.

E) Your sixteen-year-old daughter tells you that when she goes to parties there is always plenty of alcohol. Although she admits to occasionally tasting from a can of beer, she says that she knows her limit and has never gotten drunk.

4. Think It Through

When you assess each of these scenarios, what is it that upsets you most? Certainly, different levels of worry are suggested. You might consider how you learned of your daughter's behavior: directly from her, from your own observations, or from someone else? Did your daughter acknowledge and take responsibility for her decisions, deny her part, rationalize what she did, or blame others? Was your daughter's behavior impulsive? Or did she attempt to think things through but ultimately use faulty reasoning? To what degree did she take risks, and what kind? Was she aware of how her behavior affected others, including you and her father?

Probably the most fundamental issue for you is how deceptive or sneaky your daughter was. For example, did she fail to tell you the complete truth, concoct a white lie, renege on her original story and come clean, or continue to look you straight in the eye and insist on an elaborate, far-fetched fairy tale that you know is an absolute whopper? Once you are clear about your most pressing concerns, you will know how best to approach her. (For more on truthfulness, see the next chapter.)

5. Hold Her Accountable

Many a mother has thought, "Oh, well, maybe it's not worth making an issue out of after all" or "I'll just give her the benefit of the doubt." Despite such temptation to avoid your daughter's mistakes, this is when you must apply one of the main principles of parenting: not only expecting your daughter to be accountable, but modeling accountability yourself. No matter what she says, your daughter is relying on you to be her mother. She has to trust that you will do whatever you need to do, no matter how unpleasant or uncomfortable, to guide her through these adolescent years. If she thinks you will excuse or overlook her errors, you are essentially giving her license to make her own rules, to do as she pleases. Being her mother means addressing her mistakes. It requires confronting her bad judgment. Holding her accountable is the first step in teaching her to make better choices.

You may be apprehensive about making your daughter angry, resentful, afraid, or embarrassed, but this is a chance you must be willing to take. Because you are not her peer, however, you don't have to worry that your daughter will dump you. Yes, you might have to tolerate her temporary frustration, sulking, indignation, or rage. The atmosphere in your home may well get chilly for a while. But it is important that your daughter know how seriously you take your job. When she sees that you have the courage to confront her mistakes, she may be more willing to do the same.

6. Acknowledge Your Part

As always, to encourage your daughter to take responsibility, you probably want to acknowledge any part you played in the situation. However, this is not the same as accepting blame. While you did not make your daughter's decisions and cannot take that responsibility for her, perhaps there are things you might have done differently. For example, you may decide to be clearer about your expectations in the future to avoid hearing, "Oh, *that's* what you meant?" or "I didn't know you didn't want me to drive with *any* boys, I thought just if they'd been drinking." Considering your daughter's age and growing skills, you may need to adjust your limits, give her more or fewer rules, or adapt them to new situations. Maybe her errors suggest that you have not communicated your values as well as you thought you had. Or it is possible that you were not as involved in your daughter's life as you thought you were. Your openness to these possibilities, instead of merely blaming her or accusing her of wrongdoing, speaks volumes.

7. Communicate Effectively

• *Be brief.* When you do speak to your daughter, be brief. Say what you have to—and then let her be. It is unwise and unproductive to prolong a painful confrontation any longer than necessary. The more you talk, the less able your daughter will be to take in your words. While the typical teenage girl has a relatively brief attention span, it becomes even more limited when her mother addresses her bad decisions because she feels put on the spot or attacked. As suggested in *"I'm Not Mad, I Just Hate You!" A New Understanding of Mother-Daughter Conflict,* follow the "20-Second Rule." Say what you have to say in twenty seconds or less to ensure that your daughter hears your message:

NOT

> MOM: Let me tell you about alcohol, my dear. You may think you know what you're doing, but I think otherwise. I want you to have a good time, but not at the expense of your health and safety. How am I going to get through to you? Maybe I should tell you about your Aunt Bess. Do you know the story of what happened to her? I think it's about time you heard this story so you'll know exactly what choices you're making. When she was fourteen, . . .

TRY

> MOM: When I see what happened tonight, it makes me really concerned about the choices you're making about drinking when you're with your friends. We need to talk about this so I can feel that you're safe.

For the same reason it is wise to put a positive spin on what you say:

NOT

> MOM: You're so busted, young lady!

OR

> MOM: How could you have been so stupid?

OR

> MOM: Is this how I brought you up to behave?

TRY

> MOM: We need to figure out together how you can make better choices.

- *Stay in Control*

The last thing you want to do is escalate an already charged situation. So make up your mind to stay in control at all times, regardless of what your daughter says or does. If she yells, makes accusations, curses, or threatens, use all the strategies you have accumulated thus far. It is not that flaring emotions are harmful, but that you or your daughter may say hurtful things that cannot be taken back or, more worrisome, begin to express your feelings physically rather than verbally. No matter what, do not cross this line into pushing, slapping, smacking, or pulling—and prevent your daughter from doing the same.

- *Focus on the Positive*

Earlier you reminded yourself of whatever good choices your daughter made to alleviate your own distress. Now when you focus on what was positive along with her troubles, you are doing it for her sake. Commending her for partially good judgment helps her hear the other part of your message, and increases the likelihood of her making more wise decisions. Along with your reviews of her mistakes, you might want to say, "Good thinking!" or "You really used your head about that!" or "What a good idea that was!" What you want her to hear is, "I think you handled that part of the situation very well. You made a good choice there. Let's talk about what went wrong later."

8. Use Her Mistakes as Lessons

Keeping in mind your goal of helping your daughter to take better care of herself, you might think about what her troubling incident tells you about her skills. Where are the gaps that need further attention? Given too much freedom to surf the Net in the privacy of her bedroom, for example, your middle school daughter's exploration of inappropriate sites may be telling you she needs more supervision. Similarly your daughter's forgetting your family's rules while staying at friends' homes tells you she cannot yet make good decisions without more specific instructions or direct monitoring. Such mistakes point out that your daughter is not yet ready to assume so much responsibility. She needs more time, maturity, self-control, assertiveness, or other social skills. You can then direct your efforts accordingly so that she gains whatever skills she needs to enjoy more freedom in the future.

9. Take Time to Regroup

Just as contracting a virus or flu is the body's way of getting a much-needed rest, using bad judgment may be the psyche's way of carving out some time for reflection. Eventually, your daughter may look back on this time as a turning point of sorts, a pivotal moment when she learned some things and made important changes in herself. Although teenagers' mistakes—and the crises that often result—rarely occur when it is convenient, take time to regroup. Allow your family the time to recover. You may find that you are touchy around each other ("Why are you giving me that weird look?") or more apt to read into things ("What did you mean by that?"). You cannot expect an immediate turnaround or return to your former status. Give yourselves some privacy before you make an annual visit to the grandparents or have your own childhood friends to your home for the weekend.

10. Stay Connected

Above all, maintaining a respectful, closely connected mother-daughter relationship should be your priority. This is always the most important goal in guiding your teenager. David Chadwick, a minister and family life radio show host in North Carolina, likes to remind his listeners of this wise formula for parenting: $R + R - R = R$. The translation is: Rules and regulations without respect results in rebellion. How true! When your daughter finds herself in trouble, no matter her bravado, underneath she may be concerned about your feelings about her. Many a girl's worst fear is that her mother will cease to love her or may even reject her. So if your negative feelings are too strong, you may want to spare your daughter from feeling overwhelmed and desperate. Tell her you need time by yourself to think things through.

Anticipate Your Daughter's Reactions

No matter how much you prepare yourself for confronting your daughter, you cannot control—indeed you may barely predict—her reactions. Much will depend on her personality, your history, and the prevailing climate in the household. You may know, for example, that your daughter is sure to flip out if you and her father decide to speak with her at the same time because she will feel ganged up on. (Save that strategy for her most heinous crimes.) Similarly, for the same reason, you probably avoid discussing her mistakes when her siblings or friends are in earshot. Beyond that your daughter's reaction may vary according to her mood on any given day. Here is a sampling of what you might expect:

• *Relief.* When I say your daughter may be relieved by getting caught, let me qualify: She may feel this on the inside because behavior is finally out in the open. She no longer has the burden of maintaining this secret—sneaking around, hiding what she did, covering her tracks, and hoping you don't find out. All this has required enormous effort and energy. But as you undoubtedly know, it is unlikely you will see proof of this relief. She may not be able to show you that she feels apologetic or conciliatory. In fact, most of her reactions to getting caught are likely to be rather negative.

• *Anger and Resentment.* For many reasons, your daughter may become hateful and accusatory ("See? I knew you'd go crazy, so I just didn't tell you"). She may explain that, "You made me so mad by doing thus-and-such that I was just trying to get even with you." Or, she may be angry that you resorted to asking around—not to mention snooping around—to get the information with which she was busted. Her shame and embarrassment may come out as anger. Plus, if your daughter senses that you feel inadequate or vulnerable, she is likely to go in for the kill rather than focus on her own behavior. If you buy in to this line of reasoning, you let your daughter off the hook. Instead, give yourself a pep talk, if necessary, to stay firm in your beliefs. Remind yourself—and your daughter—that she is always responsible for her own decisions.

Particularly if your daughter usually makes an effort to abide by your rules or considers herself generally good, she is likely to be resentful when she is in trouble for a single incident of bad judgment. "What? You're freaking out about *that?*" she may ask. "It could've been so much worse. I'm not nearly as bad as my friends. You don't know how good I am compared to them." Your daughter feels indignant because in her mind her usually impeccable behavior should give her immunity from the occasional problem (e.g., "I just made one little mistake!"). At these times she needs your acknowledgment that this one episode has not erased her previous track record or changed the course of her entire adolescent life. She needs you to reassure her, if it is true, that typically you can count on her to make good decisions. However, this time she didn't, and that needs to be addressed.

• *Guilt.* You might think you would prefer this response when your daughter is caught. What you had in mind was her appropriately acknowledging her culpability and expressing remorse. You want your daughter to admit she was wrong and to feel genuinely sorry about what she did. Sometimes, however, she may go overboard in this department. When she denigrates herself (e.g., "I'm so horrible!" or "Now I'll never like myself again!"), you are then drawn to comfort her. You feel compelled to reassure her that "What you did isn't so bad!" Or, overly invested in displaying her guilt, your daughter will sometimes become tearful and hang her head, stating she is too distraught even to accept telephone calls. You might feel nothing but compassion—or, then again, you may be tempted to cry, "And in the category of Best Actress in an Adolescent Drama, the winner is . . ." Only you can sense the sincerity of your daughter's remorse.

• *Disbelief.* When she exclaims, "I can't believe I did that!" your daughter may be shocked by her own behavior. The knowledge that she was swept away or used poor judgment may be unsettling enough to provoke her to reexamine the situation and her own actions. Your daughter also may be surprised by the seriousness or significance of an incident she considered inconsequential at the time. Teenage girls commonly underestimate the seriousness and potential consequences of their mistakes.

Tina, fifteen, became furious with a girl who flirted openly with her boyfriend. In the cafeteria that day, she poured "a teeny drop" of nail polish remover in the other girl's soda can. When the girl became aware of the odor and/or the taste, she became upset and fled to the nurse's office. As a result of this rather impulsive and aggressive act, Tina was subsequently called to the principal's office and her parents were notified. In this era of school violence, schools are extremely cautious about such incidents and take them quite seriously. Tina had to undergo a psychological evaluation to determine whether she was dangerous to herself or others before she could return to school. She was incredulous, complaining that she could not believe that "all those horrible things" resulted from an action that she characterized as "only fooling around." Your daughter's disbelief is an invitation to enlighten her and to help her make a connection between her behavior and its likely consequences.

• *Embarrassment.* When she learns that you know about her behavior, your daughter may cringe with humiliation. If her trouble becomes a matter of public record or the grist of gossip mills, she may withdraw from her daily life. Your daughter may stay in her room, refusing to speak to her friends or to frequent her usual haunts. She may avoid particular peers whom she knows will grill her or ask for all the gory details. While a little embarrassment might be a valuable natural consequence of the incident, as well as a possible inducement to avoid repeating her behavior, excessive self-consciousness is undesirable. It is unhealthy for your daughter to isolate herself.

Finding out that her best friend was told by the other girls in her group that she gave away a secret, Lena was too embarrassed to face them. For the next several weeks, she experienced a variety of non-specific pains and physical complaints that kept her out of school. Once the furor died down, Lena recovered and returned to class. Your daughter's embarrassment is an opportunity to remind her that it is her own reaction to her mistake that matters most. She needs to pay more attention to her own inner voice than to the reactions of her peers.

• *Fear.* It is only after the fact that girls often recognize when they have been spared from terrible consequences. When LeeAnn, fifteen, was at a friend's house, she was asked to look in the friend's father's top drawer for his credit card case. No parents were at home, the girls were drinking beer, and LeeAnn was not thinking clearly. She says, "I stuck my hand in the drawer to feel around for the wallet and I picked up something big and heavy. It was a gun! What if it went off accidentally and somebody got shot?" Even in less dramatic scenarios, your daughter may be frightened that as a result of her mistake her life could have changed irrevocably. This is more than a fear of losing privileges; she is apprehensive that you will never trust or love her again. It is this deep-seated, unconscious fear that often causes girls to act haughtily or to adopt a "Who cares?" attitude when they are caught doing something bad.

Get Past the Trouble

To move on from this crisis, it is helpful to remember the larger picture. Your daughter's mistake is merely one small part of how she behaved in a particular situation on a particular day in a particular time of her life. Don't catastrophize! Stop yourself from using this one mistake as evidence of permanent character flaws ("She'll always be selfish!") or limitations in her future ("She'll never be able to support herself!" or "How will she marry a decent man?"). Your daughter will probably not be doomed forever because of this one error in judgment. Or two or three. Adolescents do change and mature.

To get past this trouble, once again you might try to be attuned to what your daughter is thinking and feeling. Even though you don't agree with her choices, you can put yourself in her position to better understand her intentions and reactions. To muster compassion for your daughter, recall how as a teenager you wanted to feel and be seen as cool, daring, and independent. Accept that because she has not yet developed enough judgment and self-control to manage these urges, she will surely make her share of mistakes.

Viewing these mistakes as part of your daughter's social and emotional education helps. Rather than expecting immediate success, over time you are hoping to see her choices steadily improving. Even if she didn't seem especially contrite or remorseful when she was caught, she may have learned her lesson. But how can you make sure? What can you do to ensure that your daughter doesn't repeat her mistakes? When problems are serious and she needs professional help, that route will be obvious. But with everyday trouble, it will be up to you and her father to decide how best to handle these matters. For this reason, the next chapter on discipline will help you to assess if, when, and how to give your daughter effective consequences.

Safeguards Against Trouble

When your daughter is a preteen or teenager, think about establishing some safeguards against future difficulties. Give her practical choices and resourceful skills to use in unsettling or confusing situations. Armed with these alternatives, she may be less inclined to make poor decisions and get into trouble:

1. *Rely on Mom.* Your daughter needs to know that she can always depend upon you to help her get out of bad or uncomfortable circumstances. Give her advance permission to blame you for having to leave a social event, to call home, or to do whatever she feels is needed. In any situation, your daughter is more likely to pay attention to her inner voice suggesting a hasty retreat when she knows there is always a way out.

2. *Establish a Code.* Because your daughter will want to save face in front of her peers, agree upon a certain procedure or code word to communicate, "There's trouble." For example, if she says she forgot her keys or complains of a headache, you will know that she wants out, no matter where she is or what she told you previously.

3. *Guarantee a Ride.* Tell your daughter that she can call you at any time to pick her up and bring her home, with no questions asked and no punishment. If you are not home while she is out, carry a pager or cell phone so that she can reach you. You will gain immediate peace of mind knowing that your daughter never has to

stay somewhere when she is uncomfortable or accept an undesirable ride. If you do pick her up and she has been drinking or using drugs, abide by your promise not to ask questions or punish her.

4. *Use Community Resources*. Many communities offer a safe rides program, usually run by high school students, which also guarantees transportation for teenagers who need a ride home. Make sure your daughter knows what services are available for her and her friends.

5. *Role Play.* Anticipate potential dilemmas and help your daughter to think of solutions. Include situations that involve adults as well as teenagers. For example, what should she do if the parent who picks her up at a sports event seems drunk? What are her options if her ride disappears and leaves her stranded? What should she do if she feels uncomfortable being alone with a father who is supposed to take her home from a baby-sitting job?

6. *Give Her Tools.* Together, think of statements that your daughter can use in difficult situations. Help her tailor the words so they feel right to her and she can say them naturally:

> "I just remembered my mom said I had to call her before I went home."
> "You think that's *cool*?"
> "My parents will kill me if they find out."
> "I'll lose my car if I do that."
> "My mom insists on picking me up."

"If I get caught, I'll be grounded for life; it's not
    worth it."
"I'm not feeling very well."
"Hey, not tonight. I'm not in the right mood."
"I've gotta get up at the crack of dawn."
"I have a big game tomorrow."
"No thanks, not right now."
"I've sworn off that stuff."

Chapter 7
Truth and Consequences
DISCIPLINE

"I don't know what's happened since my daughter started middle school, but I feel as if I'm losing control. At first, I took her phone out of her room because she was constantly gabbing, even after she was supposed to be asleep. Then she was so busy talking to her friends online that she wasn't doing all her homework and I received several interim reports. So I took away her e-mail privileges. Just last week, I found out that when Sherrill supposedly stayed after school to get extra help for her science test, she was actually hanging out with her pals in the cafeteria. That lie was the last straw! I grounded her for the next six weeks. But has she changed her ways? Not at all. She's been in a foul mood, constantly picking fights with everyone in the family. I have no idea what to do, but nothing I've been trying seems to be working." —Fern, forty-five

"My daughter has always been a rather easy kid who's just done whatever it is that I expected her to do. We've had such a good relationship that discipline has hardly ever been needed. But recently I found a beer can in the back of her closet, and when I tried to talk to her about it she blew up. I was flabbergasted, but figured she was just having a bad day. Then she was pretty rude to me and wouldn't apologize for that. Again, I felt as if I should do something, but it's my nature to avoid conflict. I just forgot about these incidents and figured she'd get back to her old self. But now a problem's come up that I can't ignore. Shannon's best friend's mother called me because the girls took her car without permission. Everyone says I have to punish her, but isn't it normal for teenagers to sneak around? I'm afraid to make too big a deal out of this. I guess I'm really afraid of pushing my daughter away." —Sheila, forty

"Eva is a very strong-willed girl who always wants to be on her own. Whenever I tell her no, that doing something is out of the question, she accuses me of not trusting her. That's usually not the case. It's just that I'm always worried about letting her take that next step. Recently, she's done a few things that definitely made me lose trust in her. It's a terrible feeling. Whenever I look at her now, instead of seeing my sweet little girl, I picture in my mind what she's done. I'd like to keep reminding her how upset I am about this, how little I can trust her. I don't, though, because I know that deep down Eva feels just as bad about all of this. It kills me that I don't know how I am ever going to trust her again, let alone forgive her. How can we get beyond this?"

—Bonita, thirty-nine

 Y our daughter's adolescence is likely to be filled with a mixture of triumphs and failures. Since her development as a social being is a process—much like the course of becoming fluent in a foreign language, executing a perfect back flip, or reaching the high notes in her solo piece—sometimes she will fall short. In theory, you accept and even anticipate this possibility. You may now be more inclined to see her unfortunate behavior as a sign that her skills need some work, rather than as an indication of permanent character flaws or a doomed future.

Still, you are faced with the challenge of knowing how to respond so that your daughter does learn from her mistakes and refines her skills. How can you give her the clear message that her behavior is unacceptable so that she doesn't do these things again? This chapter will take you though the most common dilemmas mothers face in such situations. Essentially, when must you think about doing something beyond talking to her? What should you do to make your point so that your daughter makes better choices in the future? And how can you discipline her most fairly and effectively?

A Typical Disciplinary Quandary: Should You Punish Her?

Like many mothers, as you sort through these issues you may hold a debate within yourself, first presenting one side, then its counterpoint, in your own internal argument. Suppose, for example, that your daughter and her friends made some poor decisions that got them into trouble at a recent community fair. In the hope of convincing her to see the light (that is, to agree with your view that she needs to use better judgment), your first tactic is probably to sit down with your daughter and have a heart-to-heart talk.

On occasion this approach may do the trick. But what if, despite trying out your top-notch strategies for discussions, she doesn't come around to your way of thinking? What if you are not at all reassured that were she to face the same situation again, she would make different decisions? In fact, what if your daughter becomes angrier and more defensive about her activities, even defiant about your efforts to chastise her? Or what if you remember that she got into this same sort of trouble last year, and worry that this is becoming a pattern?

Such thoughts could well propel you to take further action. You might then ask, "What will put a stop to this behavior once and for all?" You may look to make a statement that is somehow louder, more urgent, and less likely to be forgotten than in the past. Maybe you will begin racking your brain to figure out the exact right punishment, the cleverest and most perfect consequence to teach your daughter this momentous life lesson.

Before you get too far, however, other thoughts may stop you in your tracks. When you recall that previous efforts to correct your daughter's bad choices were dismal failures, you may think, "It won't do any good anyway; it never does!" More worrisome, after remembering that "Last go-round, we didn't speak for a week!" you may conclude that punishing your daughter only seems to make things worse. With this in mind, it is easy to decide that dealing with her mistake is simply not worth the risk of jeopardizing the goodwill in your relationship. Shouldn't that be your top priority?

Anyway you rationalize, her error was probably only a slight lapse of good sense. After all, she was a bit overwhelmed when this incident occurred. Maybe she was feeling rejected by her crush, or had gotten a bad grade from a mean teacher, or had just endured an unfair team loss. In light of these recent traumatic events, your daughter's mistake is perfectly understandable, perhaps not even her fault. And besides, what would punishing her accomplish other than making her unhappy—or unhappier? That doesn't seem particularly nurturing or loving to you. You prefer to give to your daughter, not to take things away.

This series of thoughts, which is based on fear and self-doubt rather than a clear sense of purpose, typically exacerbates mothers' confusion about what constitutes useful or appropriate responses to their daughters' mistakes. As a result many tend to err at one extreme or another along the disciplinary continuum, either invoking overly harsh or unrealistic punishments in the throes of distress, or letting the crisis blow over and imposing few or no consequences. The bottom line is, when mothers put off taking action while they obsess about what to do, in effect they do nothing.

This is when you might apply several of the key principles of effective parenting. Having made the important distinction between your daughter's thoughts and deeds, you recognize that she crossed a line. Your actions therefore need to convey clearly that this is unacceptable to you. Above all, in order to make her accountable for her behavior, you have to be accountable as well, even if that makes you uncomfortable or uneasy.

Let me clarify from the outset, however, that disciplining your daughter or giving her consequences does not necessarily mean punishing her. If you equate discipline with spankings, harsh restrictions, verbal cruelty, or even abusiveness, you can set your mind at ease at once. You can discipline your daughter positively, fairly, and effectively, while remaining loving and closely connected with her.

All discipline means is teaching your daughter to learn from her mistakes, to refrain from repeating them, and to make better decisions in the future. It is a way of responding to her that encourages her to solve problems more effectively. You are essentially guiding her by providing logical consequences for her actions.

But when the inevitable mistake occurs, when your daughter uses truly awful judgment or places herself at tremendous risk or smiles into your eyes as she lies unabashedly, all those rational and sensible thoughts may fly right out of your head. You may have an uncontrollable urge to do something—*anything*—rather than feel helpless. Perhaps you might scream, "You're grounded until next spring!" or something even worse, unleashing your daughter's boundless fury or provoking a domestic Cold War. To reassure yourself that you are on the right disciplinary track, you might ask yourself these two questions:

1. Am I Invoking Consequences for the Right Reasons?

• *Disciplining Out of Anger or Frustration*

Learning to avoid knee-jerk emotional reactions has prepared you to postpone disciplining until you can be most effective. Refer back to Chapters 5 and 6, if necessary, to review strategies for approaching your daughter while you are in a state. When disciplining your daughter, you convey respect by separating your feelings from your actions. As upset or disgusted as you may be, you might refrain from expressing disdain. Your seething silence will not teach her to make better choices. Belittling her will not induce her to abide by your values.

Similarly, you might question whether you are disciplining your daughter for reasons other than her crime. Teenagers in therapy often tell me about being punished because of unpleasant exchanges with their mothers. As they describe these episodes, something rings hollow; for example, the explanation given for punishment often seems particularly murky or mysterious. Although girls often are unaware of their own behavior and cannot understand their mothers' objections, sometimes I get the sense that there is truly more to these stories.

Consider the possibility, for example, that you might be upset about something else entirely, perhaps an issue that may not even relate to your daughter. If this is troubling you, unwittingly you may make a proverbial mountain out of the molehill of your daughter's minor error. You might, for example, tell her that she can't go to the long-awaited eighth-grade graduation dance just because she just talked back to you. Do you ever find yourself overreacting to something your daughter did simply because you were in a bad mood? Or, angry about something else your daughter said or did, have you fanned the flames of a subsequent argument, perhaps to justify punishing her? If you answer yes to any of these questions, you might legitimately think twice before invoking discipline.

- *Disciplining to Control*

When you feel as if you are losing all influence over her social life, not to mention your daughter herself, consider the possibility that you may assert your authority just because you want to—or think you still can. To demonstrate that you can still control her, despite her growing independence, you might find reasons to restrict her. For example, during a heated discussion with her about an unchaperoned party or a later curfew, you may suddenly hear yourself say, "It's rude to interrupt me! Now you're not going out at all!" You have effectively reduced your own anxiety by manufacturing reasons to ground your daughter—and thereby preventing her from experiencing age-appropriate opportunities. Afraid of her possible choices, you prevent her from having to make any. As always, however, aim to be noncontrolling. Consider your daughter's age and let go gradually. Discipline used for the wrong reasons will only give you the *illusion* of control, and will probably intensify her resentment or ignite a rebellion.

- *When Disciplining Is Overkill*

It is also valid to question whether it is appropriate to discipline when your daughter is already being punished. For example, if her misbehavior in school has resulted in a detention or suspension, it is probably best to let school deal with the problem, as long as you believe they are handling the situation appropriately. Stay out of the relationship between your daughter and her teachers or school administrators. Their punishment may be enough. In this case, enjoy the freedom to be supportive of your daughter while her school takes on the role of the bad guy.

You might also respect the natural consequences your daughter may suffer after she makes a mistake with her friends. For example, she may confide to you that she broke a promise, acted unkindly, or stole her friend's boyfriend. Or you may see for yourself the painful fallout of her behavior, such as having an angry, withdrawn friend, dealing with the ostracism of her group, being reluctant to return to school, or feeling terrible guilt. Again, rather than imposing your own, additional consequences, you are in a position to empathize objectively, support her understanding of the situation, and guide her in learning from her mistake.

2. Do I Tend to Discipline out of Habit?

• *Imitating What You Experienced*

To avoid reflexive but unhelpful responses to your daughter's mistakes, you might reflect on your tendencies. Your disciplinary style has undoubtedly been shaped, at least in part, by your own parents. If you approved of your parents' style, you may be comfortably following their lead. In fact, without giving this issue much thought, you may react to your own daughter's trouble just as your parents did when you were in hot water. Like your mother, for example, you may be loathe to discipline or, conversely, you may step in every time your daughter's toe crosses a line. Similarly, when you punish her, you may use a particular strategy, such as grounding, giving her chores, or taking away her phone, no matter what she did wrong, and regardless of whether this is the best approach for your daughter. It is wise to ask yourself if she needs more or less discipline than you did, or perhaps another form of guidance. When you remain attuned to your daughter, you are aware of her disciplinary needs and respect that they may be different from your own.

• *Trying to Do It Differently*

If you were disciplined in an extreme manner, you may be trying deliberately to use a whole different approach with your daughter. For example, if you believe your mother was neither aware of nor sufficiently responsive to your mistakes ("She was out to lunch"), you may be determined to stay on top of your daughter and correct her every mistake to ensure that she does not get away with murder. Of course, if you carry this to an extreme, your fears of invoking harsh or unfair discipline may be valid.

On the other hand, if one or both of your parents were severe disciplinarians, you may go out of your way to be gentle and non-confrontational. As Sheila describes her early experience, it becomes clearer why she struggles with disciplining her daughter, Shannon: "My mother was pretty critical of me, always punishing me for the slightest thing. Instead of wanting to please her, I grew up feeling resentful. I remember once she found out that I had lied to her. It was about something little, but she actually made me stay home when everybody went to see the July Fourth fireworks. I was so mad that I sat there all night thinking up ways to get back at her."

You too may bend over backward not to recreate a situation with your own daughter that you disliked as you were growing up. Being aware of these tendencies will help you to know whether or not you are hesitating to discipline your daughter for the right reasons. If not, you may well have to take action. If you follow these guidelines, however, you will be more confident of disciplining her fairly, positively, and effectively.

Guidelines for Effective Discipline

• *Be Timely*

Respond to your daughter's behavior as soon as possible after your own reactions are in control and your thoughts are clear. But you have to use your judgment here; this does not mean lambasting her the moment her face appears in the front doorway or correcting her while she is entertaining friends. Being timely requires that you deal with a situation while it is fresh in everyone's mind and the facts are still readily recalled—within, say, a day or two. By all means, wait until both you and your daughter are calmer and can think more clearly so you can stay in control. But if you procrastinate until the clamor is but a distant memory in your daughter's mind, she is likely to feel blindsided. You will know this when she cries, "You're still bringing *that* up? But it happened so long ago!" To her, a belated consequence is evidence of your spitefulness, not your loving concern. You are then likely to hear, "You're so mean! All you do is keep reminding me of how awful I am."

The most dreaded situations, according to teenage girls, are when their mothers drag it out when they are in trouble. This happens in two ways. One, they are impatient to be sentenced after committing a crime, and two, they fear being punished indefinitely. Being restricted from having fun with friends for an unspecified time period can feel as intolerable to your daughter as being exiled for all eternity. Girls need to know when they can look forward to a reinstatement of their phone and online privileges and their freedom to go places after school—in short, when their lives can return to normal. Otherwise they can become unduly discouraged, hopeless, and even desperate. So specify the exact time period you have in mind for her restriction or loss of privilege. Remember that once you have made your point, you can let up. In fact, repeatedly throwing your daughter's crime in her face will probably backfire.

• *Let Her Make Amends*

By giving your daughter consequences, you are affording her the chance to atone and make amends for her errors. This enables her to deal with her own feelings, such as guilt, embarrassment, or remorse. Ironically, making her pay for her mistakes may assuage her self-blame and alleviate her need to beat herself up. For example, she can earn the money to compensate someone for her carelessness or perform acts of kindness to atone for thoughtlessness. So if you are hesitant to make an issue out of your daughter's poor decision, you might consider that not only are you teaching her a lesson, but also you are helping her to put the incident behind her, forgive herself, and move on.

There may be times when it is possible and desirable for her to make restitution. For example, when Portia, eleven, was caught with a necklace she had taken from a store the family visited while on vacation, her mother asked that she include a detailed letter of apology when she sent it back. Similarly, Ursula, fourteen, had to do chores to earn the money required to repair a mailbox that she and a group of friends vandalized one evening. Asking that your daughter do something tangible to fix her mistake is not only potentially healing, but also a positive learning experience.

• *Be Positive*

Praise is a powerful motivator for learning. You may be amazed at how effectively you can teach your daughter when you follow the principle "Catch her doing something right." For example, when you say, "It must've been hard not to join your friends when they all went to town. That was such good judgment," you are not only validating her inner voice, but also reinforcing her internal motivation. That strengthens the sense of personal satisfaction she gets from making good decisions and, therefore, her commitment to repeating them. If you praise too infrequently, your daughter may despair of pleasing you and stop trying. Just as important, positive consequences contribute to goodwill between the two of you and a generally pleasant atmosphere in your home.

Another way you can keep discipline positive is to avoid teaching your daughter a lesson at the cost of another valuable opportunity. For example, you probably don't want to take away an activity that she needs or would benefit from. Forbidding her from participating in track or softball would eliminate a healthy way for her to reduce stress, elevate her mood, and stay in shape. Similarly, if your daughter tends to struggle with friends, you might not want to restrict her from potentially beneficial social opportunities, even if she did cave in to peer pressure. Instead, you may want to permit these activities, but only under certain conditions, or with better supervision. Find a way to teach your daughter a lesson without truly punishing her.

• *Be Specific*

When you focus on the positive, also try to be as specific as possible (e.g., "That was such a great decision to call us. I'm really proud of you"). That way, your daughter is likely to pay more attention than when you issue blanket approvals (e.g., "You're such a wonderful girl!"). Specific praise rings true to her. She perceives you as being attentive and honest in your appraisal. Thus your stock in credibility rises.

• *Reward Desirable Behavior*

Along with praising her, award your daughter more privileges when you approve of her choices. That way she will associate, quite correctly, that she gets more opportunities when she demonstrates good judgment. For example, "Since you showed great self-control by not drinking when you had the chance, I think you're ready to do thus-and-such." The privilege she earned should be related to the skill she demonstrates. In this case, if her age permits, you might allow her more leeway about unsupervised socializing. Although wise decisions are not always rewarded (in fact, it is one of the realities of life that occasionally good behavior is actually punished), whenever possible help your daughter to realize the benefits of her desirable choices.

• *Use Negative Consequences to Make a Statement*

The purpose of discipline is to communicate to your daughter that she needs to rethink a bad decision. When you use negative consequences sparingly, you make a forceful statement to that effect. For example, to make a point when your daughter messes up rather badly, you might take away what she loves most or is looking forward to doing (e.g., her telephone or e-mail privileges, a sleepover date, getting her own pet, etc.). The problem is, when such negative discipline is used routinely, its effectiveness is diluted. So choose these consequences carefully, and use them when they matter most.

• *Make Consequences Fair and Appropriate*

Effective discipline is logical rather than arbitrary. Above all, it has to make sense to your daughter. Thus consequences must fit and follow naturally from their crimes. To highlight your daughter's demonstrated lack of judgment, you might consider restricting or temporarily rescinding her privileges in that same area. For example, if she makes an inordinate number of long-distance phone calls, forbidding her from participating in her school's homecoming weekend seems unreasonable. Better strategies might include requiring her to get permission before using the phone, asking her to repay you for her inappropriate calls, and curtailing her unlimited phone usage until she demonstrates better restraint. Also, tailor consequences to her age. Treating your older teenager as you did when she was younger will surely infuriate her. If your daughter perceives her consequence as fair, she will be more apt to learn her lesson and less inclined to rebel or retaliate.

- *Factor in Her Honesty*

You may wish to assess how you want to handle the matter of your daughter's truthfulness. If this is a priority for you—as I believe it should be—you might take the position that "If I ever find out that you lie to me, you will be in far worse trouble than if you tell the truth." If you agree with this stance, you will need to follow through by being more lenient if your daughter admits that she made a mistake, holds herself accountable, and demonstrates that she learned her lesson. Conversely, if she lies about her crime, the outcome might be costlier. To communicate most clearly that lying is unacceptable to you, acknowledge and reward her honesty.

- *Be Creative*

Whenever possible, design a consequence that offers multiple benefits. For example, if your daughter has mistreated a younger brother or sister, requiring her to do a favor for her sibling may suffice as an apology, provide an opportunity to serve as a role model, and encourage closeness. Or if your daughter has chosen to be rebellious or disrespectful to you, you might ask her to do extra work around the house. Not only is she making restitution for her mistakes by lightening your workload, but physical tasks enable her to blow off steam, reduce tension, learn new domestic skills, and feel proud of the contribution she makes to the family.

- *Elicit Your Daughter's Ideas*

If you are undecided about how best to respond to her mistake, you might use a collaborative approach by asking for your daughter's input: "What do you think would be a fair consequence?" Of course you are not obligated to accept her suggestions, but you may be surprised at your daughter's objectivity and fairness. In fact, not a few mothers have told me that their daughters suggested far more severe consequence than they had in mind! By including her in this process, you are stimulating her thinking about the natural consequences of her actions, staying attuned to what is important to her at her age, and contributing to the good will in your relationship.

• *Make Consequences as Mild as Possible*

To distort a well-known Chinese proverb, "Don't use a hatchet to remove a fly from your daughter's forehead." Many times, you can accomplish your objective—that is, highlighting your daughter's mistake so that she can learn from it—by instituting a relatively mild consequence. Maddy, for example, mother to ten-year-old Ginnie, found that she did not have to cancel her daughter's birthday party when she was caught stealing candy from a classmate. Instead, after much discussion about this episode and what it meant to Ginnie, she asked her daughter to write an essay about all the reasons why it is a bad decision to steal. You too may realize that harshness does not underscore a lesson, but rather disheartens the soul of the pupil.

• *Be Realistic*

Mothers often get into trouble when they institute a consequence they are ambivalent about, or that will be difficult to impose. Discipline can be effective only if it is realistic enough to be enforced. For example, if your daughter will be doing homework or research on a computer located in her bedroom, it will be nearly impossible to forbid her from responding to instant messages from her online buddies. You would have to become the full-time guardian of your daughter's computer monitor. If you don't follow through, all you will teach your daughter is not to take your discipline seriously. Jamie, fourteen, for example, who frequently locks horns with her mother, scoffs, "She threatens all kinds of stuff and I get all sorts of punishments, but I don't care. I can do whatever I want 'cause she just sorta forgets about them."

• *Be Clear*

It is important to avoid the possibility of miscommunication about consequences, which only complicates matters and intensifies bad feelings. For example, if you tell your seventeen-year-old daughter that she has lost her car privileges this weekend, clarify whether she may still go out if she gets a ride, or if you are expecting her to stay in. Otherwise, it is likely that you will find yourself mired in no-win land:

> DAUGHTER: But you never said I couldn't go to that dance!
> MOTHER: You know darn well what I meant!
> DAUGHTER: No, you didn't say that at all. You're changing your mind. It's so unfair!

• *Trade Consequences*

Modifying a consequence is not the same as rescinding it or failing to enforce it. For example, it is reasonable to substitute one consequence for another if you decide that doing so is in your daughter's or the family's best interest. You may come to believe that she should attend a concert, after all, so as not to disappoint a friend to whom she made a commitment, or that her restriction should not interfere with her participating in a long-planned event. In such cases, make it clear that you are not forgetting her consequence, but merely modifying it. You can still make your point even if you change the terms.

• *Maintain Your Relationship*

As always, don't lose sight of your relationship with your daughter. Her teenage breach of trust should not be permitted to damage the connection between you. Beneath your daughter's demeanor, whether she is blasé, unrepentant, sanctimonious, or on her high horse, she may fear losing your love more than she can acknowledge to herself, let alone express to you. Upon hearing that her mother found out about an indiscretion, many a teenage girl has anxiously asked, "Do you hate me now?"

When your daughter is bad (or, more to the point, is caught), she may fear seeing a different, now-tainted reflection of herself in your eyes. In essence she is not pleased with herself and is attributing to you her own guilty feelings. Not too long ago, I received a poignant note from one of the middle school students with whom I spoke at an all-girls private school. She wrote: "I am the youngest of two and I am the angel of the family. Recently my parents discovered that I am not perfect. Now I feel my parents look at me differently and see me as a bad kid. I don't know how to deal with it because I am fine with what I do but I still want to feel my parents love me." This is one of the central quandaries of every teenage girl: reconciling who she is and wants to be with the ideals of her parents.

The Universal Consequence: "You're Grounded!"

For many mothers the staple of discipline is grounding daughters— that is, keeping them at home rather than allowing them to go out by themselves or with friends. If you are inclined to use this consequence, it pays to be aware of why it is useful, how it works best, and what pitfalls you might want to avoid.

• *Advantages of Grounding*

It is true that grounding can be a powerful, no-nonsense consequence for bad decisions. As an occasional, short-term restriction, grounding your daughter seems to make a point. You are basically telling her, "I'm not comfortable with what you did. For this time period, you are not going to socialize so you can think about making better decisions in the future." By keeping her from certain social situations, you may also be preventing her, at least temporarily, from repeating her mistakes. Presumably, your daughter's intense desire to socialize will induce her to use better judgment so she can avoid being grounded again. Yet grounding is rarely that simple. There are some rather compelling issues that you might want to consider.

• *Effects on the Family*

It could be that you are among the rare but fortunate mothers who enjoy their daughters' company when girls are forced to stay at home. More likely, you may ask yourself who is actually being punished when your daughter is grounded. When teenage girls are miserable, as you surely know, they are extraordinarily gifted in spreading their discontent to everyone around them. Thus rather rapidly they make their mothers, fathers, and siblings feel just as wretched as they do. There is actually no incentive for them to do otherwise. In fact, grounded girls often think, "Why should I be good? I'm stuck at home anyway." Before you decide to impose this restriction, ask yourself how you will handle your daughter's possible reactions, such as sullen moods, martyrlike behavior, aggressiveness, or retaliatory silent treatment.

- *Modify the Terms, as Needed*

To get the most out of keeping your daughter at home, reduce her negative reactions, and prevent your family from suffering along with her, you might consider how to fashion the terms of her being grounded. In his book, *How to Behave So Your Kids Will, Too!*, psychologist Sol Severe offers this advice: Restrict for an even number of days (e.g., four, six, eight, or a maximum of twelve), but deduct one day of punishment for each day your daughter behaves well during the grounding period. That way, she is more inclined to see the arrangement as fair and flexible.

Similarly, you might modify the terms of the grounding as circumstances change. Alexa's daughter, Victoria, was a freshman in high school when she hosted a party for upperclassmen while her mother and father were away. Alexa not only wanted to punish her daughter for an outrageous infraction of an obvious rule, but also, considering Victoria's age, she wished to make the point that she was not ready to handle socializing with older students. At first, Alexa grounded Victoria for a few weeks, but told her specifically how she could prove she was more responsible. When her daughter fulfilled those conditions, Alexa then allowed her to invite friends over while she or her husband were home. In other words, she provided only as much supervision as she thought her daughter needed. Gradually, in small steps, she allowed Victoria to have as much additional freedom as she proved she was able to handle.

- *Beware of Severing Lifelines*

Another potential danger of too many or too severe restrictions is cutting off your daughter from friendships she sees as vital to her continued existence. Of course, as a result of her mistakes, you may be tempted to ground her to protect her from undesirable friends. As you will see in the next chapter, however, that goal is not ideal. Your real objective is to help your daughter to make better choices when she *is* being social. But when mothers are alarmed about their daughters' bad choices (especially, it seems, in the academic realm), their immediate response may be imposing ever more restrictions—until girls feel trapped in their rooms, unable to contact the outside world.

As Fern described in one of the stories that opened this chapter, she first forbade her daughter, Sherrill, to use the telephone and when that did not work, rescinded her e-mail privileges. When that too failed, she tried grounding her. Cut off from all social contacts, however, teenage girls often feel isolated and may even become depressed. Like Sherrill, they may also feel panicky and desperate. Girls need to hear the reassurance of their best friend's voice each night and get caught up on all the news since school let out at two-forty. Otherwise, they can feel left out or even discarded and rejected by peers. When Fern recognized how these consequences were adversely affecting her daughter (and also were ineffective), she eased up.

Even when you must make a thunderous point, if you ground your daughter you might allow her to connect to her friends in some other way. This is both humane and beneficial to her well-being.

Downward Spirals of Discipline

Punishment: When Less Is More

Mothers are sometimes confounded by teenage daughters whose behavior not only fails to improve with punishment, but actually deteriorates. It is as if they are so outraged at being punished that their behavior becomes even more defiant or atrocious. In response, mothers usually impose further restrictions. In fact, each time girls refuse to abide by consequences, additional penalties are given, until they pile up at an astronomic and alarming rate.

For example, if two weeks of grounding proves insufficient, mothers extend the punishment to four weeks. If restricting the telephone fails to do the trick, mothers also eliminate e-mail privileges. On and on they search for new and different ways to punish daughters in desperate attempts to finally get through to them. This negative cycle self-perpetuates, until there is nothing else to take away. Because this hardly inspires girls to improve skills and change their behavior, discipline has lost its meaning and effectiveness, and mothers are understandably at sea.

Of course in dire situations it may be prudent and reasonable to keep your daughter under lock and key. In such cases, you are likely to be working closely with a professional counselor, who can advise you about what conditions are most sensible. In everyday circumstances, however, it is good to detect and interrupt patterns of mounting punishments as soon as possible. Your daughter may be

one of many girls who does not respond well to negative consequences. You may find that instead of being vigilant for mistakes
and instituting punishments, it is better to correct her behavior by
looking for and acknowledging signs of her compliance and good
decisions. You might be on the alert for successes rather than failures, provide incentives for desired behaviors, and reward them
accordingly.

This was Fern's solution to the downward disciplinary spiral she
found herself in with her daughter, Sherrill. Finding herself at wit's
end to make her point, Fern decided to call a cease-fire. She sat
down with Sherrill and suggested that they erase all previous restrictions and start over with a clean slate. Fern then described how she
would do her part to keep the household running smoothly and
take steps to help Sherrill get better organized. When Fern promised
to have dinner ready by six-thirty every evening, Sherrill agreed that
she would start her homework before dinner, and finish any remaining assignments before doing things for pleasure.

Then they negotiated a period of time each evening when Sherrill could use the phone or talk to her friends online. Initially, Fern
reinstated Sherrill's privileges for a minimum amount of time, but
provided an additional proviso: For each week that Sherrill got to
the school bus on time, maintained specified grades, and completed
her household chores, the following week her phone and online
time would increase by ten minutes, up to a certain maximum. For
failure to live up to any of these expectations, Sherrill would lose ten
minutes of phone and online time the following week. They put this
agreement in writing and signed it.

Thus Sherrill was given incentives and rewarded for successes.
Within these parameters—achievable ways to gain privileges, along
with clear-cut, defined consequences for not doing so—Sherrill felt
both motivated and empowered to improve her behavior. Fern appreciated her daughter's efforts, as well as the more positive atmosphere in their home.

Hard Transitions

It is no coincidence that downward spirals often begin when girls
start middle school or high school. In fact, these transitions often
provoke developmental crises for teenagers and their mothers. As

girls anxiously try to adapt to sharply heightened social and academic demands, they often make abrupt, radical shifts in both attitude and behavior, all of which can alarm their mothers. Although
mothers then issue consequences to try to restore equilibrium, this
strategy often backfires. What occurs instead is a steady stream of
deteriorating behavior, lengthy discussions, and unpleasant scenes
between girls and their mothers.

Describing a typical scenario, Felice, forty-four, laments that her
thirteen-year-old daughter has gotten off to a bad start in junior
high by becoming overly precocious: "Christine is so driven to socialize that she frenetically makes plans with friends, gets phone calls
at all hours, tries to wear more sophisticated and provocative clothing, puts homework on a back burner, and wants to venture into
areas she knows are forbidden." Many mothers complain that girls
begin to lie, usually about where they are and whom they are with.
One hallmark of this developmental crisis is that mothers are struck
by their daughters' telling relatively petty, even obvious, fibs that are
easily discovered.

Similarly, mothers describe how daughters starting high school
suddenly begin to act as if they expected to shed all vestiges of
parental authority at the main entrance. Instead of asking for permission, girls begin to *tell* their mothers they are going out. They
demand use of the family car, or act as if they consider their whereabouts to be classified information. Even if teenagers are actually behaving appropriately, this attitude is enough to send their mothers
into a panic.

During transitions, when mothers' anxieties are already running
high, they may be inclined to impose even steeper punishments for
their daughters' poor choices. In fact, in this cultural climate of increasing alarm about substances, sexuality, and violence during adolescence, mothers may react to relatively minor or common mistakes
as if they were certain indications of serious problems. They are desperate to halt what they fear may be a pattern of rapidly deteriorating behavior. On the other hand, failing to take appropriate action
when girls struggle with transitions may also exacerbate or escalate
problems.

Rather than immediately treating your daughter like a prisoner,
try to recognize the likely developmental reasons for her unfortunate behavior. What is she trying to accomplish, and how can you

guide her to do it more effectively? Consider her age; is she attempting to feel more grown-up and taking steps toward independence that you would consider appropriate if she were older? Is she caught up in trying to do what her peers are doing, but showing you she is not ready to handle the pressure?

When your daughter messes up as she switches schools or makes other important changes, she may be letting you know she is experiencing too much too fast. View her broken rules, poor communication, dishonesty, and other bad decisions as ways of saying, "I can't admit it, but I need your help. Even though I think I want this, I'm not quite ready for it." Despite her protests that you should let go, she may be asking you to pull her back a bit. That way, she can avoid social situations that are too sophisticated, complex, or uncomfortable for her without losing face. In a word, she may be asking you (indirectly, of course) to supervise her more closely.

You will know you are on the right track when your daughter responds positively to your setting stricter limits. For example, Sybil found out that instead of staying at football games on Friday nights, her fourteen-year-old freshman daughter, Rae, had been sneaking around, attending unchaperoned parties, drinking alcohol, and smoking cigarettes. As Sybil said, "There is no way we would tolerate this kind of behavior, especially at Rae's age. She was forbidden to go out for the next month. We expected that she would become hysterical when she heard that news." In fact, Rae's protest was so weak that her mother interpreted it as obligatory. Sybil concluded, "She didn't spend those weekends glaring at us or holed up in her room with the music blasting. When she sat and watched videos with her dad and me, we knew she had been in way over her head. Her reaction was very telling."

Similarly, Ruth tells of her daughter, Madelaine, getting off to a wild start in middle school: "Madelaine was only twelve, but she looked about sixteen and, in many ways, wanted to act as if she were eighteen. We were suddenly fighting about wearing makeup, going out with friends at night, and staying out late. 'This is ridiculous,' I thought, 'she's not even an official teenager yet!' " Although she struggled to impose limits, Ruth watched in vain while the situation escalated.

"It came to a head when we came home from dinner one night," she says, "to find a note saying Madelaine and her friend had gone down the street to another friend's house. When we checked, they weren't there. We were absolutely livid that she had told such an outright lie, and told her she had totally lost her freedom. She pitched a fit, but a much milder one than we expected. That weekend, she wanted to play games with me. It was as if she needed to be nine again and beat me at Monopoly." Getting caught stopped the downward spiral and forced Madelaine and her parents to reevaluate what activities she was really ready for.

If your daughter's social life suddenly accelerates or veers off in a worrisome direction, it is wise to take a broader look.

NOT

> MOTHER: I can't believe how awful you've become!

OR

> MOTHER: That's it, I'm withdrawing your application to gymnastics camp. You're not responsible enough to go away this summer.

TRY

> MOTHER: This is a big transition for both of us. I know you want more freedom, and that's perfectly understandable. But it's my job to make sure you're ready. We need to work together so we can both feel comfortable that you have all the skills you need. Here's what we need to do . . .

To plan better for the future, you two may need to figure out what basic skills she will need for each new step toward independence. Then your daughter will know what you think she needs to do to deserve privileges. For example, before she gets to go out with friends who drive, she may be required to prove that she can respect your house rules, tell you honestly what she is doing and where she is going, and be responsible for herself. To earn more privileges, she first has to earn your confidence. Until then, she may harbor a secret delight in being restricted because it allows her to reexperience the benefits of being treated as a younger girl. Briefly she gets more of your attention and, especially, the sense of feeling safely grounded again.

Too Good to Be True

No discussion of discipline would be complete without addressing good girls. By this I mean girls who even during adolescence are unusually mature, responsible, conforming, and perhaps even highly achieving, to boot. They seem to do everything right. Eventually, sometime during their teenage years, however, even these good girls may feel the need to be bad. That is because obedience eventually seems too juvenile, too reminiscent of the goody-goodies of elementary school.

Lauren, fourteen, who had barely given her mother a moment of trouble, was caught sneaking off with some older friends to a pep rally at the high school when she was supposed to be at the movies. Her mother, Stella, fifty-two, says, "That made no sense. Of course I found out; her friend's mother knew, and she couldn't even tell me who starred in the movie she supposedly saw." Lauren explains, "My mother thinks she can control every little thing about my life, but she can't." Breaking rules and defying parental desires seem cool, a badge of teenagers' evolving independence. Another mother says, "Last year I overheard my daughter telling a friend, 'I got into big trouble. I'm so grounded!' Oh, really? She didn't get grounded. In fact, she didn't get into any trouble at all!"

Sheila, the mother who found a beer can at the back of her daughter's closet, now believes that Shannon was attracted to girls with troubled behavior and conflictual relationships with their mothers because they seemed more precocious and worldly. She understands why her daughter was drawn to the camaraderie of her cafeteria group, whose main topic was commiserating about the trials of being a teenager forced to live with parents. During middle school Shannon needed to experience, even vicariously, what it felt like to be bad. As Sheila reflected on that year, she saw the beer can episode in a new light. She says, "I wonder if Shannon was trying to break out of her mold of being almost too compliant. Maybe she needed to test how far she could push her independence—and how far she could push me."

If your daughter suddenly and uncharacteristically gets into trouble, at least consider the possibility that she perceives her behavior as a required rite of passage for any self-respecting teenager. You still may need to issue consequences so your daughter gets the full experience she is seeking. But you can go lightly. Whatever you do, in fact, may be less important than your doing something, which acknowledges and marks her indiscretion. If you decide to ground her, your daughter would not be the first girl to complain to her friends with equal parts outrage and barely concealed pride. She may view this event as her initiation into the sorority of bona fide teenage girls.

A Matter of Trust: It's a Big Deal
Trust Affects Both of You

Your daughter's errors never touch your love for her, which is pure and constant, but they can certainly demolish your trust. That is because her unfortunate decisions and bad behavior affect you too. Although her mistakes may occur somewhere out in the world, they reverberate palpably throughout your relationship. After all, the cornerstone of your mother-daughter relationship is mutual trust and respect. So when she lies, breaks a rule, makes a poor decision, or uses bad judgment, you may lose trust in your daughter's willingness to follow your advice and adopt your values. Besides feeling disappointed, worried, or angry, your trust in your ability to guide and teach her may also be shaken. With every mistake your growing belief in her evolving abilities is chipped away. Thus you may be overtaken with worry about your daughter's ability to take good care of herself.

Your daughter too feels the repercussions of your broken trust. One of the biggest complaints I hear from teenagers is "My mother doesn't trust me." Most of the time, girls know full well what caused that breach of trust. It is heartbreaking, however, to hear a girl such as Janine, fourteen, say, "I have never done anything to break my mother's trust, but she still doesn't trust me. I don't know what to do." Of course, girls often cannot discriminate between their mothers' wariness about the world at large and lack of confidence in their abilities. Teenagers' youthful idealism and sense of immortality prevent them from appreciating their mothers' realistic fears for them.

Whenever possible, help your daughter to see that your worries are not always about her. Sometimes you will be uneasy about the situation, distrust other people, or simply see her as too young and inexperienced for the activities she desires. Bonita, one of the mothers who told her story at the beginning of the chapter, tried to explain to her daughter, Eva, that her decisions were not always based on Eva's shortcomings or failures. Although Eva bristled with indignation whenever her mother refused a request that involved a greater degree of independence, Bonita attempted to assure her that the circumstances were to blame: "Once I told her that no woman in her right mind would drive around by herself in that neighborhood at night. So why would I let my only daughter do that?"

When you truly do not trust your daughter (whether or not she has given you good reason to doubt her), she is probably going to feel keenly your lack of faith in her abilities. If your mistrust is chronic she may not develop the skills you want her to have. For one, she needs to mingle with a variety of individuals and experience many different social situations. This helps her to learn more about people, solve problems, rely on herself, and make good choices. Second, if she begins to mistrust herself, she won't push herself to deal with social challenges, overcome the obstacles to her feeling successful, or work through conflicts with others.

Conversely, trust in your daughter's good judgment and her ability to make mature decisions is mutually beneficial. For you, feeling comfortable with how your daughter manages her social life is like sipping chamomile tea while cuddling in front of a blazing fire. You are not frantic every moment she is out of your sight, wondering, "What is she up to now?" Instead, you are soothed by the confidence that your daughter can make her way competently.

For your daughter the realization that "my mom really trusts me" is like getting the gold medal of compliments. What could be more affirming to her? When she got her driver's license, Michelle's mother said to her, "You've done everything we've asked. You're responsible, get your work done, seem honest with us, you're reliable about getting home on time. Now that you're driving yourself, we'll have no way of knowing exactly where you are when you leave home. But we trust you to do what is right." Michelle nearly glowed with pride. Believing her efforts had been noted and appreciated, she was determined not to do anything that would risk losing her mother's trust.

Re-Earning Trust

If your daughter breaks a rule or disappoints you, it is crucial not just to enforce a consequence, but to provide the means for her to earn your trust once again. Becky, a fourteen-year-old eighth grader, says, "Sometimes I feel like my mom doesn't trust me. I know that I have messed up, but after a period of time I don't really think it's necessary for her to check up on every single thing I do." Your daughter needs to prove that she is trustworthy.

Explaining precisely how she might go about re-earning your trust is key. You might say, for example, that you will regain trust in her "When I see that you follow through on your chores responsibly" or "When you are straightforward with me about where you are going" or "When you show me that you can manage your time better, such as by respecting curfews and getting ready for school in the morning." If your relationship is strong, the more you express your confidence in your daughter's ability to regain your trust, the harder she will work to be reinstated in your good opinion.

Getting Over It

As Bonita expressed in her story, mothers often fear that they will never recover from their daughters' mistakes, especially the serious ones. Not only is their trust shaken, but they believe they will never again look at their daughters in quite the same way. Perhaps this is true. Both of you may be changed irrevocably by her deed, as well as by your response to it. You realize that your teenager is not the little girl who used to hang on your every word and obey your instructions to the letter. You can no longer take for granted her absolute truthfulness. You may vow never again to be so naïve as to think that your daughter would avoid such behavior. In turn, your daughter may now see you as someone who will always question to some extent who she is, doubt whether she is honest, ask if she is protecting herself, and remind her to use good judgment.

Though your discipline demonstrates that you do not forget, condone, excuse, minimize, or deny your daughter's undesirable behavior, over time you will come to forgive her. Be patient with yourself. And be patient with your daughter. Although she may still blame you and your stupid rules for many of her adolescent disappointments and regrets, at some point she may begin to appreciate your abiding commitment to her and her well-being. Although it may be hard to imagine, these incidents, for better or worse, will gradually become part of the fabric of your mother-daughter relationship. You will both learn to acknowledge, live with, and grow from imperfection.

This is a good thing, because throughout her teenage years your daughter will face a myriad of temptations and challenging situations. She will be forced to negotiate the mercurial personalities of girl and guy friends, the sometimes treacherous dynamics of friendship circles, and the intricacies of romantic relationships. The next three chapters will give you an inside look at this occasionally formidable world of teenage friendships, socializing, and dating.

Chapter 8

Circling of the Wagonettes

FRIENDSHIP

"My daughter's social life is getting out of hand. Greta is constantly on the phone with her friends instead of doing her schoolwork or chores. She's either rehashing what they just did or making still more plans. All she seems to care about is speaking to her friends. And yet, these best friends often seem to switch. One day, Greta's closest to so-and-so, but soon they've had a falling out and she's replaced by someone else. Because I'm kept in the dark, I never really understand what's happening. Why are these friendships so volatile? This is so different from how it was when I was her age. Basically, I had the same group of close girlfriends all through school. We stuck by each other, no matter what. Greta is flitting about rather than forming what I would consider true friendships. Shouldn't I expect these relationships to be deeper and more loyal by the time she's a teenager?" —— Delia, thirty-six*

"It breaks my heart to see my daughter come home from school looking so beaten down and discouraged. I know she's having a hard time with her peers. A few of the girls like to tease her and say some pretty nasty things. Or else they ignore her, like during lunch. Allie is obviously hurt by all this. Although she refers to one or two girls as her friends, I don't think there is any real relationship there. Allie pretty much stays in her room. I don't know what to do because when I try to talk to her about this, she insists, 'I'm fine, Mom,' and tunes me out. Sometimes when I see her looking sad I get so upset that I'm tempted to do something about these awful girls, like calling their parents or reporting them to the school. Surely, they should be taught to treat others with decency. But I also get upset with Allie because she seems so passive, as if she's given up and is willing to accept mistreatment; I wish she'd learn to stand up for herself. My daughter is being damaged by their meanness and I don't know how to help her." —— Flora, forty-two*

"Pasha is an only child who has never been afraid to express strong opinions, but I was hoping she would learn to be more discreet. Unfortunately, she can be rather blunt in telling her friends what she thinks about them. Sometimes I am actually appalled at how she talks to them. Recently, she had an argument over a trivial issue with a girl who's been a neighbor and friend since preschool. My daughter is still furious, refuses to talk to her, and will only say that this girl is being ridiculous. I wonder what is really going on, and if my daughter is being fair to her. It's awkward, to say the least, when I see this girl's mother on our street. Pasha is so harsh and critical sometimes; is it awful to say I wish she would be sweeter and more tolerant?" —Penelope, forty-three

Girlfriends, precious to women of every age, are absolute lifelines to adolescent girls. Your daughter's sense of herself as okay and overall contentment during her teenage years are determined largely by how well she thinks her peers like her. She may fret about the shifting alliances among her best buddies, worry about having enough friends, and do all sorts of finagling to feel closer to the right friends (e.g., the most popular or coolest or nicest or most awesome girls, etc.). In response to the goings-on in her peer group, your daughter might get hurt, be upset, act furious, or feel rejected, sometimes keeping these reactions to herself, at other times making obvious her distress to anyone within a two-mile radius.

Since you are watching your teenage daughter's friendship dynamics from a front row seat, it is unlikely you will always be completely comfortable with her choices. The question becomes, however, what can you do about them? What is your role? Thus far, the issues you have been examining have been between the two of you—for example, your parenting approach, rules, discussions, responses to her troubles, discipline. Sure, you have focused on helping your daughter to develop a strong sense of self and social skills so that she would choose her friends wisely, deal with conflicts in healthy ways, and resolve any dilemmas she encounters. But when the problems are between her and her friends, how can you continue to guide her and teach her important skills?

Although you cannot join your daughter as she socializes and certainly won't be able to make decisions for her, she is not completely on her own. This chapter will demonstrate how applying a collaborative approach will help you to influence the choices your daughter makes in her friendships. Being flexible and considering both your daughter's age and maturity, you can find new ways to communicate your values about relationships, what you find acceptable, and how you expect her to be accountable. Being Attuned to her desires and needs and Respectful of her preferences, she'll be more receptive to your interest. Above all, being Noncontrolling enables you to remain appropriately Involved with her so that you can be most influential. Now that she is a teenager, you may have to adapt your strategies, but your input is more needed and valuable than ever. You are still her mom.

A Mother's Concerns

You too may use the quantity and quality of your daughter's peer relationships as a gauge of her adjustment. Most often mothers fear either that their teenage daughters are being harmed by undesirable friends, or that they are socially isolated.

Some of you will be delighted to notice that your phones are suddenly ringing constantly or at ungodly hours, there are whispered confidences behind closed doors, online time is increasing sharply, your daughter is frantically attempting to coordinate convoluted social plans, there are inked names and numbers on her hand and notebooks, and she speaks in the new language of "Teenglish." These are surefire signs that your daughter's friendships are now in high gear.

Your daughter's busy social life assures you that she is okay, that she is a normal teenager. Plus you realize that during this developmental stage her peers contribute to her sense of who she is and, at the same time, help her to distinguish herself from you. If your daughter has ever struggled to fit in with her class or to find a special chum, you might be especially gratified to see that she is now socially active. But as many mothers have warned, "Be careful what you wish for."

Delia, who worries that her daughter is too preoccupied with her social life, described the disconcerting flip-flop of her own feelings. "You'd think I would be happy because Greta used to be rather shy and isolated but now seems to be at the center of a social flurry," she says. "I used to fret that she wasn't popular enough, but this situation isn't so great, either. It's hard to deal with her being out all the time—or wanting to be. And I'm afraid if this kind of involvement with friends continues, she'll be distracted from her schoolwork, music lessons, and other activities."

Mothers also worry if their daughters are not especially involved in the teenage social scene. Girls may be more comfortable hanging out at home, show little interest in friendships outside of school, or, like Flora's daughter, Allie, struggle to connect with peers. In fact, I have noted this truism: During the teenage years, mothers usually are unsure exactly *what* to wish for. Either their daughters seem to be too social, or not social enough—and each has its own share of worries and potential problems.

Beyond this, there are subtler concerns about the nature of a teenager's relationships. For example, have you ever wondered: Is my daughter able to keep friends over time? Can she get too bossy? Is she comfortable making new friends? Does she tolerate hurtful or disloyal behavior? Does she replace friends as blithely as she gets new jeans? Or maybe you think your daughter maintains her social ties by acquiescing too readily to the demands of her friends. Can she be strong and assertive in friendships, yet flexible and accommodating? Is she tolerant of individual differences without compromising her own values? Can she be a steady friend without becoming possessive?

Even when things seem to be running smoothly, you may question if her friends have much to offer her or whether her relationships are balanced. When you glimpse hints of potential trouble—i.e., your daughter pursues the best friend who repeatedly drops her, she gossips shamelessly about one close pal to another, she hangs out with scantily clad, unkempt, chain-smoking girls at the local fair—you may be prompted once again to ask yourself, "Has my daughter lost her mind?"

The trials of your daughter's social life are painful not only because you love her and want to protect her, but also because they evoke memories of your own teenage friendships. In this way, your history can influence enormously your reactions to your daughter's social woes, prompting you to deny or minimize her concerns or, conversely, to overreact to them, jumping in prematurely or unhelpfully. Being aware of your sensitivities will help you to be more attuned to your daughter's experiences and to respect her feelings and desires, especially when they are different from your own.

Your Friendships

Despite admittedly enormous differences between your generations, you and your daughter probably share at least some of the age-old teenage social worries and struggles. At various times, both of you may have had concerns about being accepted, ridiculed, or betrayed by peers. There may also be regrets about your indiscretions. Your memories of such experiences all leave their indelible mark on you as a social being. While this can potentially help you to be more attuned your daughter, at the same time it may be all the more difficult to ensure that your reactions are based on her experiences rather than yours. This can surely be confusing. Terri Apter and Ruthellen Josselson, authors of *Best Friends: The Pleasures and Perils of Girls' and Women's Friendships,* say, "Old dynamics, reflexive responses, are branded on us by past suffering."

As a teenager, were you as socially included as you would have liked? Were you content with your friendships? Were you part of a group of girls? Did you prefer to have a few close pals, or did you enjoy a large cast of friends and acquaintances? Did you have a best friend? Can you remember times when you felt isolated, slighted, or mistreated? Did you have issues around competition or trust? Similarly, how would you describe your present, adult friendships? What do you model for your daughter in terms of the importance and intimacy of your relationships? How assertive are you in initiating friendships, resolving differences that arise, and setting limits? Perhaps most important, what would be your wish for your daughter in terms of her friendship patterns? What would convince you that her friendships are healthy?

Delia, who is concerned that her daughter Greta does not keep friends for very long, is the first to admit that she struggles with the same issue. "My problems are not so different," she says, "especially at work. When I look back, I seem to get only so close to people, and then things just fizzle. It's not like we have a fight or anything, but I start feeling uncomfortable. For instance, right now a colleague I've been pretty friendly with has started insinuating herself with our boss for a promotion we'd both like. I hate those dog-eat-dog tactics, so I've kind of distanced myself. I wonder if this is what Greta is feeling sometimes."

When daughters' experiences reopen their mothers' old wounds, women often cope by reducing the pain any way they can. To avoid both your own distressing recollections and the acute sting of your daughter's anguish, you might ignore evidence of her social troubles or make unhelpful comments. The pages that follow will encourage you to examine the potential pitfalls of these approaches and offer more constructive responses to your daughter's predicaments with both cliques and individual friends.

The Meaning of Her Friendships

As you know, your daughter's friendships are a lot more to her than just lacrosse teammates, companions in the school cafeteria, or classmates in French II. As Apter and Josselson put it, "Friends are never 'just friends.' " They describe a variety of emotional and developmental needs served by friendship. For example, your daughter probably looks to her friends for reassurance, comfort, empathy, feedback about herself, and protection against loneliness. Even teenage behaviors that seem on the surface to be silly or superficial, such as borrowing T-shirts, replaying and dissecting conversations, and giggling over in jokes, reflect subtle but significant and often complex dynamics, all of which serve a purpose.

During the adolescent years, when insecurity, self-consciousness, and hypersensitivity probably peak, girls frequently ruminate about their relationships and what others think of them. In fact, a survey of sixth-, eighth-, and tenth-graders by psychologists Susan Nolen-Hoeksema and Joan S. Girgus demonstrated that relative to boys, teenage girls worried more about friends, romantic relationships, what kind of person they are, and being liked by peers. This preoccupation was observed in girls as young as eleven or twelve!

As the typical preteen or teenage girl ponders what she likes and dislikes about herself, on a bad day the negatives can appear to loom over the positives. The belief that everyone is looking at her—even staring critically—only adds to her insecurity. Your daughter probably fears that gossip and rumors about her will spread, much like vicious computer viruses, through the halls of her middle or high school. There is only one elixir for these collective horrors, and that is a friend.

All it may take to transform your daughter's life from a living hell to perfectly okay is just one phone call.

Flora, whose daughter struggled to feel accepted by her peers, described the dramatic change that took place one afternoon when Allie was invited to another girl's house: "She had been in her room nearly all day, sulking, listening to this awful melancholy music, and probably writing gloomy poetry again. I was feeling so sad for her when suddenly the phone rang. Several minutes later, an entirely different girl emerged from that room—all smiles, a new outfit on, a bounce in her step—on her way to see a friend." In minutes, that one phone call converted Allie from a self-proclaimed loser to a girl who felt worthy and desirable.

To describe a friend as the potential lifeline of a teenage girl is no exaggeration. Whenever girls feel shaky, there is no more effective confidence booster than attention from friends. In the face of disappointment, friends can be marvelously soothing as well as much-needed champions. When girls feel wronged, a friend's validation can instantly deflate their outrage and boost their self-esteem.

Being attuned to what friendship often means to a teenager helps you to respond more empathically and effectively to your daughter's social problems. Even when you cannot fathom why she would want to be friends with a particular girl, or would choose to maintain a relationship with someone who continuously disappoints or even torments her, you can remind yourself of what such friendships may offer. This insight may inhibit you from blurting out well-meaning but unempathic responses such as, "Don't you worry about her! You don't need friends like that!"

What You Can't Do: Be Her Best Friend

Despite your vast social experience, which gives you plenty of wisdom to offer your daughter, you will probably find that she does not always invite or welcome your input. When she struggles with friends who disappoint her or aren't as supportive as she would like, you may wonder, "Why doesn't she ask for my advice about these things?" This is one question that has an easy answer: She prefers to turn to her peers.

Since you are her mother, you probably can't—and shouldn't—be your daughter's best friend, at least not until after the adolescent years. Collaborating with her does not make you peers, but preserves your roles as mother and daughter. Even if intellectually you accept this, on some level it still may be painful when she replaces you as her confidante. When you ask about your daughter's bad mood and she tosses over her shoulder a mere, "Oh, nothing!" as she rushes off to confide in her best friend, it can feel like a slap in the face. After all, you know her best.

There are actually many valid reasons, however, why mothers cannot fulfill the role of their daughters' best friends during adolescence. They can be boiled down to a few essential points:

1. *She needs a mother—i.e., you—to convey values, set limits, and say no, when necessary.* During the teenage years, being your daughter's friend conflicts with your primary goal of being her mother. While friends are free to placate her by saying whatever they think she wants to hear, your priority is different. Your maternal decisions are designed to keep your daughter safe, not to please her. Although you are always concerned about preserving your closeness, you do what you think is right even if that risks her occasional irritation or unhappiness. If you are unduly worried about losing your daughter's friendship as a result of setting limits with her, you will not stick to your guns.

2. *You are the mother from whom she wants to feel separate and autonomous.* The very act of confiding in you makes your daughter feel babyish and dependent. For many teenagers, therefore, choosing to keep information from parents or to share it only with peers reassures them of precious autonomy. The social tidbits your daughter decides to keep from you are rarely vital. They may just be private.

3. *You are a primary authority figure.* It is also possible that your daughter is not particularly proud of what she confides to a girlfriend. She may predict, quite rightly, that telling you would make you anxious—and provoke a lecture. How would you respond, for example, if she mentioned that her best friend was angry because she flirted with her boyfriend? Or what if she told

you that she skipped her science class to work things out with a friend who was acting aloof and snippy? Your daughter is apt to protect herself from your anticipated reactions by justifying to herself, "Why should I upset Mom?"

4. *You don't know as much as you think you do.* This is not your fault; you lack firsthand information and experience. Regardless of how much you care, you are not part of her teenage social world. Your daughter may become hysterical about an incident you consider inconsequential. Her best friend, on the other hand, who probably shared this experience in some way, can better appreciate its subtleties and likely ramifications; unlike you, she knows without being told what the big deal is.

For example, suppose you learn that your daughter is furious because a girl in her group suddenly began acting like a snob. Since her close friend actually heard the girl's remark, she is a better judge of whether it was said as an intended joke, gentle tease, or nasty dig. Because this friend was part of the group's recent history, she may more accurately sense why the girl might be singling out your daughter. Undoubtedly, your daughter is also looking for certain reactions from this friend—loyalty, support, sympathy, fury, or whatever—that are only meaningful because they come from a peer.

Because you did not hear the offensive interaction, your daughter may dismiss altogether the possibility that you could be helpful. But even if you tried your best to be attuned to how she felt about the incident, she still may regard your most empathic and insightful comments as frustrating or annoying. Many a mother has given what she considered her wisest analysis, only to be told, "You just don't understand!" That is because it may be impossible to appreciate the innuendoes and subtleties that mean so much to your daughter—much like trying to understand native South Americans while clutching your high school Spanish-English dictionary.

Peers Versus Parents: You're Both Influential

Just because you can't be your daughter's confidante doesn't mean you're no longer needed. You continue to have tremendous influence on her. It is just that her friends do too. A 1999 *New York Times* poll found that in the previous five years, the percentage of teens reporting peer pressure as their biggest problem increased significantly. At the same time, a recent article in *American Psychologist* underscored the importance of parents. At issue is not whether parents or peers have the greatest impact on teenagers; both do. In fact, contemporary researchers now examine how parents and peers are conjointly influential. As you sort out the impact of your daughter's friends, these points may be helpful:

The Quality of Your Relationship with Your Daughter Affects Her Susceptibility to Peer Influence

It is hoped you have already laid the groundwork. The close, respectful mother-daughter relationship you developed in your daughter's early years is a strong foundation for her social choices as an adolescent. Approaching your teenager collaboratively, you continue to be interested in her friends (e.g., "What does Amanda enjoy doing?" or "How is Francesca adjusting to her new school?"), but refrain from evaluating their credentials (e.g., "What do Amanda's parents do?" or "Is Francesca in honors classes?") or trying to control her relationships with them. This open-minded attitude, which conveys respect for your daughter's right to choose her own friends, adds to the goodwill in your relationship. Your daughter therefore has less reason to abandon your values for those of her peer group.

If Your Daughter Identifies with a Troubled Peer Group, Don't Automatically Blame Her Friends

Years of clinical experience have demonstrated over and again that girls who are most vulnerable to negative peer influences are desperate for acceptance. Invariably, they are lonely and despondent because of either a severe falling-out or a chronically poor connection with their parents. This estrangement makes girls highly dependent on peers for attention and reassurance. Thus if you and your daughter are usually distant or at odds, she might settle for the guidance of peers who are the least capable of advising her.

If your daughter's friends tend to have serious problems, you might consider the possibility that she herself is more troubled than

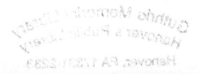

you had wanted to believe, or is having difficulty in her relationship with either you or her father. When she abruptly changes friendship groups and shows signs of deteriorating functioning across many aspects of her life (e.g., in school, at home, in activities, etc.), this is a red flag for potentially serious problems. In this case, professional counseling for your daughter and possibly the entire family could help reopen communication, address the issues, and restore cohesion.

You Do Influence Your Daughter's Choice of Friends

When your daughter was in elementary school, you managed her entire social calendar, effectively guiding her toward some peers and away from others. During middle school, you continue more subtly to endorse certain friendships by offering to drive your daughter to a particular friend's house, agreeing to pick up other girls, taking them to activities you support, and welcoming some of them into your home. At the same time, you also deny certain requests and invitations. In this way, your choices affect your daughter's social choices.

Now that she is a teenager, your methods of influence change. You are less able to make decisions for her because she has more autonomy and probably is less dependent on you for rides. But speaking more openly about social topics stimulates her thinking about relevant issues, communicates your values, and encourages her to solve problems. Since her inner voice has taken on many of your standards, without quite realizing it your daughter probably asks herself, "What would Mom say about this girl?" She also notes your subtle, nonverbal reactions to her various friends, taking in your unspoken approval or disapproval. Finally, your daughter learns much from carefully observing how you conduct yourself in friendships.

Your Daughter's Attitudes and Motivations Are Less Affected by Peers Than You Would Think

According to researchers, peers have more effect on transient adolescent attitudes and everyday behaviors than on enduring values such as educational plans, religion, and occupation, which are more influenced by parents. (However, it is true that the consequences of early sexual or antisocial activities can affect—and limit—long-term plans.) In a study surveying ninth- and eleventh graders, psychologist Harold D. Fishbein and sociologist Neil Ritchey found that friends' attitudes did not affect adolescents' prejudices or stereotypes. Observations of students in middle or high school corroborate this. Just as the lackluster student is unlikely to develop a burning desire to excel in school just because her friends are high achievers, a well-adjusted, well-behaved girl is unlikely to turn into a delinquent because she associates with one.

Your Daughter Does Not Necessarily Approve of Her Friends' Values and Behavior

Remarkably, your daughter can be friends, even close friends, with peers whose values and behavior she condemns. Not a day goes by when a teenage girl in therapy doesn't vent about a friend who behaved in a disappointing, worrisome, or even disgusting manner. Lainie, for example, a fifteen-year-old high school sophomore, says, "I have no respect for Chris, even though she's one of my best friends. She has no morals. Saturday night we were all at this party except for Yvonne, who's our other best friend, and Chris went for the guy that Yvonne's been going out with!"

Similarly, Chloe, another fifteen-year-old, complains about the selfish and disloyal behavior of her best friend: "When our friend drank too much the other night and got sick, Clarissa refused to baby-sit her. She tossed her some crackers and shut the door, but when *she* was sick, she was like, 'Stay with me. Don't leave me alone!' What a hypocrite!" Mothers who worry that their daughters will imitate the behavior of their closest friends often needn't. Even if girls staunchly defend friends to others, publicly circling the wagonettes, privately they are more discerning and critical of them than their mothers would imagine.

What You Can Do: A Five-Part Plan

Beyond these general influences, you can have an enormous impact on your daughter's choices whenever she faces predicaments with her friends during the teenage years. For example, you will have to decide whether or not to give your daughter advice, to tell her how you feel about her friends, to find ways to keep her from girls who may be a bad influence, or to allow her to work things out for herself. At times you may struggle to know when you should remind your daughter of your values—and when the wisest tactic is keeping your thoughts to yourself.

Before we get into the specifics, though, there are basic guidelines you can use in just about any situation that arises. However you become aware of your daughter's social woes—whether you observe them yourself, she confides in you, or she's been caught in a major transgression with her friends—you might try:

1. Listening

This suggestion is based on two simple but often neglected principles: (a) If you want your daughter to talk, you have to keep quiet; and (b) If you are listening well, you cannot be talking. Teenage girls often have trouble expressing their feelings and ideas, but it is impossible for them to do so when their mothers are speaking. Refraining from talking also enables you to resist unhelpful, knee-jerk comments. Listening attentively conveys your interest in your daughter and your willingness to try to understand her perspective. You, it is hoped, will learn more about your daughter's feelings about her social life. Perhaps more important, so might your daughter. As you recall, she is using her discussions with you as a sounding board for her own ideas.

2. Empathizing

For over twenty years, teenage girls have complained to me that their mothers "just don't understand!" For the reasons described, it is unrealistic to expect that you *could* understand completely the nuances of your daughter's social experiences. But you can make a concerted effort to get a clearer picture of the situation from her viewpoint. What are the facts *as she sees them*? What makes the situation difficult for her? Your daughter needs to empathize with others, become more aware of her own feelings, and manage them well to make the best decisions. That is why even if you think her reactions are overblown, off the mark, or inappropriate, it is important to understand them. How is your daughter trying to solve the problem?

3. Refraining from Giving Swift or Unsolicited Advice

Hasty judgments about your daughter's friends and unsolicited suggestions often backfire. You are apt to hear "Just forget it, Mom," as she stomps out of the room. Girls usually say they perceive such advice as uncaring, unhelpful, and uninformed. Plus this way of intervening essentially cuts off the very process you want to encourage—that is, helping your daughter to be active in assessing and resolving her own social predicaments. Besides all that, you would not be the first mother to discover that she cannot always offer perfect, Solomon-like solutions to her daughter's dilemmas.

4. Stimulating Her Problem Solving

Suppose your daughter has shared an issue or difficulty with you. To your delight, you believe she has opened the door for discussion. After listening carefully for further information and empathizing with her perspective, you remind yourself not to offer quick advice. So what should you do? You might encourage your daughter to think through the situation herself. Help her brainstorm ideas, imagine the potential consequences of her various solutions, anticipate how to get around obstacles, and pick the best option. Finally, convey your respect and confidence by allowing her to live with her decisions, for better or worse.

5. Respecting the Learning Process

Being noncontrolling requires respecting the process by which your daughter learns about having and being a friend. Over time she must figure out how to deal with girlfriends who have various personalities, interpersonal styles, and pressing needs. This enables her to develop her own ways of maintaining a strong sense of self while getting what she needs in relationships. Unless the situation is dire, consider stepping back and allowing this process to unfold, even though it may entail watching her suffer bumps and bruises along the way. It is not just that she will reject your intrusion into her business. There are real limitations to what you can remedy. Many social issues can best be addressed by your daughter learning, slowly and gradually, how to manage them.

For example, your daughter may be faced with friends who are unreliable, aggressive, or competitive. She may have to confront girls who bruise her self-esteem, get on her nerves, demand exclusivity in friendship, ask her incessantly for favors, or expect her to follow their every whim. At the same time, she may have to learn how to respond when friends resent her bossiness, get impatient with her stubbornness, bristle at her jokes, or are taken aback by her candor.

Sometimes your daughter will make needed changes deftly, without a wrinkle in the friendship. When a friend calls her repeatedly, for example, demanding more attention than she wants to provide, she may simply say, "I've got to go now" until her friend backs off. At other times she may achieve some temporary distance by pushing her friend's buttons in order to pick a fight. Occasionally your daughter may decide she has to sever a friendship. Pasha, whose mother is concerned about her hard-edged nature, describes her neighbor as unbearably intrusive: "I couldn't stand how annoying Juliana was, and she wouldn't take the hint. Did she think she'd actually get on my good side by talking to one of my friends about me behind my back?" Clearly, Pasha felt desperate to unlatch herself from the clutches of a girl whom she saw as increasingly bothersome and inappropriate.

Even if you respect and support this learning process, it will be difficult to see your daughter cope with betrayals, put-downs, and rejections; tolerate mistreatment; give up activities; and slight kinder friends in the hope of befriending girls who snub her. That is why you may need to remind yourself that you may not be able to appreciate what your daughter is getting out of a situation you perceive as harmful or intolerable. So great may be her need to ally herself with a group or maintain a particular friendship that she is willing to accept whatever conditions these girls require. When you can step back and refrain from attempting to rescue her, you are giving your daughter a chance to learn for herself how to improve these situations. Her awful friend may in fact be a necessary but temporary stop along the road to better relationships.

Girls on the Outs

Although most teenagers occasionally feel excluded or rejected by their peers, some girls truly have few attachments, either to a single girl or to several, loosely recognized as a social group. Several reasons could account for this.

Struggling to Fit In

Many times, girls are isolated because they have yet to find a social niche that feels comfortable to them. Ask any teenage girl about the social strata of her school and she will rattle off a list of well-defined, mutually exclusive groups whose names change over time (e.g., brains, jocks, freaks, nerds, heads, thespians, populars, druggies, goths, etc.). While some girls penetrate the invisible boundaries of these cliques, moving in and out freely to socialize with various friends, other teenagers don't mix well at all. Recognizing that your daughter's connection with one or more special friends would be insurance against seeing herself as a social outcast, you may offer what you consider reasonable, common-sense suggestions for making friends. And your daughter may repudiate each and every one of them.

NOT

> MOTHER: Why don't you call that girl Emmie from art class?
> DAUGHTER: Are you kidding, or what?
> MOTHER: She seems nice.
> DAUGHTER: Yeah, right, Mom. She's so Goth!

OR

> MOTHER: How about getting together with your lab partner?
> DAUGHTER: She's joined at the hip with this other girl, Mom.
> MOTHER: So why can't all three of you hang out?
> DAUGHTER: You just don't get it, Mom.

TRY

> MOTHER: Is there anyone you've met lately you'd like to get
> to know better?

OR

> MOTHER: Who might be interesting to spend some time
> with?

It is helpful to recognize why her perception of not fitting in among her peers may keep your daughter from taking positive action. She is reluctant to make an overture to a potential friend because this girl not only could reject her, but may also act as if your daughter was insane to think she might ever want to be her friend. This would be the ultimate humiliation. Thus it is important to remember that reaching out to a possible friend is a thoroughly risky social enterprise for the typical teenage girl.

However, counting on someone else to make the first move is hardly an ideal strategy either, because a potential friend may be equally reluctant to make herself vulnerable. Yet your daughter is unlikely to attribute other girls' apparent unfriendliness to their being shy or insecure. Rather she will interpret this as evidence that she is undesirable as a friend. Trying to break through this barrier of self-consciousness and fear is not easy. It is tempting to offer quick, reasonable advice that nonetheless dismisses your daughter's apprehension and interferes with her generating her own solutions.

NOT

> MOTHER: Just go up to her and be friendly.
> DAUGHTER: No way!
> MOTHER: What's the big deal?
> DAUGHTER: Leave me alone, Mom!

TRY

> MOTHER: What happens when someone you don't know well
> starts talking to you?
> DAUGHTER: They usually just say hi and stuff.
> MOTHER: What is that like for you?
> DAUGHTER: I don't mind. It's fine.
> MOTHER: Is there anyone you would feel comfortable
> chatting with?
> DAUGHTER: I guess so. There's a new girl in my Spanish class
> who seems nice.

MOTHER: Good idea, she might be looking for a friend too. What do you think you might have in common to talk about?

DAUGHTER: Everybody thinks the teacher's being a jerk for giving us another project.

MOTHER: Well, it sounds like you found a great topic to start off with.

Teenage girls, who typically lack time perspective, often believe that because they don't have a best friend at a particular moment, no one will ever find them interesting. Within an extremely brief period, they can become convinced they will never have a soul mate again. In addition to helping your daughter find her own strategies for making friends, you can also offer some perspective on the nature of friendship. And, if possible, remind her of times when she did have a terrific friend.

NOT

DAUGHTER: Everyone hates me.

MOTHER: Don't be ridiculous. You know that's not true.

TRY

DAUGHTER: Nobody likes me.

MOTHER: It often takes time to find a special friend.

DAUGHTER: I'm never going to a have a best friend.

MOTHER: Remember how you and Mary Lou were great friends when we lived down South? You and she were two peas in a pod! You just have to find the right person.

Girls who are on the outs in their middle or high schools are often perceived as not having the right looks, accessories, friends, or degree of coolness. Your daughter cannot possibly appreciate how artificial and, thankfully, transient adolescent standards are. She may scoff at but secretly welcome the perspective your experience can provide.

NOT

> DAUGHTER: Everyone thinks I'm a dork.
> MOTHER: So, what's so bad about that?
> DAUGHTER: (leaves and slams the door)

TRY

> DAUGHTER: If one more person tells me I look brainy I'm
> going to scream.
> MOTHER: What does that mean, anyway?
> DAUGHTER: It means I don't look cool.
> MOTHER: You know, things that seem so important now
> won't in a few years. When I was your age we made fun
> of a girl because her hair was kinky. How silly was that?
> Now we spend hours perming and crimping our hair! But
> maybe it would make you feel better to change
> something about your look.

The all-important and often elusive qualities that label some girls as cool make them highly appealing to peers. Your daughter may be in awe of the popular girls—the seemingly self-assured, attractive, and precocious clique whose acceptance she craves to dispel her own fears of being terminally uncool and boring. Your daughter's desperation to improve her self-image by associating with this group can be puzzling or disconcerting to you. There is no way she would believe that the girls she idolizes express the very same insecurities!

The all-or-none thinking characteristic of this age group may convince your daughter that if she can't be friends with so-and-so or be part of a particular, desirable group, her social life is a failure. It must be this group of girls—or none. But this is when you can prevent her from growing up too fast and remind her to be her own person. This is when, despite your daughter's dire predictions of social doom, you remain true to your own values and communicate clearly what you find acceptable.

NOT

> DAUGHTER: If you would just let me go the Teen Center, I could be friends with Jessica and Jasmine; they're so amazing!
>
> MOTHER: Not on your life! The kids at the Teen Center look trashy and they're bad news.

TRY

> DAUGHTER: You give me such a ridiculous curfew that nobody cool invites me anywhere. If you don't stop treating me like a baby I'm never going to have any friends, Mom.
>
> MOTHER: I know it's hard for you because some girls can come and go as they please, but this isn't a competition to see who does things first. If you're responsible, you'll get more privileges when you're older. Years from now, nobody will care if you were thirteen, or fifteen or seventeen when you did something.

Your daughter may be more reassured by biographies of famous women than listening to her mother's reassurances about popularity, fitting in, and being accepted. Such stories can be powerful teachers. Teenage girls typically assume that successful women have always been successful, but reality can be quite eye-opening. For example, psychologist Barbara Kerr's studies of such eminent women as Nobel Prize–winning scientist Marie Curie, the writer Gertrude Stein, human rights activist Eleanor Roosevelt, anthropologist Margaret Mead, artist Georgia O'Keeffe, actress and activist Katharine Hepburn, and writer/dancer/activist Maya Angelou are illuminating.

These extraordinary women share a similar history—in particular, a difficult adolescence. Coming from odd families or lacking families entirely, many of them were isolated from others. In general, these women looked different, felt socially awkward and unpopular, and were ignored or rejected by their peers. According to Kerr, the nonconformity of these young women resulted in their spending enormous amounts of time alone, usually reading voraciously, thinking, expressing themselves creatively, and furthering their intellects. Without social distractions, they successfully pursued their goals. Furthermore, as a result of being lonely, many of the women identified with and ultimately became advocates for those who were unaccepted, suffering, or oppressed. Your daughter's appreciation for others' plight can help to put her own in perspective.

While you are having these conversations with your daughter, remember to keep her isolation in perspective yourself. Though your heart may break for her, this is probably a temporary problem that will disappear the moment she and even one girl find each other. If you are concerned about what may be happening in school and why your daughter is having such difficulty, you might ask her guidance counselor for feedback and constructive suggestions. There may be a group or club she can join. When you remain confident that she can make new friends, your daughter will too.

Self-Imposed Exile

In some cases, social isolation is self-imposed. There are girls who enjoy their solitude, who relish being in their rooms listening to music or writing poetry, and who seem not to require so much companionship. This preference is not a problem unless their mothers see it as a problem. When you are sensitive to loneliness or invested in your daughter being a highly social teenager, her seclusion can set off alarms. This is a situation that calls for you to separate clearly your needs from your daughter's.

Using Good Sense

For reasons that mystify their mothers, some girls choose to remain outside the social inner circle. When your daughter announces her intention to skip her school's spring fling ("I hate those stupid dances!") or uses a flimsy excuse for missing a classmate's party ("It's not gonna be any fun!"), your knee-jerk reaction may be to coax her to participate anyway. Perhaps you want her to overcome her customary shyness or trepidation, which you assume to be the cause of her reluctance to join in.

Many times, however, if you try to understand and empathize with her perspective, you will learn that such decisions are based not on maladjustment or social inhibition—but wisdom! Unlike you, your daughter is aware of what really transpires at these social events. If you are doing a good job of building her sense of self, her inner voice will help her to avoid situations she is uncomfortable with or not ready for. In these cases, respect your daughter's judgment, and count your blessings.

NOT

> MOTHER: Why don't you go? Everyone will be there.
> DAUGHTER: I don't want to, Mom, okay?
> MOTHER: You'll have fun.
> DAUGHTER: NO!

TRY

> MOTHER: You really don't want to go, huh?
> DAUGHTER: That's right, I don't.
> MOTHER: Well, you must have a good reason. Want to talk about it?
> DAUGHTER: No, maybe later.
> MOTHER: Okay, I trust you to make the right decision.

Not Keen to Grow Up

In rare instances, girls' deliberate social isolation is part of a more pervasive inhibition of maturation. They may have the impression that growing up—participating in normal teenage activities—will deprive them of maternal love and attention. Consciously or unconsciously, they essentially choose to avoid the increasing demands of a social life. Sometimes girls even retain their childlike appearance and delay puberty through starvation—that is, by developing an eating disorder. If you observe this kind of immaturity in intellectual, physical, or emotional areas, consider seeking professional help so that your daughter can work through her ambivalent feelings about growing up.

Undesirable Friends

Regardless of the reasons for your daughter's befriending undesirable girls, which were touched on earlier, when it happens you need to know how to respond most helpfully. What might you do, for example, when your first glimpse of your daughter's new best buddy makes you think, "Uh-oh, this girl is bad news"? It could be her look, her demeanor, her behavior, or even her associations that set you off. For example, Delia's daughter came home with a friend whose overdone makeup and tight skirt suggested sexual precociousness. Penelope's daughter gravitated to a girl whose lack of manners and indifference to adults conveyed disrespect and possible defiance.

Whatever the reason, you may want to tell your daughter plainly and urgently how you feel about this friend. Considering your daughter's age, however, you might think twice. The older she is, the less control you truly have over her friendship choices. In fact, although you may be tempted to forbid this connection, remember that such a tactic usually has the opposite effect. Trying to pry your daughter away from this friend is almost inviting or daring her to cement the relationship. It is probably better to respect the process by which your daughter learns for herself which friends share her values. It is not that you will close your eyes; by remaining involved and vigilant, you can help your daughter to evaluate the friendship herself.

NOT

> MOTHER: How could you be friends with that girl?

OR

> MOTHER: I do not want you associating with that girl again. Is that understood?

TRY

> MOTHER: What is it that you like best about Johanna?

Despite your best attempts at maintaining a poker face, your daughter may astutely sense your trepidation. If she asks outright if you dislike her friend, you might aim for a reply that is somewhere between complete dishonesty and utter condemnation. A moderate stance will discourage your daughter's defensiveness, encourage her consideration of your concerns, and, when appropriate, compel her to correct any misconceptions you have.

NOT

> MOTHER: How could I like her? She's hardly the sort of girl I'd think you'd want to be friends with.
> DAUGHTER: How can you say that? You don't know what you're talking about.

TRY

> MOTHER: I don't know her as well as you do, but I wonder about the impression she gives.
> DAUGHTER: I know what you mean, Mom. She wears the skankiest clothing and looks like a slut, but actually she doesn't drink or fool around with guys.

When you think your daughter's friend is bad news, rather than confronting her directly and ineffectively you might subtly limit the relationship. For example, when she is a younger teenager, you can ask that your daughter invite the girl to your home rather than going to hers. You can encourage your daughter to see this friend mostly in school as opposed to on weekends. It may be possible to structure activities so that they are accompanied by other girls or supervised by adults—as opposed to, say, going on solo excursions. If your daughter herself becomes less enthralled with the friendship, you can coach her to disengage slowly and sensitively. She can always blame you: "Sorry, but my mother said no" or "She'll only let me invite one friend."

Of course if your daughter's choice of undesirable friends becomes a pattern, you may want to refer back to the possible reasons and suggestions mentioned earlier in this chapter.

Conflicts with Friends

Although you know in your own mind that conflicts are normal and even inevitable in close relationships, your daughter's fights with her friends may challenge you in any number of ways. Your own struggles with conflict may emerge, your daughter may actually ask for your opinion, or your heart may break as you see her moping miserably around the house. As Apter and Josselson expressed, "Inconstancy in women is hard enough, but for girls new to friendship, the abruptness of change in the emotional climate of friendship can be shattering and incomprehensible."

Mothers can be confused, upset, and worried when they don't know the cause of friction in their daughters' friendships. Asking why you often hear, "I don't know." In the rapidly shifting winds of adolescent friendships, your daughter probably has no more idea of the reasons behind the sudden chill between her and her best pal than why a cold front turns up in July. Your role may be to comment gently on what you observe in a way that encourages your daughter to think or talk more about the conflict. At the same time, you are conveying both the inevitability and transiency of discord between friends.

NOT

> MOTHER: I don't understand how you two can be friends if you fight like this.

OR

> MOTHER: What is wrong with you girls? Can't you get along?

TRY

> MOTHER: I've noticed you haven't gotten together with Nan for a while.

OR

> MOTHER: So you and Corinne are on the outs right now?

OR

> MOTHER: It seems that you and Brenda need a little time apart.

It is important not to assume too much about your daughter's culpability. For example, even when you think her behavior has been awful, it is unwise to ask, "How could you act this way to Tracy?" or advise, "Tracy probably feels slighted and hurt by what you did." Your teenager will be crushed that you are defending her friend and taking her side rather than supporting your own daughter. Instead of assuming or second-guessing her friend's role and feelings, it is better to wonder aloud how your daughter might react if Tracy behaved in a similar manner toward her.

One, you can never be sure of what is really going on between your daughter and her friends. Two, even if you could, you probably would not be able to affect the course of their conflicts. Penelope recalls painfully what occurred when she and her neighbor tried to take their daughters for ice cream to facilitate a reconciliation: "They refused to so much as look at one another. We could have cut the silence with a knife, it was that agonizing." Your daughter has to discover for herself what she can tolerate in a friendship, and where she draws the line. What does she do if she objects to how a friend treated her? How does she react if a friend finds her annoying? When does she decide that trust is irrevocably broken? Where do your daughter's loyalties lie?

Delia, for example, remembers an incident that highlighted her daughter's determination to navigate friendships her own way. Greta had felt torn between two offers: "I didn't know what to do when I was supposed to go with my two good friends to a basketball game, but then the day before my other best friend got tickets to an awesome concert. I guess I should've gone to the game, but I knew I'd have a better time at the concert, mostly because I feel closer to Alana right now." Her mother, Delia, says, "I don't think that was any way to treat friends. Greta basically ditched them at the last minute. It was like something better came along."

Wisely, Delia chose not to scold her, but respectfully asked Greta about how she arrived at that decision and how she thought her friends would react to her change of plans. Greta replied, "I guess they'll be mad at me for a while, but I can deal with that." This would not have been Delia's solution. In fact, she admits she was disappointed in her daughter, but "I knew I couldn't control her; I couldn't force her to go to the basketball game. And even if I could, what would that have accomplished—other than making her angry at me?" Instead, Delia felt Greta learned the hard way when she had to live with the consequences of her decision.

Hurtful Friends

Almost every teenager is the occasional victim of another girl's meanness, spite, jealousy, or hostility. A best friend has enormous power to inflict pain. It is hard to sit back and watch while your daughter is hurt by girls whose trustworthiness she relies upon. In fact, when your daughter is injured, you may hear comments impulsively leave your mouth, prompted by fierce maternal protectiveness.

NOT

> MOTHER: I'd like to strangle that horrible girl!

OR

> MOTHER: If you let that girl hurt you, it'll be your mistake.

Despite your intention to be reassuring and comforting, girls usually perceive such comments as minimizing the significance of situations they consider disastrous (if only briefly). Thus your daughter may feel that you are dismissing her and seeing her concerns as trivial. Moreover, she may experience you as being critical of her.

NOT

> MOTHER: Why do you care what someone so foolish says about you?
> DAUGHTER: You think it's my fault because I care that Karla is accusing me of stuff?

Another common knee-jerk response is to defend your daughter by condemning her friend.

NOT

> MOTHER: I don't know why you hang out with that awful girl in the first place.

OR

> MOTHER: Someone like that will never be your true friend.

OR

> MOTHER: Don't you think you should find some better
> friendships?

As described above, despite the occasional hurtful episode, your
daughter may be bound and determined to be friends with this girl
for reasons you cannot possibly contemplate. For one, she may believe that this girl represents her last chance for friendship. Your
daughter may fear being alone more than she fears arguments,
episodes of unkindness, or the hurt feelings that result. In addition,
she may be benefiting from the relationship in ways that are not obvious to you, for example, through connections and opportunities
the girl provides.

Suggesting that her friend is unacceptable not only inflicts further pain, but may also make your daughter feel that you are insulting her choices—not to mention her friend, whom she will then feel
compelled to defend. In the future, when she remains close pals
with this girl, she may continually remind you, "I know you don't
like her, Mom." Instead, model for your daughter how not to judge
or react too quickly. Show her how getting further information can
enable her to make the best possible decisions. Encourage her to use
her reasoning, analyze possible motives, and assess this episode of
hurtfulness in the context of the entire relationship.

NOT

> DAUGHTER: I hate her. If she thinks I'm going to be her
> friend, she's crazy.
> MOTHER: That's right. You don't have to put up with that.

TRY:

> MOTHER: Is this the first time something like this happened
> with you and Lizzie?

OR

> MOTHER: This isn't like Ursula, is it? Is she having some kind
> of problem right now?

OR

> MOTHER: Why do you think Willa might have said that?

It is not that you are ready to excuse bad behavior or tell your daughter to let her friend off the hook. You would prefer that she develop friendships with good people. You are teaching her that she should expect to be treated well in relationships. When you point out what you like about certain of your own friends and, conversely, why you choose to avoid other people, you convey these values most effectively.

Your response when your daughter is hurt by a friend is tricky when you think she is overreacting to the situation. For example, suppose your daughter feels slighted when she is not invited to a party given by a girl she considered a close friend. Pointing out the extremity, fallacy, or hypocrisy of her reaction will probably enrage and alienate her.

NOT

> DAUGHTER: She's such a bitch for not inviting me.
> MOTHER: But she can't invite everybody.

OR

> MOTHER: But you wouldn't have invited her, would you?

TRY:

> MOTHER: That really hurt you, huh?

OR

> MOTHER: Suppose you had a party and didn't invite her. If she was hurt, what would you say to her?

OR

> MOTHER: It really stings when you don't get an invitation you want. This is something we've all had to deal with.

One of the most potentially devastating experiences for girls is being dropped by a best friend—or, worse, their entire group. Although boys seem to move on after such events, pragmatically changing their lunch period or hanging out with another group, girls more often ponder and obsess about why this happened. Lynette, seventeen, spoke of being depressed all summer when her best friend of many years "just stopped talking to me. I try to ask her what is wrong, but she ignores me and never tells me. I can't get over it." Years later, the poignancy of her loss was still apparent. While some girls eventually shift gears, others react passively and helplessly, sometimes experiencing such humiliation that they can barely muster the courage to return to school.

Even when you cannot offer answers, your daughter would probably welcome your empathy and support. It is always wise to tell her that you understand how hurtful it is to lose a friend. Assuring her that such experiences are painful but not uncommon can help her keep the episode in perspective. It is also important that your daughter learn the tough social lessons: that not everyone will like her, and that she can learn to cope when friendships end painfully. A story from your own life that illustrates these points may offer a respite from her own misery.

NOT

MOTHER: Well, there's nothing you can do about it, so stop thinking about it.

TRY:

MOTHER: That really hurts.

OR

MOTHER: Sometimes it can seem so unfair.

OR

MOTHER: A similar thing happened to me when I was about sixteen . . .

Bullies

It is astonishing how many girls are victims of bullying in school hallways, on buses, and even in classrooms while teachers are present. Boys more often fight physically, but girls pummel each other with subtle sniping remarks and insults. Their bruises are internal. In a study of fourth- and fifth-graders, researchers Nicki Crick and Maureen Bigbee found that more than 10 percent of girls (as opposed to less than 4 percent of boys) were victims of rumormongering, exclusion from peer groups, and other forms of nonphysical aggression they dub "relational aggression." Speculating that girls' manipulation and emotional threats could cause long-term scars such as submissive, depressive, or hostile behavior, these researchers suggest teaching children to be assertive and to negotiate without aggression.

Several years ago, an overweight thirteen-year-old girl reportedly took a fatal overdose of painkillers because she could no longer endure the chronic taunts of her peers. For the previous three years, at least four neighborhood teenagers allegedly had thrown food at her house, put salt in her school lunches, called her names, and teased her regularly about her weight. Her community as well as her parents were at first incredulous that she killed herself.

Bullying occupies a continuum from verbal cruelty and abuse to physical assault and violence. Research demonstrates that such aggression is a learned behavior that develops through observation, imitation, direct experience, and rehearsal. L. Rowell Huesmann, Ph.D., a psychologist and researcher on violence at the University of Michigan, recently told a Senate committee that television, movies, videos, the Internet, and electronic games have "assumed central roles in socializing our children while parents have lost influence. Mass media are having an enormous impact on our children's values, beliefs, and behavior." Launching a youth antiviolence initiative in conjunction with MTV, the American Psychological Association developed a warning signs program to help teenagers recognize violent behavior and take steps to deter it.

Your daughter may not tell you directly that she is the target of teasing or abusive peers. Instead, you might be alert to cues such as reluctance to go to school, avoidance of certain places, changes in her schedule, or symptoms of depression. A girl who is different, who stands out in some way, is most vulnerable to bullying. Witnesses to bullying are also affected. A girl who sees others being bullied may feel guilty about not stepping in, failing to support the victim, or not stopping the episode altogether—all because she is afraid that such actions could result in her becoming the next victim.

Here are some pointers on coaching your daughter to deal with bullies:

• *Support Her.* Assure your daughter not only that you believe her, but that you also believe in her. You think she is terrific and does not deserve to be mistreated by anyone. Moreover, you will help her to do whatever needs to be done to stop it.

• *Educate Her.* Although bullies come off as ultraconfident, their aura of superiority actually originates from a lack of confidence. The bully is as insecure as they come. What your daughter needs to understand is that a bully preys on weakness, intimidating and making others feel awful in order to make herself feel better. When she acts as if she is superior to everyone else, she is merely trying to convince herself of this fact. Teach your daughter that at the core of every bully is a knot of inferiority and rage that she expresses as criticism, hostility, and ridicule of others.

• *Help Her Portray Confidence.* Since bullies exploit vulnerability, help your daughter to present herself as strong. Discourage her from skulking around bullies, looking down to avoid eye contact, acting hesitant, or giving off other nonverbal signs of weakness. Instead, encourage her to stand tall, walk with confidence, and go about her business in a take-charge manner.

• *Teach Her Self-Coaching.* Your daughter may benefit from saying to herself, "This is her problem, not mine" or "She must be really insecure to do this" rather than taking personally the bully's behavior. She can remind herself, "I don't want to be friends with someone who is this mean, anyway."

• *Give Her Practical Tools.* To console herself, she can talk to old friends, make new friends, write in her journal, or even write a letter to the bully, whether or not she mails it. Teach her that when she does not react to a taunt, she deflates the bully's satisfaction. Have her practice saying, "Yeah, right" or casually responding, "That's not your concern." In response to an insult, coach her to say, "Well, I like (my hair, this outfit, my friend)." Or she can find another retort that feels right to her. Yet another approach is to laugh off a barb, which deprives the bully of the satisfaction of seeing her hurt.

• *Guide Her to Protect Herself.* Encourage your daughter to ward off bullies by sticking with a buddy or staying in larger groups. Tell your daughter that you support her standing up for herself. Urge her to say something like, "I want you to stop this right now, or I'll tell someone" or "I'm not going to let you get away with this." Help her to follow through on these statements.

• *Support Your Daughter's Taking Further Steps.* Refrain from immediately confronting the girl, her parents, or school personnel. Not only can't you assume your daughter's perceptions of the situation are accurate, but you also cannot predict how others may react. Instead, first encourage your daughter to take appropriate action on her own behalf (e.g., to tell a teacher, guidance counselor, or school psychologist, vice principal, principal, etc.), giving her the necessary tools and skills to do so.

• *Intervene When Necessary.* If the bullying continues despite your daughter's efforts, you may need to get more involved. Start with school personnel. Assure your daughter that you will follow appropriate channels and not give up until the bullying stops.

• *Get Her Help.* Enroll your daughter in a confidence-building group or self-defense course that will facilitate her feeling stronger and more confident. Arrange for her to speak to her guidance counselor or a private counselor.

Your Daughter, the Meanie

It is the rare mother whose daughter is always an angel. Yet when you observe a particularly virulent episode of insincerity, nastiness, duplicity, or exclusion, you may think, "Can this really be my little girl?" or, alternatively, "What is my daughter thinking?" Alarmed if not aghast by these revelations, you might demand of your teenager, "Why did you say/do that horrible thing?" However, you do not always know what motivated your daughter's behavior and what might have led up to or prompted her action. In addition, what may seem like the actions of a monster are probably just her efforts to figure out how she can be a friend and still be true to herself.

For example, how can she say how she really feels without being cruel? How can she get through to a friend who repeatedly makes insensitive remarks but refuses to acknowledge her behavior and apologize? How can she explore new or different friendships without being disloyal to her old buddies? Where does she draw the line between being a good friend and compromising her values? At times your daughter may engage in behaviors that even she knows are petty, mean, or over the top simply because she feels too much resentment, anger, or frustration to do otherwise. Although loathsome to many mothers, this is all part of the process by which she learns how to have and to be a friend.

Many times your daughter's meanness, which stems from fears of being ousted from a particular peer group or friendship, is designed to jockey for a better social position, more power, or greater security. In the movie *Beaches*, eleven-year-old Cici and Hillary meet for the first time when Cici auditions for a part in a children's show. Observing the acrobatic performance of Cici's adorable new rival, Hillary declares, "Personally, I think walking on your hands is creepy." In those nine words, which profess Hillary's disdain for their now-shared enemy, she clearly and emphatically pledges her staunch alliance to a new friend. The grateful, radiant expression on Cici's face seals the promise of their lifelong bond.

Does this mean you should ignore your daughter's meanness? Do you accept her explanations of "I was just kidding" or "It doesn't mean anything, Mom"? In an isolated incident, you can try to understand your daughter's social needs without condoning her behavior, for example, by asking, "What were you hoping for?" You can convey your values without condemning her by asking, "How would you have felt if she had done that to you?" or "Is there a less hurtful way to accomplish that?"

On the other hand, it may be difficult to admit (even to yourself) when your daughter is involved in ongoing meanness or bullying. Like many mothers, you may try to justify or explain away her behavior to avoid recognizing her aggression. Yet it is imperative that you intervene—both to make her accountable and to help her. If her behavior reflects emotional problems such as unresolved anger or low self-confidence, you might get her counseling. If she needs to channel her aggression into more positive pursuits, you might encourage sports, music lessons, drama, or creative writing.

This is not, however, the same as condoning her actions. As always, make distinctions between her thoughts and deeds. While you might understand her perspective, you draw the line at destructive behavior. In the same vein, help your daughter to be accountable rather than blaming her victims (e.g., "She was asking for it" or "She kept annoying me even though I told her to quit it"). Nobody made her do anything; she must take responsibility for her own actions. Reminding your daughter of times when she was teased or hurt by peers reinforces the idea that even the girl who looks weird or acts differently has the same capacity for feelings as she does. In addition, point out that bullying can scar girls with lasting physical ailments and promote high absenteeism from school, low self-esteem, and depression.

As you have seen, your impact on your teenage daughter's friendships may be gentler and subtler than when she was younger, but it is still vital. As she matures, you hope your daughter has learned the important lessons about having and being a friend so that she can enjoy the rich relationships women often share with girlfriends. As challenging as it has been to guide her in her friendships while respecting her growing autonomy, it is far more complex to deal with your daughter's romantic relationships, which are the subject of the next chapter.

Safety Nets

Sometimes, despite mothers' best efforts, daughters still struggle to have satisfying friendships with other girls during the teenage years. If this is the situation in your house, take heart. Here are some strategies that can help your daughter to feel more connected to her peers and experience being part of a peer group:

Family Friends. Your daughter may feel more comfortable with the children of your friends, particularly when they have known each other a long time, they go to different schools, and they have developed enjoyable rituals and shared experiences.

Nonschool Friends. The girls your daughter meets at summer camp, religious youth groups, acting and music programs, or other organizations are potential respites from the classmates with whom she struggles during the school week.

Boys. Some girls find that they are more comfortable hanging out with boys, whom they see as less intense, catty, and manipulative than girls at this age. When a teenage girl's best friend is male, this is often the reason.

Activities. Participation in after-school activities, including sports, not only may introduce your daughter to different girls, but also will teach her constructive skills, build self-esteem, and offer outlets for reducing stress.

Volunteering. Many kinds of volunteer work can tap into your daughter's strengths, talents, and interests, as well as encourage her to feel valued and appreciated. Plus interacting with people who are struggling in various ways can help her to keep her social problems in perspective.

Chapter 9

Love and Lust

ROMANCE

"My daughter's been unusually sullen and down on herself lately, and I'm wondering if it has to do with the boy-girl frenzy in her grade. Unlike her friends, Suzy hasn't been involved with boys much, and I think it's beginning to bother her. A few times she's hinted about feeling unattractive or being the oddball. Some of the other girls are pretty comfortable talking about boys and even calling them, but Suzy isn't. She may sense she's not ready, or maybe she's just confused or scared. Part of me is glad, but I'm a little worried that something may be wrong with her. Suzy's a bit different, maybe a little behind her friends. I wonder when she'll feel easier around boys. When will she be ready for a boyfriend? And meanwhile, is she feeling pressured to act like her friends? What can I do to reassure her—and myself—that she's okay?"

—Marge, forty-five

"Ever since Courtney started going out with John, I've been concerned. When she spends hours upon hours talking to him at night or argues that she should be allowed to see him whenever she wants, I worry that she's making him the center of her universe. I don't want Courtney to be one of those girls who drops her friends because she has a boyfriend. I tell her why this would be unhealthy, but my words seem to fall on deaf ears. And, of course, I worry that if they continue like this, Courtney will get into sex. All this makes me look for a reason to restrict her from seeing him, or start pointing out his faults. I just don't want Courtney to get herself into bad situations that she'll regret in the long run. Maybe some of my fears have to do with a disastrous relationship I had in high school. How can I help my daughter to avoid my mistakes and develop healthier, more balanced relationships with boys?"   —Zelda, fifty-one

"My daughter, Lynette, is not yet an official teenager, but already I'm worried about what's ahead. She's absolutely boy crazy! She and her friends talk constantly about who they like. Some girls have had several boyfriends already, and they're consumed with issues that I thought were years off. For example, I've overheard comments about some of them breaking up and others messing around. What is going on? I can understand Lynette having crushes; but does she actually expect to date in middle school? Maybe my own social life is affecting Lynette, since I'm a single mother. Is she trying to imitate me? Some parents consider this harmless puppy love, and think it's cute when children date, but I don't think so. How can I know when she's truly ready for dating and heaven knows what else she's dying to do?"   —Ginger, thirty-five

*J*ust as your daughter's friendships are one gauge of her overall adjustment, you may also look to her romantic relationships as an important indicator of her social success. In fact, in your mind the teenage years may be virtually synonymous with consuming infatuations, eager kisses, and the thrill of first dates. Nevertheless, reassuring yourself about your teenager's amorous relationships is even more complicated than assessing if she has the appropriate number and kind of girlfriends.

How do you begin to sort out the many beliefs, values, feelings, and experiences about dating and sexuality that you bring to mothering your daughter? By what scale do you measure whether your daughter's decisions are advancing her along the path to mature, healthy romantic relationships? Where is the mark that tells you if she is dating too much—or too little? By what criteria do you decide whether your daughter is finding the right boys? Although such standards will vary from mother to mother, the more closely your daughter's dating pattern matches your own vision of the ideal, the more comfortable you will be.

Just as you may have misgivings about your daughter's friendships, you can torment yourself about just what sort of romantic relationship you should hope for. On the one hand, seeing that your teenager is involved may reassure you of her healthy desires, capacity for warmth and connectedness, and ability to attract young men. On the other hand, you may worry about excessive dating or relationships that are too intense, too exclusive, too on-again-off-again, or too something. In other words, for any number of reasons you may believe your daughter's decisions could result in unhealthy attachments. With this realization, you run headlong into the all-too-familiar predicament of how to intervene most effectively.

Fears of girls' dating mistakes are magnified astronomically, of course, by the specter of teenage sex—with all its complexities and risks. In fact, anticipating or imagining daughters being sexual often casts a mammoth, hair-raising shadow on the already challenging adolescent years. Rather than ignoring or putting off thinking about teenage sex, however—which, admittedly, is preferable to heart-thumping panic—it is actually beneficial to survey your own beliefs as early as possible. What attitudes do you want to instill in your daughter about her sexuality? Which decisions would you like her to make? Are you confident that you are doing all you can to guide her in this area? What are your worst fears for your daughter (i.e., the ones that visit you at four A.M.)?

In this chapter you will explore your desires and expectations for your daughter in the context of what she may confront in her world. You will hear from the experts—both researchers and girls themselves—to learn about teenagers' thinking, motivations, and actual dating practices. These facts, however surprising, disappointing, or even upsetting, will help you to stay informed and realistic about what your daughter's peers are doing, not to mention what she may be experiencing firsthand. Of course guidelines will be offered to help you approach the intricate and often confusing dilemmas of teenage dating in ways that encourage your daughter to make good decisions.

She Needs Your Guidance

As described in an educational pamphlet published by the American College of Obstetricians and Gynecologists, one of the essential tasks of parenting daughters is to help them relate to others in healthy ways. This is far more than imparting traditional facts about reproduction and general lessons about the birds and the bees. Your daughter's sexuality includes her sense of what it means to be female; how she dresses and carries herself; and how she acts with boys. It also consists of her attitudes and feelings about intimacy, her values and expectations about love and relationships. If the prospect of addressing all this seems formidable now that your daughter is a teenager, be assured that in some ways you have been attending to this business for a long time—in fact, almost since the moment of her birth.

Your daughter's sense of her own body and sexuality develop from: the affection you have shown her; the way she has been spoken to and touched—even how you handled diapering her in infancy; your reaction to her use of bathroom words and self-exploration; the labels you provided for her body parts during the toddler years; your explanations when her cat, Roger, had kittens; the way you handle nudity in your home; your instructions about who should and should not touch her private parts; and countless other interactions. Many child-rearing moments, each in their own way, have contributed to your daughter's sexuality.

Yet your work is far from finished. She needs you to remain appropriately involved in this aspect of her development for many reasons:

She Wants Information from You

This may be hard to believe, but it's true. According to a recent study by the Kaiser Family Foundation and Children Now, about half of ten- to twelve-year-olds want to know how to handle pressure to have sex, how alcohol and drugs might affect decisions to have sex, and how to protect against HIV/AIDS. Many preteens named their mothers as one of their top sources of information about sex. Yet about half of parents surveyed had steered clear of these difficult conversations. Your input is crucial to supplement the knowledge your daughter receives in school, gets from books, and, especially, picks up from more educated peers in the cafeteria or on the school bus. Although a National Campaign to Prevent Teen Pregnancy survey reported that parents typically believe their teen-gagers' friends affect their sexual choices more than they do, don't be fooled. This same study found that teens ages twelve to ninteen say parents are more influential than friends in their sexual decision making.

She Needs Accurate Information

Although you may be astonished about what sexual phenomena even your young daughter is aware of, don't be fooled: Girls' information is rarely accurate or complete. Many schools have dropped sex ed in favor of an abstinence-only curriculum. Your daughter needs you to fill in the gaps in her knowledge and correct her misconceptions (e.g., "You can't get diseases from oral sex!"). This may be the twenty-first century, but it is still necessary to debunk myths about contraception (e.g., "If I jump up and down, I won't get pregnant" or "It's only my first time, so I'm safe!").

She Needs Emotional Education and Support

The emotional aspects of dating and sexuality are just as important as mere facts. Though she may get the mechanics from books and hearsay, you want her to understand the deeper, value-laden aspects of romantic relationships. Plus as your daughter struggles with wanting to be attractive and desirable to others, she desperately needs your unwavering support and the reassuring wisdom of your experience.

She Needs to Hear About Your Values

Your daughter needs you to counterbalance the assumptions about sexuality that she gets from television, movies, music lyrics, and the kids who congregate at the mall. Even when she protests, "But we covered all that in health class!" take every opportunity to enrich your daughter's understanding with the values most important to you.

Strategies for Approaching Conversations

No matter how successful your strategies for approaching most discussions with your daughter, they may not be enough when you broach these topics. In my experience, however, it is usually trepidation rather than lack of knowledge that mangles most well-intentioned mother-daughter chats about dating and sex. If you are generally uncomfortable with these issues, if sexual words stick in your throat, or if your past or present sexual experiences are emotionally loaded, not only will you be reluctant to tackle this subject but also, sensing this, your daughter will avoid talking to you when she has questions and problems. As always, however, a collaborative approach works best. Here are ten practical guidelines that can smooth the way:

Admit When You Are Uneasy

Since girls perceive your feelings far more than your words, it rarely works to plant a brave smile and plunge ahead. Many a teenage girl has reported in exquisite, rather humorous detail her mother's nervous mannerisms when this topic is addressed. Rather than denying your discomfort, try admitting: "This is hard for me to talk about, but I'll try my best" or "I'm not used to discussing this, but it's really important to me."

Don't Get Bogged Down by Details

Try not to worry about saying the wrong thing, answering questions too precisely, saying too much, or not saying enough. If you listen carefully, your daughter's responses and further questions will guide you. What is key is conveying your respect, openness, and availability when your daughter needs more information or reassurance.

Use Everyday Opportunities

Invariably, the most effective talks are not the ones you spend hours plotting and agonizing over, but the spur-of-the-moment comments after watching movies, observing people, hearing gossip, reading books, listening to music, etc. Rather than, "Okay, Missy, it's time we had a serious talk about sex," try: "What do you think of the relationships between young men and women on this show? Do they seem realistic?" or "What do you think about the sexual trend among teenagers reported in that magazine article I cut out for you?"

Strive to Be as Truthful as Possible

No matter what, make it a priority to maintain the basic trust between you and your daughter. Your credibility with issues of dating and sexuality matters a lot. When you prefer not to divulge information, rather than lying, say "I'm uncomfortable talking about that because it's really private."

Know the Facts

Keep up to date on important subjects, including slang terminology, or do some research, if necessary. When you don't know something, it is perfectly okay to say so. Try, "I have to say I'm not sure of that answer. But I'll find out and get back to you right away" or "Let's investigate that together."

Avoid Scare Tactics

Not only are scare tactics a turnoff, but they are generally ineffective because teenage girls cannot relate to extreme examples. As described, your daughter's "not me" viewpoint prevents her from imagining that she would ever be the statistic, for example, the one who gets pregnant or contracts a sexually transmitted disease (STD).

Ask for Her Thoughts and Opinions

Rather than issuing controlling proclamations such as "You're way too young even to think about sex," try asking, "How will you know you are ready to take that step?" or "Think about what you want a sexual relationship to mean to you." Consider giving your daughter permission to keep her thoughts private if she wishes: "You don't have to give me an answer, but I'm interested if you'd like to share your thoughts."

Stimulate Her Problem Solving

Again, instead of giving her directives (e.g., "As soon as you get out of the movie, you should say you want to go right home" or "If you let him do that, you're a fool"), it is better to elicit your daughter's thinking (e.g., "How will you handle it if Kurt wants you to go somewhere alone?" or "What will you do if you're not having a good time?").

Emphasize Planning

Over and again, you may need to stress that sound decision making is preferable to impulsive behaviors, which can have far-reaching negative consequences. Try, "What do you think could happen if you drank with your boyfriend at that party?" or "What is likely to happen if you agree to go to the dance with a boy you don't really like?"

Encourage Accountability

Rather than colluding with the idea that things just happen, help your daughter to see her responsibility. To encourage her to see how her decisions set events in motion, try "How do you think you contributed to that situation?" or "What would you do differently next time?"

These guidelines can certainly assist you with challenging conversations, but they can't guarantee success. In general, if you can convey to your daughter that you are not trying to "tell her what to do," but wish to sit down together with her and discuss important issues about romance, you will be better able to influence her decisions.

Rethinking Your Past

To manage your own anxiety and be most effective during these conversations with your daughter, you might reflect a bit about yourself. Your past and present experiences, beliefs, and values are critical to how you respond to her. During their own teenage years, most mothers experienced some degree of romantic involvement. Maybe you were shy, uncomfortable around boys, and reticent to date. Perhaps you were attracted to boys who were, for a variety of reasons, unavailable or failed to reciprocate your interest. Some of you may have struggled with feeling desirable and attractive, or felt left out of the teenage dating arena. Or you may recall forming a string of intense crushes, being consumed by one passionate first love, or experiencing the agony of being dumped. Some may remember adolescent relationships that, in retrospect, you can only consider ghastly mistakes (aka learning experiences).

Recalling the physical or intimate aspect of your romantic relationships, picture the age at which you first kissed someone. How extensive was your youthful sexual experimentation? When did you begin to touch a boy or allow him to touch you? Under what circumstances did you first have intercourse? Looking back, how do you evaluate the wisdom of these behaviors? Which choices would you make differently, and why? It is important to realize that these memories of your past, including the range of your feelings—from contentment to regret to euphoria to devastation—can permeate your responses to your teenage daughter's romantic life.

In their book, *Things Will Be Different for My Daughter,* Mindy Bingham and Sandy Stryker advise women to think through and refine their own values about sexual behavior in preparation for speaking to their daughters. Specifically, they suggest that mothers ask themselves a series of questions to clarify their beliefs about premarital and extramarital sex, and consider how their values compare to their own parents'. Women are asked to reflect on their hopes for their adult daughters in terms of cohabitation and/or marriage, and the messages they wish to give their teenage daughters about the appropriateness of various sexual behaviors.

Unless you deliberately examine these issues, your unconscious feelings can intrude upon or even interfere with your ability to guide your daughter. For example, your observations and potential empathy for your daughter may be dimmed if you see her experiences through the murky lens of your own unexplored history and unresolved feelings. As Zelda admits, "I can't really be objective about Courtney's relationship with John. I always have these horrible memories of being exactly her age and getting involved in a relationship I couldn't handle. At first I loved the idea of being a couple, but soon I felt awfully trapped and unable to be myself. Maybe I'm relating too much to Courtney. Maybe it's not even fair, but I'm just so worried for her."

The more fervent your feelings about your past, the more likely they will insidiously influence your mothering. Josie, a twenty-eight-year-old single mother, had become pregnant with her daughter, Renatta, as a young teenager. At fourteen, Renatta is now the exact age of her mother when she was born. She speaks poignantly of this legacy: "My mom is terrified that what happened to her is going to happen to me. I know she works hard to support us and she's a great mother, but sometimes she doesn't see that she's putting this whole thing on me. She doesn't let me do anything." Josie's unrelenting warnings and intense vigilance have made Renatta feel defensive and resentful. She pleads with her mother to see her for who she really is and treat her accordingly. As Renatta put it, "I'm not her. I'm not gonna have sex and get a baby before I'm ready."

It is crucial to clarify in your own mind when your parenting decisions are based on valid, realistic assessments of your daughter's situation or, in contrast, are governed by unconscious wishes to protect your daughter from the slights, hurts, rejections, and poor decisions of your youth.

Exploring the Present

It is not only your past, but also your present, issues that affect your parenting around romantic relationships and sexuality. If you are middle aged or nearly so, you may be apprehensive about the consequences of advancing years, such as declining vitality, attractiveness, and libido. Given this developmental vulnerability, your teenage daughter's blossoming sexuality can add to your insecurities and create sensitivities. As a mother of three teenage daughters puts it, "Sometimes, I look at all the firm thighs and perky breasts around here and I just want to hide!"

There is nothing shameful about experiencing an occasional competitive or envious twinge; these are normal human emotions. What matters is what you do with them. When permitted to influence your mothering unchecked, these responses can be unhelpful. Lily is a forty-nine-year-old mother who struggled with her upcoming birthday as she brought the older of her two daughters to therapy. Cindee, a bright, strikingly attractive fifteen-year-old girl with deteriorating grades, was increasingly depressed and turning to substances. Her mother, a professional actress who had worked hard to achieve success, was puzzled and put off by her daughter's apparent apathy and lack of motivation in school. Distancing herself, she adopted a hands-off approach to both Cindee's academic problems and social life, asking few questions and setting minimal limits. In fact, Lily appeared to overlook clues of her daughter's casual sexual activities.

Cindee reported that one night when she returned home after

"getting drunk and hooking up with a guy at a party," her mother nonchalantly pointed out that her shirt was buttoned incorrectly. Cindee expressed amazement that her mother acted clueless about the meaning of her disheveled state. As Lily struggled with fears of waning physical beauty, which had been central to her identity and success as a performer, she couldn't seem to recognize the signs, much less address, her daughter's sexual behavior. In fact, on some level she may have gotten vicarious pleasure and reassurance from her daughter's involvement. Sometimes mothers react in the opposite way, by becoming watchful, accusatory, disapproving, or rigidly restrictive, ostensibly to protect their increasingly womanly daughters from undesired sexual activity.

Your marriage or intimate relationship is also an important factor. The quality of your own partnership influences how you deal with your daughter's progress in this area. At a minimum, if you are preoccupied with a relationship that is unstable or unhealthy, you will have fewer resources to focus on your daughter's issues. It gets more complicated when you and your daughter are dating at the same time. This is not to say you shouldn't have a social life, only that you might be aware of the complexities that may arise. For example, don't be surprised if your daughter is aghast at aspects of your dating. The average teenage girl would prefer to be grounded for a year than to envision her mother going out and, heaven forbid, acting on sexual desires similar to her own!

Your relationship also offers a powerful model of how men and women interact. Your daughter makes it a point to note the balance of power and affection, how effectively you communicate, and the ways in which you and your partner deal with anger and conflict. Although mothers often go to great lengths to hide tension in their own relationships and cover up patterns they consider undesirable, teenage girls frequently see through these efforts. They are astute observers of others. Consequently, it is not only what you say about healthy relationships but what you do that is important.

Be aware of biases and prejudices that can somehow influence your daughter's attitudes and behavior. For example, you may make assumptions about your daughter's friends according to whether or not—and whom—they are dating, or judge adult women on the basis of their marital status. Those who were raised to think that women should be wives may unwittingly communicate to their daughters disparaging opinions of those who never married. Consider too the attitudes you convey about alternative lifestyles, the subtle ways in which you and your family perpetuate or refute this culture's prejudices against those who are different.

Gay Teenagers

It is especially important to think about your attitudes about homosexuality. The fact that an estimated 10 percent of the population is gay means that your daughter will probably encounter this issue in some way during her adolescence. Whether she learns that a good friend is gay or struggles with her own orientation, you can be pivotal in this process. You have the opportunity to influence and perhaps counteract the earliest, destructive messages she is likely to get about gay and lesbian individuals—for example, scathing put-downs heard on the school bus, nervous tittering in response to locker room jokes, or newspaper accounts of gay bashing. As your daughter works through issues of her own sexuality, your knowledge, understanding, and acceptance can keep her from feeling overwhelmed or isolated.

It may be difficult to consider that your daughter might come to believe that she is bisexual or gay. Mothers nearly universally want girls to be not only all right, and doing okay, but also familiar and understandable. For many parents, anything different from heterosexual dating is too unsettling or frightening even to contemplate. Imagine how it is for teenagers! This period of life, which is synonymous with desires to fit in and intolerance for those who dare to deviate, could not be less conducive to grappling with this issue.

Mothers and daughters alike often report confusion about how homosexuality is first recognized. During the early teenage years, intense, crushlike relationships between girls, often accompanied by possessiveness and loyalty conflicts, are considered developmentally appropriate. Curiosity about each other's developing bodies is normal, and sex play in girls who later are strictly heterosexual is also rather common. Although girls can be baffled and frightened by early same-sex experiences, this culture's hostility to differences often prevents them from asking important questions and getting much-needed information.

This is one reason why the process of self-discovery for lesbian teenagers is typically so painful. In retrospect, many girls describe first denying their homosexuality, trying to convince themselves that they are "normal," and then becoming depressed. Although teenagers almost never cite their sexual orientation as a cause for seeking treatment, they describe feelings of isolation, perceptions of being different, and resultant despair. Some do not know if they are, indeed, lesbians, many are not ready to address the issue directly, and others do not even have a word for it.

Jacki, sixteen, was brought to therapy by her mother because of vague feelings of unhappiness and loneliness. Eventually, she began to associate with known drug users and wore a baggy, disheveled style of clothing considered extreme in her community. While her fourteen-year-old sister was a freshman cheerleader who read teen magazines and imitated the trendiest styles, Jacki often watched videos and played computer games alone in her room. Fortunately, her mother was not only perceptive about but open to and accepting of the vastly different ways in which her daughters defined themselves as teenage girls. Strongly suspecting the possibility that her daughter was a lesbian, she actively encouraged her self-discovery and was prepared for her eventual disclosure.

Mothers are crucial to the process of girls' discovering and claiming their sexual orientation for several reasons. The average teenager is highly unlikely to share such information with peers, as middle and high school environments are infamous for verbal and physical harassment of openly gay students. Other teenagers are often afraid of associating with known homosexuals for fear of being labeled. Keeping this secret, however, is arduous and exhausting. If they cannot unburden to mothers, girls may soothe themselves and escape inner turmoil by turning to alcohol or drugs. In her paper entitled "Coming Home to Self, Going Home to Parents: Lesbian Identity Disclosure," a Work in Progress of The Stone Center of Wellesley College, Lennie Kleinberg, Ed.D., says, "Lesbian women rarely grow up feeling good about themselves."

Regardless of her orientation, it is imperative to build a relationship with your daughter that encourages her to share any thoughts, feelings, and confusion she has about her sexuality. According to Dr. Kleinberg, young lesbian women usually struggle with whether to maintain their secret and remain in conflict themselves or, conversely, to risk hurting their parents and creating disharmony in their families. Fears of inciting negative reactions in their mothers, such as homophobia or feelings of personal rejection, typically stop girls from expressing their true selves.

Since most lesbians disclose their orientation to their mothers first, your receptiveness to her news and your ability to advocate for her may well determine your daughter's ultimate path, especially how and when she shares this information with her father and other relatives. Chris, a seventeen-year-old high school senior, told her mother her secret in a fit of rage during an argument. Her mother's response, "Don't tell your sister; we don't want her to get any ideas," was devastating to her. In contrast, when Nan, also seventeen, finally disclosed that she was homosexual, her mother helped her to brainstorm how to tell other family members and to anticipate their possible reactions.

Your daughter must maintain an authentic sense of who she is, both for her own well-being and in order to enjoy a genuine, close connection with you. Secrets create barriers.

If your daughter speaks of alternative lifestyles, the women's movement, homosexuality, or lesbianism in the context of other people, pay close attention. Similarly, many young women speak of leaving out books, articles, or music about lesbian women where their parents would find them. While these tactics are hardly proof of a teenager's inclination, they could be means of testing the waters of tolerance. If you suspect your daughter might be bisexual or homosexual, or if she comes out, you might check out PFLAG (Parents and Friends of Lesbians and Gays), an organization that many parents find both supportive and informative.

Modern Dating: Revised
New Words for a New World

Once you have weeded through your own past and present circumstances, you might turn to what is going on in your daughter's romantic world. As you probably know, dating patterns have definitely shifted. There is less formal, one-on-one, boy-asks-girl dating, and more casual pairing off within groups. Increasingly, teenagers meet somewhere outside the home to attend a party or event together. This means they spend less time around parents, who don't always meet boyfriends—or, in some cases, even know about their existence! So when your daughter goes out with a bunch of male and female friends, you cannot assume that she is part of one big platonic group.

To understand her dating world, you may need to buy a brand-new dictionary, as the pertinent terminology has also changed. You might wonder what your daughter means, for example, when she announces that she was "with" Wynn on the class trip, or that she and Danny are "going out," or that she and Fred are "together" now. Is she saying she has a boyfriend? Are any of these terms similar to the antiquated concept of going steady? Or do these expressions convey subtle differences in commitment or seriousness? It is hard to respond appropriately when you are not all that sure what your daughter is talking about.

The sexual lingo has also undergone a metamorphosis. You may have heard terms such as "hooking up" or "random hookups." Not too long ago, I had the chance to speak with a group of high school girls during a morning assembly, prior to giving a lecture that same evening for their parents. "Please," the girls begged me, "Straighten our mothers out! They read a [national] magazine article and now they're convinced hooking up means having sex. But around here, when we say that we just mean kissing." I am passing along these girls' sage advice: When your daughter uses unfamiliar jargon, check it out instead of making assumptions.

Apparently, the age-old bases of physical intimacy have changed as well. (Hint: Third base is not necessarily what it used to be; those experiencing "sloppy third" are engaging in oral sex.) In some circles, too, girls and boys no longer advance around the bases as their relationship progresses, but often skip first and second and go right to third, which they perceive as less intimate.

But before you call 911 or order a security device for your daughter's bedroom door, remember that there are a whole host of ways you can influence her to become well informed and capable so that she approaches dating and sexuality as wisely as possible. Here are some of the major issues teenage girls confront in the contemporary dating world, along with pertinent information and possible helpful interventions:

Can't Wait to Date

You might apply the general parenting principle of considering your daughter's age to counteract the tremendous cultural pressure she experiences to be involved as soon as possible in an exclusive, one-to-one dating relationship. Indeed, elementary school children are often portrayed by the media as boyfriend and girlfriend. Contemporary music lyrics promote romantic notions of intense passion and exclusivity. Magazine and television advertisements show young girls dressing provocatively and being sexy to appeal to the opposite sex. As Ginger, mother of Lynette, described, some parents find it adorable when fifth- and sixth-graders go on dates and even equate this with popularity. Other mothers don't set limits because they want to be seen as cool or to avoid conflict with their daughters.

The fact that your young daughter's peers may be interested in boys or dating enormously affects her views of herself. Like Marge's daughter, Suzy, if your teenager is not keeping pace with her friends, she may be filled with silent self-doubt. Feeling different, she may be confused or sad or angry and not even know why. If she joins the dating frenzy before she is ready, she may be confused or sad or angry for different reasons. But somehow, during adolescence, that seems preferable to sitting outside the dating arena. As Suzy says, "My friends who have boyfriends are in the popular group; they're always invited to the cool parties." Girls who are unattached often see themselves as less attractive, less successful, and, sometimes, out-and-out losers.

In her essay "The Age of Beauty" Nancy Friday describes attending a dance as an early adolescent, and experiencing herself as exceptionally unable to succeed with boys: "I watched my friends, whose leader I had been for years, watched them happy in the arms of desirable boys, and I recognized what they had that I lacked . . . By morning I had buried and mourned my eleven-year-old self, the leader, the actress, the tree climber, and had become an ardent beauty student. From now on I would ape my beautiful friends, smile the group smile, walk the group walk and, what with hanging my head and bending my knees, approximate as best I could the group look."

This essay poignantly portrays many girls' experience. When her daughter's school sponsored a "Moving Up" banquet for eighth graders, Marge became increasingly aware of the strain this put on Suzy and her friends. "These girls obviously felt enormous pressure to have a date for the banquet," she explains. "Although many of Suzy's friends were frantically asking boys to go with them, Suzy could not bring herself to do this. When I spoke to her she said it wasn't a big deal, but I had a feeling she was worried about what would happen if no one asked her." In fact, Marge found out later that just before the banquet Suzy approached a boy who had been her neighborhood friend since preschool. So nervous that she was trembling and nearly in tears, Suzy begged him to go to the banquet with her as a friend. When Marge heard this from the boy's mother, it confirmed all her concerns.

Why the rush to date? It is probably stating the obvious that many girls merely long for affection, a simple hug or holding hands. But according to a recent national survey of *Girls' Life* magazine readers, another significant reason many younger girls want boyfriends is to gain popularity with other *girls*. Apparently, your daughter's social status skyrockets when other girls are eager to hear the details of her dating experiences. Plus saying they are going out with someone affords added security. As one eleven-year-old put it, "I really need a boy to lean on." Although these early relationships are as fleeting as a breeze, for the moment at least girls can feel connected to someone. Tomorrow, it may be a different someone. Thus the *Girls' Life* survey reported that by age ten or eleven some girls already had dated eight or ten boys!

When Is She Ready?

In your discussions with your daughter, arm yourself with the known hazards of dating too early. Although many girls enjoy the flurry of attention and requests for advice from their friends, they risk a bad reputation if they become *too* experienced. Even those especially keen for dating often find themselves disappointed or uncomfortable in one-to-one situations. "It was fine when we were with our group, but I didn't know what to say when we were alone," one girl confided. Another said, "Once I said I'd go out with him, I didn't know how to get out of it. I got my friend to tell his friend. It was so stupid." Many girls describe how perfectly good friendships with boys were strained or ruined forever after they turned into brief romances. Thus girls who date early almost always say they regret doing so and wish they had waited.

Shared with your daughter, this information may percolate and have an influence on her decisions. As always, when you approach her in a respectful, collaborative manner, she is more apt to consider your ideas about teenage romance and the kind of relationship you think is right for her. Don't hesitate to say what you think is and isn't appropriate. If you think she is too young, you might try "I can see why you'd want to date, but I think it's better to wait because . . ." Although she may protest, deep down your daughter may benefit from hearing "You don't need a boyfriend to have fun and be happy" or "First concentrate on getting to know and love yourself, and you'll be better able to love someone else later on."

How will you know if your daughter is ready for one-on-one dating? Her age is only one important criterion. As always, you probably want to assess whether she has the requisite skills. Although there are no hard and fast rules, you might consider using these questions as a rough checklist of your daughter's readiness:

- Is she at least fifteen?
- Has she enjoyed friendships with boys?
- Is she generally at ease around boys?
- Is she assertive in speaking her mind?
- Has she demonstrated general trustworthiness?
- Is she a good problem solver?
- Can she say no and mean it?
- Is she reliable with curfews?
- Are you comfortable with her values and beliefs?
- Is she responsible with alcohol and drugs?

In preparation for dating, discuss important issues well in advance. Once there is a particular boy on the scene, your perfectly reasonable concerns will be registered as utter condemnation: "What? You don't trust my boyfriend!" or "You must think I'm an idiot!" Brainstorm situations that may arise in the future. You might ask her, for example, "How will you handle it if your date has a beer before driving you home?" and "If you don't want to go where he suggests, what will you do?" Give your daughter permission to tell white lies to extricate herself from sticky situations. For additional strategies, you might want to refer back to the sidebar, "Safeguards Against Trouble" in Chapter 6. Communicate clearly how you expect your daughter to behave during a date, including whether she must call home during the evening and abide by her usual curfew.

The Healthy Relationship

How will you evaluate your daughter's romantic relationship with her boyfriend? In various families there will be a different emphasis on the young man's age, family, socioeconomic status, intelligence, level of achievement, athletic talent, etc. What probably matters most in terms of a healthy relationship, however, is how he treats your daughter and the degree to which the connection allows her to be true to herself. Rather than completing the following quiz for your daughter, you might suggest she give these questions a whirl herself:

• *Is He Good to Her?* Are her needs for companionship, understanding, and support being met? Does her boyfriend respect her wishes? Does your daughter feel appreciated and safe? Can she trust him? It is usually unhelpful to say, "He pays a lot more attention to his friends than he does to you!" or "How can you let him treat you that way?" but try "Do you feel cared for?" and "Does being with him make you feel special?"

• *Is Power Balanced?* Your daughter should be comfortable expressing her desires and expect that decisions will be mutual. When you see her letting a boyfriend take control, instead of asking, "Why do you always let him make the plans?" try "Are you able to choose the movie too?" Similarly, she should not feel compelled to accommodate her boyfriend's wishes at the expense of her own. If you overhear your daughter saying, "Sure I can go. It's no big deal to blow off my friends, they'll understand," you will know she needs support in pursuing her own interests and plans. Coach her to think, "I have a right to do what I want. I shouldn't have to drop everything to keep a boyfriend. If he really cares for me, he'll understand." Some of the most reassuring words a mother can hear are, "Sorry, I already have plans for Saturday. Maybe we can go another time."

• *Can She Be Herself?* Does your daughter's romance encourage rather than inhibit her personal growth? Is your daughter comfortable being her smart, zany, exuberant, or quick-witted self around her boyfriend? Does she speak up and voice her own opinions and feelings or, conversely, does she keep quiet so as not to scare him off? You might ask, "Any thoughts on why you're so reserved when your boyfriend is here?" or "What will happen if you tell him how you feel about that?" When you see her holding back, try "How might going out for the team jeopardize your relationship?" or "How does he feel about your doing that community service project?"

• *Is She Learning to Resolve Conflict?* Especially with their overly romanticized, fairy tale or sitcom mentality, teenage girls often expect instant perfection with boyfriends. They may be surprised that maintaining a relationship is an ongoing process, or that getting along can take some work. To avoid conflict and the risk of a breakup, some are perpetually agreeable. Help your daughter to respect her own wishes along with her boyfriend's. Empower her to face misunderstandings and disagreements head on. When she complains that her boyfriend invites his pals along on their dates or that he teases her too much, use this opportunity to suggest better communication and negotiation. Try "You and Justin need to discuss this. Can each of you talk about your point of view? Then you can figure out how to deal with this together."

• *Is Aggression Kept in Check?* Teenagers must learn how to handle anger and conflict without engaging in name-calling or insults that can escalate into physical altercations. Teach your daughter to expect people to treat her well even when they are upset with her. She needs to know that it is never okay, even during an argument, for her or her boyfriend to be nasty, to mistreat each other, or to be hurtful. Coach her to argue respectfully; to avoid mean, hurtful criticisms; and to harness her own temper. Your daughter needs to hear what you might consider obvious, that violence is never acceptable.

Teenage Sexual Behavior

Eagerness to Shed Virginity

Along with earlier dating, some teenagers are experimenting sexually at ever-younger ages. Dr. Robert Blum reported in the *Journal of the American Medical Association* that 17 percent of seventh- and eighth-graders have had intercourse. Others report higher rates, depending on race and gender. But regardless of the exact number of sexually experienced youngsters, experts generally agree on the causes. With some girls experiencing hormonal surges at earlier ages, biological urges and cultural pressure for sexual activity are occurring before teenagers are emotionally capable of managing them. Adding to this powder keg, parents are generally providing less supervision and granting greater autonomy before their teenagers' reasoning and impulse control have fully kicked in. No wonder precocious sexual behavior is on the rise!

You may wonder how prevalent sex really is during high school. According to the Centers for Disease Control, 38 percent of freshman and 60.9 percent of seniors are sexually experienced. Interestingly, through national, state, and local surveys conducted biennially, the CDC's Youth Risk Behavior Surveillance System (YRBSS) determined that from 1991 to 1997 there was a 15 percent decrease in sexual experience among males, but an insignificant decrease among female students. In a climate of educating teenagers to abstain from or delay intercourse and to protect themselves against disease, why would today's teenage girls—as opposed to boys—remain just as sexually active?

Rather than assuming your daughter's innocence or seeing her as a victim of hormone-ridden adolescent boys, consider the possibility that she may desire sexual experiences. Marge tells of hearing stories from women whose sons have been pursued by Suzy's girlfriends: "They have apparently become very brazen, not only calling boys and asking them out, but also putting pressure on them to fool around. Some of these boys are clearly not ready for this, but when they refuse the girls ridicule and humiliate them." Because boys mature on average two years after girls, they often have no idea how to distance themselves gracefully from girls' pressure. When they manage intense, uncomfortable emotions by ignoring girls or behaving cruelly to them, a vicious cycle is perpetuated. Girls feel rejected and are doubly determined to find another boyfriend to prove they are desirable.

One subgroup of girls, in fact, is virtually preoccupied with losing their virginity or getting it over with. Perhaps they are driven by their own curiosity, the stigma of virginity in some groups, and the desire to be included in conversations among the initiated.

In your discussions with your daughter, you can cite compelling facts. According to the National Center for Health Statistics, the younger a teenage girl when she has sex for the first time, the more likely it is unwanted or involuntary. Of sexually active girls fifteen to nineteen, 31 percent say their first experience was not really desired. Listening to their stories in therapy, it is obvious that intercourse is rarely enjoyable for teenage girls. Feelings of shame, being rushed, the chance of being caught, and fears of pregnancy or contracting sexually transmitted diseases, including HIV, interfere with relaxation and pleasure. Most girls have never had an orgasm or are unsure what that is. They often admit, somewhat reluctantly, that their partners were not overly attentive to their needs.

The girls I see in therapy typically report many symptoms of depression and speak of feeling terrible about themselves as a result of regretted sexual experiences. When relationships end, they feel used and discarded. After losing their virginity, girls often choose to have sex with later partners simply because "it was no big deal 'cause I already did it." When they discover their powers of attraction, some even begin to dress differently and to relate to males provocatively. Others withdraw when they believe that people, especially mothers, know what they have done. No wonder 80 percent of sexually active girls say they wish they had waited!

"It's Not Really Sex, Mom!"

Much has been said about the observed increase in oral sex among teenagers, beginning as early as the middle school years. In fact, the latest studies report that half of boys ages fifteen to nineteen have received oral sex from girls—a significant increase in the last twenty years. This suggests, of course, that there are a significant number of girls who are performing oral sex on boys. With the widespread publicity of a recent presidential sex scandal, the name for this act has become a household word, familiar even to elementary schoolchildren.

What concerns mothers and professionals alike is not just that oral sex is on the rise, but the anonymity, impersonal nature, and almost mechanical quality of this act. It is girls who perform oral sex on boys—some of whom are not boyfriends but mere acquaintances. Because girls are giving rather than receiving pleasure—

essentially servicing boys—their subservience and demeaning position is alarming. Research confirms that some girls report feeling exploited. If you wonder what could motivate girls to give oral sex, you might be interested in their stated reasons:

- "I was curious about what it was all about."
- "It was a coup; this guy's really hot and everybody wants him."
- "I was drunk."
- "I just wanted to see if I could get him."
- "I don't know; I'm not sure."
- "I'm still a virgin"
- "It's not a big deal."
- "I don't have to worry about getting pregnant."
- "It's not really sex!"

Many girls seek the status or popularity that often accompanies this act. In many groups, oral sex is considered so acceptable, if not desirable, that girls do not fear damaging their reputations. Remarkably, girls who have intercourse are more likely to get negative reactions from peers than those who give oral sex. What some teenagers cannot yet understand or express is that oral sex also enables them to get the male attention they crave, to please boys, and even to gain power over them. Others are unconsciously expressing anger and rebellion. A few are repeating earlier traumas, such as sexual abuse. Still others use the excitement and forbidden quality of oral sex as a defense against despair. The sense of connection, however brief and coarse, can be an antidote to frightening loneliness and isolation.

The strategies you have been using to bolster your daughter's sense of self, to underscore her personal dignity, and to empower her to build relationships, as discussed in previous chapters, are all effective inoculations against these less-than-ideal motivations. Girls who know who they are and what they stand for, who feel valued, and who are confident that they deserve to be treated well, are less inclined to give oral sex.

In addition to correcting misinformation—for example, dispelling the myth that STDs, including HIV, cannot be contracted by oral sex—you need to counteract what your daughter hears. Ginger, for example, reported having this conversation with her daughter when Lynette asked to go to the movies with a small group of friends:

> MOTHER: I've heard some rumors about what some middle schoolers are doing at the movies.
> DAUGHTER: You mean oral sex? What's so bad about that?
> MOTHER: This is not a question of what adults who love each other decide to do in the privacy of their own home. It's not okay in middle school, and it's certainly not okay in a public place. I expect you to respect yourself, to make good decisions when you are out with boys, and to act responsibly.
> DAUGHTER: Oh, Mom, don't worry, I would never do that!
> MOTHER: What do you suppose would make a girl want to perform oral sex for a boy? What's in it for her?
> DAUGHTER: I really don't know, Mom.
> MOTHER: Well, I wonder about how a girl who does that at your age feels about herself. I want you to know that in a mature, loving relationship there is mutual caring and commitment, not one person trying to please another.

Birth Control, Pregnancy, and STDs

Whenever your daughter decides to be sexually active, you hope that she will be protected from pregnancy and disease. According to the National Campaign to Prevent Teen Pregnancy, this country has the highest rate of teenage pregnancy in the western industrialized world. Although public education has increased condom use among teenagers from 46 percent to 57 percent, each year one million girls become pregnant. In fact, at least half of all sexually active teenagers who do not use birth control become pregnant within two years.

Of course nowadays, mothers' greatest fears run to sexually transmitted, often lethal, diseases. It is alarming to learn that half of all new HIV infections occur in people under age twenty-five, and HIV is the sixth-leading cause of death among fifteen-to-twenty-four-year-olds. The infection is growing fastest among straight girls, who make up nearly half of all new teenage HIV cases, most of whom contracted the disease from having sex with older guys. In fact, the number of female adolescents with AIDS more than tripled in the ten years from 1987 to 1997. With their infamous belief in immortality, however, it is the rare teen girl who admits to being concerned with this possibility.

Your discussions with your daughter about making good decisions, planning, and avoiding impulsive actions can go a long way to prepare her for these situations. How you handle the delicate issues of birth control and protection from disease, however, depends upon your own background, religious beliefs, and values. Be aware of the philosophy and curriculum of your daughter's health or sex ed classes as well. Is she being taught abstinence only, safe sex practices, or a combination of both? What is your own philosophy and that of your family?

It is possible that your daughter will decide to take a path different from the one you recommend. In this case, some mothers take the position "If you do, don't tell me. What I don't know can't hurt me." Others, however, more wisely say, "I would much rather that you wait until such-and-such a time to be sexually active, but if you choose otherwise please tell me so that I can help you to be safe." Such a statement conveys to your daughter your clear preference, but is also (a) highly respectful of her right to be her own person, and (b) noncontrolling because it recognizes that she may make her own, different decision. You are also confirming that your priority is her well-being, not her obedience. This approach would make a teenage girl more comfortable coming to her mother without fears of recrimination, especially in the event of a problem.

Even if you approve of her using birth control, however, clinical experience suggests a striking impediment to teenagers doing so. Essentially, girls are in somewhat of a bind. Plagued by ambivalence or guilt, they typically cannot bring themselves to acknowledge their intent to be sexual. When it happens, usually as a result of getting carried away or drinking too much, they feel less culpable and bad than if they had planned or arranged it. Obviously, it is hard to disown complicity while obtaining birth control in advance!

This is not unlike the quandary some mothers feel about whether to put their teenage daughters on birth control pills. Is this a mixed message condoning—or even inviting—sexual experimentation? Or when girls are sexually active or planning to be, should this be viewed an appropriate and realistic precaution against pregnancy? Remember too that birth control pills offer absolutely no protection against STDs, including the HIV infection. Resolving the dilemma of contraception will of course require weighing all the factors, including your religious and moral values, medical issues, and your daughter's unique situation.

Influencing Your Daughter's Choices

When you and your daughter discuss the issue of sexual behavior, you might use the following guidelines to help her make the wisest possible decisions:

• *Counteract the Media.* A University of Michigan study showed that females who actively identify with characters on television are more likely to see sex as recreational, as a game, rather than as a relationship. That is one reason why it has been crucial to monitor and discuss television shows that create a heightened sexual atmosphere and shape (or, more likely, distort) your daughter's impressions of real-life sex. Convey to your daughter that things are not always simple, fun, or no big deal. The entertainment industry does not always present accurately the complexity, challenges, or pitfalls of sex, all of which require considerable emotional maturity.

• *Differentiate Between Desire and Doing It.* This is yet another opportunity to apply the principle of differentiating your daughter's thoughts from her deeds. Her sexual feelings do not make her bad. They are perfectly normal and expected. Although you may be uneasy about her sexual arousal or fantasies, she needs to know that they hardly brand her a slut; it is how she handles them that counts. With the aid of her sense of self, she learns to value herself and set long-term priorities that help her manage physical desires. Anticipating possible consequences, she can delay rather than give in to her sexual impulses when it is in her best interest to do so.

• *Clarify the Difference Between Love and Lust.* Today, sexual behavior among young people is often detached, unemotional, and rather mechanical. When teenagers hook up at parties and perform sexual acts, a sense of anonymity often prevails. Boyfriend or no boyfriend, many girls want to kiss and practice sexual acts. This is a disturbing notion to mothers for whom deep affection is a prerequisite for physical closeness. If you believe that sex should be meaningful rather than casual, you will want to differentiate lust, which is a biologically based, physical urge, from love, which is an expression of deep affection and intimacy. You will also want to teach your daughter that emotional intimacy should be a foundation for and precede physical intimacy. According to the CDC and Kaiser Family Foundation, research shows that 34 percent of teenagers surveyed never talked to their partners about birth control, and 40 percent never spoke of STDs. Try "Get to know someone well before you become intimate. Share your hopes, secrets, and dreams before you share your body." Excellent guidelines for gauging girls' readiness for intimacy are offered in *Girltalk*, by Carol Weston.

• *Explore Other Motivations.* Help your daughter to question other reasons, besides physical arousal, that tempt her to be sexual. You might suggest she consider whether she is hoping merely to gain acceptance among her peers or to achieve popularity. If she believes she truly has intense feelings for her intended partner, you might wonder with her if there are other ways she can demonstrate her affection.

• *Encourage Decision Making.* Why not ask your daughter outright, "How far do you want to go with sexual feelings?" This emphasizes that this is her choice, not something that just happens. To prevent unplanned sexual activity, discuss high-risk situations that might be avoided, such as attending unchaperoned parties and being alone in an isolated setting with her boyfriend. The role of alcohol and drugs is pivotal. According to MADD (Mothers Against Drunk Driving), a survey of sixteen- to-nineteen-year-olds found that they were 49 percent more likely to have sex if they had been drinking. Your daughter should understand that this is because drinking lowers inhibition and affects judgment. In fact, in therapy the words "I got drunk" are echoed throughout the week by girls who justify the previous weekend's unplanned sexual activity. When they first make the decision to drink, it is as if on some level they are also deciding to engage in sexual behavior.

• *Don't Hesitate to Share Your Values.* When you discuss sexuality with your daughter, it is okay to share your beliefs even if you anticipate that she will not agree with them. For example, you might say, "I think it is important to be in a committed, mature, adult, long-term relationship before you have sex" or "I don't believe in premarital sex" or "I want you to be engaged before you have intercourse," or whatever it is you do believe. It is acceptable to state that before such-and-such age, young people are not ready to deal with the complex emotions and potential problems that can arise with an intimate sexual relationship. Above all, your daughter needs to hear over and over and in many different ways, "I think you are a wonderful young woman who deserves love, romance, and commitment."

• *Build in Delays.* The research suggests several aids to delaying sexual intercourse. Since 39 percent of teenage girls' first sexual partners were three or more years older, this suggests one guideline about dating. Also, maintaining a close emotional connection with your daughter and monitoring her daily activities, which are emphasized in the collaborative approach to parenting teenagers outlined in this book, are protections against early sex. In addition, girls who are studious and stay busy with hobbies and extracurricular activities tend to put off sexual involvement. A recent study by psychologist Carolyn Tucker and her colleagues determined that teenage girls of higher intelligence were two to five times more likely to postpone intercourse, and significantly less likely to engage in a range of transitional, partnered sexual activities, such as holding hands, kissing, and various petting behaviors. For example, for each one-point increase in I.Q. score, girls were 1.6 percent less likely to neck. Whether your daughter is at the top of her class or struggling to keep up, these findings offer valuable guidance. Factors associated with postponing sex included teenagers' perceptions of how their mothers would feel about their having sex, their notions of the consequences of pregnancy, their estimated probability of going to college, grade point average, participation in school clubs and sports activities, and attendance at religious services. These data are consistent with other reports of girls postponing premarital intercourse because of clashes with their religious and moral values. So use your daughter's long-term goals as deterrents to unwise behavior. Teach her how the consequences of making poor choices may be the forfeiture of those dreams.

• *Anticipate Pitfalls.* To further demystify idealized sex, remind your daughter that the double standard is alive and well. While girls who are too sexually active are classified by negative names like slut, ho, and skank, to mention just a few, boys are dubbed players—a term that is tinged with admiration for their conquests. Ask your daughter, "How did your friend get a bad reputation?" or "Did she flirt too much, change boyfriends too quickly, go too far?" In addition, mothers may remind girls to consider what might happen if their boyfriends are indiscreet. As one mother bluntly asked her daughter, "Do you want a boy to touch your body and brag to his buddies in the locker room or compare your breasts to all the others he's touched?"

• *Decode the Mysteries of the Sexes.* Teach your daughter to interpret the plea "If you really loved me you would have sex with me" as a form of emotional blackmail, a line whose aim is simply to manipulate. Convey that agreeing to have sex is never proof of love, maturity, or desirability. You might also share this wise adage: Girls often have sex to have relationships, while boys often have relationships to have sex.

• *Coach Your Daughter to Respond Effectively.* Especially in the awkwardness of a moment, girls sometimes know how they would like to respond but need the actual words. Your daughter may be willing to brainstorm effective retorts, or she may be receptive to your suggestions, such as "I'd rather not do that tonight," "I'm not ready for that," or "I'm not comfortable. We should talk about this." Even if she anticipates that her boyfriend will be displeased or upset, by dealing with the issue directly and clearly, and avoiding being critical or insulting, she is effectively managing the situation.

• *Remind Her of Her Value.* Everything you have done to build your daughter's sense of self will contribute to her seeing herself and her body not as giveaways, but as gifts she will choose to share at some point when she is truly ready with someone highly deserving. The more she believes in herself, the more selective she will be.

When you and your daughter can talk about sexual issues with honesty and mutual respect, you know that you have done many things right. Although you may not see eye to eye about either your beliefs or practices, the fact that you trust one another enough to sit down together and speak about this highly personal subject is remarkable. For many reasons, mothers and teenage daughters are often unable to have such an intimate discussion; this does not necessarily suggest difficulty in the relationship. But if this is the case for you, consider arranging for your daughter to speak to another adult, such as a physician, counselor, godparent, favorite aunt, or friend of the family, whose values and knowledge you respect.

Potential Pitfalls of Romance

Since your daughter is still living at home, you have the advantage of being able to monitor her developing relationships and intervene, if necessary, if you become concerned about any problems that arise. The most common examples are a breakup and a relationship that seems unhealthy.

The Breakup

It is rather unlikely your daughter's high school boyfriend will become a lifelong relationship. In fact, since most teenage romances have a short shelf life, if your daughter has a boyfriend in high school or middle school, it is likely she will experience dumping or, usually more distressing, being dumped. When your daughter appears heartbroken or devastated, it can be difficult to know how to help.

Perhaps sensing her waning interest in him, John suddenly broke up with Courtney. Her mother, Zelda, says, "I thought I'd be thrilled, but actually I was pretty worried about her. She cried for hours on end and didn't want to come out of her room." Afterward, Courtney had difficulty concentrating on her schoolwork, her grades suffered, and she was caught skipping classes to look for John to discuss their breakup. Some girls review over and again their previous conversations, talk endlessly about what went wrong with their ex-boyfriends, and rehearse what they will say to them in the future.

It is ideal to have visited the topic of breakups, along with the sadness that often follows loss, prior to the first broken-hearted experience. Talk with your daughter about dating as practice for a more intensive, permanent relationship. It is hoped she will learn something from each relationship, including something about herself, as well as what she likes, desires, and dislikes in a prospective partner. Help her to anticipate the heartbreaking "my life is over" feeling of a lost love, as well as to go on with her life, learn from her experience, and grow.

No matter how short-lived or even inconceivable your daughter's feelings, it is important to convey genuine empathy. For example, you might try "I can see that you're really sad" rather than "How can you be so upset when you only went out for three weeks?" Elicit her thinking by asking, "What is it that you didn't like about your relationship?" or "What have you learned from this experience?" Even if you are actually relieved, it is better to avoid statements such as "I never liked him anyway!" or "You can do better!" If your daughter and her boyfriend make up by the end of the week, you may feel sheepish or defensive about your comments. And, regardless of how devastated she may feel, don't be shocked if in a few weeks or even days your daughter breathlessly reports, "There's this really cute guy on my bus . . ."

The Unhealthy Relationship

Regardless of her age, you may be worried if your daughter seems obsessed with a romantic relationship to the exclusion of other needs and interests. Farther along the continuum, unhealthy relationships may be characterized by girls being overly controlled, isolated, and even emotionally or physically abused.

According to her mother, Adelaide, fifteen-year-old Penny's interest in boys was excessive; she hoped her daughter would eventually find a boyfriend so she would settle down. Soon after meeting Jeremy, however, Adelaide had new worries. Jeremy began calling Penny numerous times every day, sometimes late at night. When she wasn't at home when he called, he asked her mother questions about where she was and whom she was with. Adelaide began to get concerned about the intense neediness she sensed in Jeremy's behavior. Other boys may give girlfriends beepers or cell phones. Although girls are often thrilled when their boyfriends call in repeatedly to say hi, interpreting this behavior as evidence of their love and commitment, they often do not perceive the true desire to track girls' whereabouts and/or to keep them readily available.

Another red flag for potentially harmful relationships is possessiveness. Initially this may take the form of boyfriends' keeping girls from friends, family, and their usual activities. Eventually they exert additional control by maintaining secrecy. It is therefore important to teach your daughter the difference between choosing to keep aspects of her relationship private, and being threatened or ordered to do so by her boyfriend. Similarly, there is a big difference between opting to act and dress a certain way, and feeling compelled to do so to follow a boyfriend's guidelines. In abusive relationships, there are often escalating hints, criticism, and threats of rejection if girls do not conform to boyfriends' wishes.

At the extreme end of this continuum are violent dating relationships. According to Richard Gallagher, Ph.D., director of the Parenting Institute at New York University's Child Study Center, about 15 to 20 percent of teenagers experience insidious violence in dating relationships. Either girls or their boyfriends can begin the pushing, shoving, or slapping, sometimes playfully, but teenage boys can turn the behavior up a notch. Dr. Gallagher suggests that while even a single violent incident should be a cause for concern, if it occurs more than once it is unlikely to stop. Yet girls typically make excuses for their boyfriends, such as "He lost his temper" or "He was under so much stress," and try to convince others that "He said he was sorry and it'll never happen again."

If you believe your daughter may be in danger, it will be clear that you need to seek help from mental health professionals, a women's crisis center, or law enforcement personnel. It is the less extreme situations that can be more confusing. You should know that berating your daughter or forbidding the relationship is likely to backfire by eliciting defense of her boyfriend (e.g., "He's so great, but you never liked him!") and an oppositional attitude ("You can't make me break up with him!"). Instead try to limit their contact to more supervised conditions. Invite them to spend more time with your family so that you can continue to observe and assess the situation.

Adelaide, for example, reports, "The more I lectured Penny, the worse things got. But when we kept inviting Jeremy to dinner and on family outings, Penny definitely seemed less obsessed with him." Enforce reasonable limits, such as specific phone hours and times when dates may occur. At the same time, encourage your daughter to maintain other interests or to reconnect with friends and activities. This is not the same as trying to control her, harping on this theme, or lecturing about what she *should* be doing. Rather, I am suggesting that you notice and gently support those moments or occasions when she is engaged in other activities.

Eventually, teenagers need to learn to evaluate their own relationships and come to their own conclusions so that they can learn from these experiences. As your daughter matures, you hope to see her progress in this area. You will delight in seeing her put her developing skills to good use in order to form healthier romantic attachments that encourage her to thrive. Whether or not she has a boyfriend, however, how your daughter chooses to socialize is also important. The next chapter will explore how you can guide her in the many decisions she makes when she spends time with groups of friends.

Warding Off Harassment

Based on research, nearly 90 percent of girls ages nine to nineteen years are victims of suggestive jokes, intimidation, innuendoes, leering, comments, gestures, or looks, and 83 percent are touched, pinched, or grabbed. These data are the result of a survey of 4,200 girls conducted as a joint project of the NOW Legal Defense and Education Fund and the Center for Research on Women of Wellesley College. Clearly, this subject hits a nerve in young girls. When my article "Back Off" was published in the February/March 2000 issue of *Girls' Life* magazine, helping girls to recognize and deal with inappropriate actions of some boys, a record number of readers wrote appreciative letters to the editor.

As a mother, it is important to be aware of the prevalence of harassment so that you can do as much as possible to help your daughter cope with unwanted attention and prevent her from being victimized.

The most critical issue is helping your daughter to discriminate between flirting, which is fun and makes her feel good, and hurting, which makes her uncomfortable, confused, or scared. This is where your coaching her to pay attention to her inner voice pays off. Girls must decide for themselves what feels unwanted and unwelcome. It does not matter what your daughter's friend thinks, how her teacher reacts, or, truthfully, even how you see the situation. If your daughter does not think a remark is funny, it is not. If she finds a gesture inappropriate or offensive, take that seriously. If her sense of self is strong, she will know in her gut the difference between flirting and hurting. Labeling unwanted behavior as harassment gives the problem a name and validates her feelings.

This empowers your daughter to stand up for herself, which is the next step in handling harassment effectively. Two-thirds of girls in the above study told their harassers to stop, one-third using physical force. An emphatic "Stop!" may not do the trick, however. Your daughter may have to threaten, "If you don't stop that right away, I'm going to tell someone." Then, of course, she must follow through.

The third step is seeking help. According to this same study, two-thirds of harassment occurs in public (which is more humiliating because of witnesses). Three-fourths of girls told at least one person, mostly friends, but 20 percent told parents, a teacher, or a school administrator. Such complaints are too readily dismissed by adults, however, who think "Boys will be boys" or view girls as troublemakers. When adults do not believe their complaints, girls feel understandably abandoned and angry. They may feel cheap and become preoccupied with revengeful fantasies. They also fear a backlash of rumors and, especially, being blamed by those who think victims provoke harassment.

You might refer to the section on bullies in Chapter 8 for more suggestions about empowering your daughter to deal with tormenters. If the harassment is occurring in school, however, her guidance counselor, school psychologist, or principal should respond swiftly and decisively to her complaints. A U.S. Supreme Court decision in May 1999 held that schools can be held financially liable if they are aware of but do nothing to correct student-to-student harassment that is an impediment to education. An important message for your daughter is that you will support her by doing anything and everything necessary to stop the harassment. A note of warning, however: Girls should also be taught never to underestimate the potentially devastating effects of exaggerating or falsely accusing others of harassment.

At home, create an environment that prohibits unwanted teasing. For example, forbid relatives or family friends to ridicule your daughter (e.g., about her body, weight, habits, etc.). In fact, teach her to stand up to them and ask them herself to stop. Model this behavior for daughters who are not ready to do so on their own. You might also give some thought to family principles such as "Be polite" and "We welcome our guests." While on the surface these requirements seem simple good manners, too often I have worked with girls who feel compelled to socialize with and pretend to be nice to visitors who in some way torment them. Be alert to this possibility and act swiftly to eliminate it. Finally, facilitate your daughter's confidence in protecting herself by providing lessons in martial arts, sports, self-defense, assertiveness, and coping skills.

Chapter 10

Parties and Partying
SOCIALIZING

"All my daughter wants to do is go out with her friends. I know that's supposed to be normal, but it doesn't seem healthy that she's hardly ever at home. I know it's not healthy for me, because I'm always worried about where she is and what she's doing. I just want to know that she's safe. I didn't do this when I was her age; I did things with my family. This is causing a lot of problems between us. Every time Jackie wants to go to a party we fight because I think I should speak to the parents to see if they'll be home and, of course, she thinks I'm being ridiculous. She says she's humiliated and feels I'm treating her like a baby. She thinks she's old enough to be on her own, without any supervision. But just because Jackie is a teenager doesn't mean my job is over. I think calling the parents of whoever is having a party is the right thing to do."

—Margot, forty-five

"My family has had its share of substance problems, so I'm all too aware of how devastating drinking can be. In fact, maybe I'm too sensitive to it. I'm scared that my daughter, who probably has a genetic predisposition toward addictions, has started to experiment when she's out with friends. A few times I've suspected that Darcy has been drinking, and she recently admitted that she has a few sips of beer at parties. She and her friends consider it a given that everyone drinks in high school, and that a couple of beers every now and then is perfectly acceptable. But it is illegal—and dangerous. Even though she seems responsible in other ways, I would prefer that she not drink at all, or at the very least, postpone drinking until she is in college. Would her social life really be ruined if she decided not to drink?"

—Theresa, forty-one

"I don't care what anyone says, but teenagers today have way too much freedom. My daughter may be sixteen, but she's still living in my home,

and I have a right to tell her what she can and cannot do. I was not allowed to go to parties when I was her age, and I have no intention of allowing my daughter to. Mary Ann can go to her friends' houses to sleep over if I know the parents. She can go to appropriate movies and to school functions—there's plenty to do—but I won't have her driving around to homes where the parents are probably away. That's the same as inviting teenagers to drink and take drugs! My friends are amazed that Mary Ann doesn't protest our rules, but she doesn't. I think she understands that's just the way it's going to be in our house."

—Lynne, forty-seven

Your adolescent daughter has probably said good-bye to afternoons of bowling and roller skating, snowball fights, and kick-ball games. In fact, ask a teenage girl about her favorite activity, and you will probably not hear about dancing, cartooning, reading, tutoring, or even shopping, but "being with my friends." Much to your chagrin, what may have become one of your daughter's most cherished hobbies is simply hanging out. This does not mean that all the lessons you have given her were for naught or that her brain has turned to mush, but just that your daughter desperately wants to be in the company of her friends. As you know, this is not only her favorite amusement, but her ideal strategy for dealing with everyday stress, boredom, despair, and self-doubt.

It is the form that adolescent socializing takes, however, that often causes mothers to hyperventilate. What is happening in our culture hardly helps. It is nearly impossible to read a newspaper today without learning about the latest designer drug to hit teenage circles, the most recent teenage driving fatality, or the frightening incidence of substance use among children who have yet to cut their last molars. Who would *not* be worried? And yet, once again it is crucial not to become intimidated either by what you read or by your own teenager's blasé, indignant, or incredulous attitude when you address how she socializes. This chapter will give you the hard facts about parties and partying, along with some helpful strategies, so that you can add to your daughter's knowledge, effectively influence her values, and guide her toward smarter decisions.

Teenage Hangouts

Anywhere That's Private

Along with her best friends, the typical teenage girl is on the look-out for privacy (from parents and nosy siblings), independence (or at least the perception of that sought-after state), and possibly access to favorite activities (e.g., shopping, computer and e-mail, movies, music, or television). If all else fails and your daughter is destined to face a boring afternoon or evening at home, you can thwart this near-death experience by allowing her to invite a friend—even if all they do is sit on her bedroom floor talking, giggling, or poring through magazines. If you are like many mothers, this alternative is far preferable to your daughter being out and about heaven knows where. In fact, to entice your daughter and her friends to stay at home, you may find yourself providing goodies such as movie rentals, piles of junk food, and the promise of sleepovers.

Anywhere But Home

Unless your daughter is unique, however, *she* may prefer being prac-tically anywhere to being at home. Her options (and yours) are probably determined by the geographical convenience of her friends' homes, the hospitality of their parents, the availability of entertain-ment facilities and youth programs in your community, and the teen-friendliness of local merchants. Especially when your daughter is younger, the greater the supervision provided and the more struc-tured the program she attends—whether offered by schools, sports facilities, religious groups, or civic organizations—the greater your comfort. As she gets older and these possibilities dwindle, you will need to find other ways of ensuring safe socializing.

Your daughter, on the other hand, probably has a less ambitious goal: to go wherever she and her friends will be tolerated, if not wel-comed. When she was younger, you may have recoiled from scenes of teenagers hanging out at the local pizza place or ice cream store, the gas station parking lot, or the most secluded areas in the vicinity. If back then you pledged "My daughter will *never* do that when she's a teen," this is one vow you may end up retracting.

It's a Mall World

One place your daughter may be eager to frequent is the local shopping mall. Teenagers have practically become denizens of large, indoor malls that have replaced downtown environments of small towns, suburbs, and cities. In the past, parents could better monitor teenagers who frequented the five-and-ten-cent stores or delis owned by neighbors, and routinely bumped into their parents' friends and acquaintances at the public park or post office. Essentially, this was an informal neighborhood watch of youngsters that is made nearly impossible by today's malls. And malls are not necessarily harmless places. Besides offering the temptation of shoplifting, they often draw a whole culture of teenagers who may be different from your daughter's usual associates. Some girls, in fact, feel adventurous hanging out at malls specifically because they want to meet boys who may be older, live in surrounding towns, are virtual strangers and, therefore, seem more exciting.

Robin, fifteen, a bright girl who was brought to therapy because of underachievement in school and despair over the marital strife of her parents, says: "Whenever we have nowhere else to go, we get one of our parents to drop us off at the mall. Last weekend, we met some guys from [a town fifteen miles away] who took us driving around until midnight. It was so cool. Then they drove us back to my friend's house, but I told my mom we got a ride back from her parents."

These and other imagined scenarios typically cause mothers to struggle with when it is okay to grant permission for daughters to go to the mall. At what age should girls be allowed to shop by themselves for a limited time while a mother remains on the premises? When can a mother feel comfortable merely dropping off and picking up a daughter and her friends? Like many other predicaments described so far, the answer will depend on your daughter's age, experience, judgment, and trustworthiness. When you discuss your concerns directly and hear how she would handle them, as described in Chapter 4, you will either be reassured enough to say yes, or you will be more aware of areas where your daughter needs more practice and guidance.

One word of caution, however, about transportation. Whenever you are uneasy about your daughter's plans, you might consider providing rides yourself. This also enables you to get to know her friends better and to assess whatever social situation they have arranged. Clinical experience suggests that before your daughter is a high school sophomore or junior, it may be asking for trouble to allow her to drive around with older teenagers. Although it may afford you a welcome respite from endless chauffeuring, the risk of her getting rides from teenagers significantly older than herself is early exposure to parties, isolated locations, and substances. Even when she protests, insist on dropping off and picking up your younger teenager, or permit her to carpool with a parent whose judgment you trust implicitly. You can say, "You can get a ride with your friends when you have your own license."

Parties and Get-togethers

When daughters bring up the idea of hosting or attending parties, women describe getting instant mental images of hordes of teenagers descending upon a home, drinking excessively, becoming sloppily ill, engaging in sex, destroying property, and blasting cacophonous music that eventually results in neighbors calling the police, who break up the event and make arrests that appear in the local newspaper. Anticipating this is how you probably think, your daughter's proposals to socialize with her friends may be phrased something like "It's not a party, Mom, it's just a little get-together" or "I just want to have a few people over" or "We're only hanging out, it's not a big deal."

Although you know in your heart of hearts it is normal for your daughter to want to be with her friends, how can you allow her to do so unless you are comfortable? Here are some guidelines to use when your daughter proposes hosting and attending parties:

When She's the Host

The first question is, at what age are boy-girl parties appropriate? Some fourth- and fifth-grade girls are eager for coed outings. However, it seems wise to wait until middle or junior high school, when socials and dances are first sponsored by schools. Another reasonable guideline is: The younger the girls and boys, the more structured the event. For example, rather than allowing preteens to hang out or invent their own amusements, it seems sensible to provide group activities in which everyone can participate, such as volleyball, swimming, movie rentals, dancing, etc. In this age group, remember that eating is a favored activity too. But this is not the time to create nutritious, well-balanced meals; girls especially prefer nibbling on finger food and junk throughout the event rather than eating a more traditional, heavier entrée.

You and your daughter will need to negotiate in advance the parameters of the party. Keep in mind that at this age, her definition of inviting only her closest friends may include every boy and girl in school who has ever smiled at her. Help her to anticipate that the size of parties can quickly get out of control. She may intend to invite only fifteen friends, but if each of these guests invites a few more people, eighty or a hundred teenagers could show up at your house on Friday—through no fault of your daughter. Word of a party spreads like wildfire. But make it clear that teenagers who are not on the guest list (i.e., who try to crash the party) will not be admitted. Also, as your daughter gets older you may need to decide how to handle any guests who should arrive under the influence. Will you call their parents or police to arrange safe transportation home?

In the same vein, determine beforehand the exact hours of the party. Although your daughter may think a reasonable time period is, say, from six P.M. until midnight, you might lobby for as little time as possible. Unless you have chaperoned a gathering of thirty or forty lively teenagers, you have no idea how slowly 180 or 240 minutes can pass. The theory is, you want teenagers to be as busy, involved, and content as possible to avoid restlessness, boredom, and the trouble these conditions inevitably provoke. But having said this, don't be amazed if some guests are dropped off long before you are prepared to greet them, others scramble for rides home at the eleventh hour, and a few are picked up by parents long after you wish to be asleep.

Parental supervision is another important consideration when your daughter has friends over. While some parents hire older teenagers or college students to act as chaperones, such parental surrogates are rarely as effective as parents themselves. If your daughter is hosting a party, being accountable requires that you be present. If you are fortunate, you will have the support and company of other adults. When your friend's teenager has a party, consider volunteering to help supervise—so long as your own daughter is not on the guest list—and ask your friend to reciprocate.

Before your daughter's party, be sure to clarify how you will supervise her guests. For example, whereas she might prefer that you go into hiding for the duration, you might say that you will take a little peek around the crowd every half hour or so while replenishing soft drinks and food. But ease your daughter's fear that her worst nightmare is not about to come true: You would never plunk down on the couch with her pals all evening to catch up on what's new and exciting in their lives.

You and your daughter should also establish beforehand clear rules for her party. A no-substance policy is obvious, since it is illegal to serve alcohol to those under twenty-one and to allow people to use drugs in your home. Prior to the party, in fact, your daughter and her close friends might want to put out the word: "My parents are really strict, so don't bother to bring anything." Know your legal liability for any alcohol- or drug-related injury or death that occurs as a result of alcohol consumption in your home, and have a plan in mind should you discover any guests using substances they brought in. In fact, for this reason many parents refuse to readmit guests who leave a party, even to get something from the car. One mother sensibly hired an off-duty policeman simply to stand at the door of their daughter's sweet-sixteen party, which was held in a public arena. You also might want to think about what degree of boy-girl contact you feel comfortable with. Specify ahead of time the consequences for guests who break rules.

When She's a Guest

When your daughter asks permission to attend a party away from home, trust in her safety is even more paramount. The more you can be assured that the hosting parents plan to supervise their party as you would, the more relaxed you will be. But if you ask your daughter whether the parents will be at home that evening, several possibilities exist. One, she truly might not know. Two, she might not say because she knows you would then forbid her from attending. Three, she won't say because she fears that you will tell other parents, her friends will get in trouble, and she will be labeled a tattletale. Therefore, if it is important to you that the parents know about the party and are planning to be home, you may need to call them yourself.

This situation is so common that if you and your daughter have not faced it yet, you probably will at some point in the not-too-distant future. In fact, you might have a conversation that goes something like this:

> DAUGHTER: Why are you calling Dawn's parents? Don't you trust me?
>
> MOTHER: It's not about trust, it's about my keeping you safe.
>
> DAUGHTER: Nobody else's parents call.
>
> MOTHER: I have to do what I think is right.
>
> DAUGHTER: You'll humiliate me.
>
> MOTHER: Don't worry, I'll just call and ask about the particulars and offer to bring something.
>
> DAUGHTER: You can't treat me like a baby!
>
> MOTHER: You have a choice: If you want to go to the party, I'll be calling the parents.

Some mothers feel uncomfortable calling the hosting parents because they fear conveying mistrust or looking like they're checking up on them. The truth is, parents who host teenage parties are often surprised and even dismayed when they *don't* hear from guests' parents. To get a sense of what is going on, you can verify the hours of the party or the address, ask for directions to their home, gently inquire about plans, offer to help out or bring a refreshment, and thank the parents for inviting your daughter. At the very least, this call may expand your parent network, offering a new source of information about your daughter's social world.

Having assured yourself that the parents are home, can you feel certain your daughter will not be exposed to alcohol, drugs, or sexual advances? Not really. Even when hosting parents conscientiously take precautions, your daughter can never be guaranteed protection from these risks. Statistics tell us that 60 percent of teen drinking occurs at home. Some teenagers, in fact, have been known to drink to the point of alcohol poisoning right in their own homes while their parents are present.

Another possibility is that the hosting parents may tell you of their intentions to chaperone guests, but then be less vigilant than you would expect. For example, a fourteen-year-old in therapy relayed that she was truthful when she assured her mother that her friend's parents would be home on New Year's Eve. But the parents subsequently decided to go out to dinner. They arrived home at ten-thirty to find quite the party scene, their home littered with beer cans, and the sounds of intoxicated teenagers either laughing boisterously or getting sick in bathrooms. Yet the parents nonchalantly offered the guests snacks and sodas as if they were oblivious to what was going on.

Still other parents deliberately decide to serve alcohol to minors because they think, "It's going to happen anyway, so I'd rather it be in my house." By taking car keys away from those who are drinking, these parents believe they are ensuring teenagers' safety. However, this approach clearly raises numerous legal and moral issues.

The bottom line is, you can never truly place the onus of protecting or supervising your daughter on other parents. Regardless of whether host parents are home, alcohol and drugs are available, or what her friends are doing, she must decide for herself how she will act. It will always be her choice whether or not to abide by your rules and standards. At the end of the day, it is your daughter herself who bears the ultimate responsibility for her own safety.

This does not suggest that you breathe a sigh of relief that there is nothing you can do and turn your attention elsewhere. For example, even if you have arranged for your daughter to be picked up from a party, it is wise to see her when she arrives home. If you go to sleep, ask your daughter to awaken you when she returns. Seeing that she is all right will be reassuring. For this same reason, you might want to be wary of last-minute sleepovers, which are often hastily arranged to hide telltale signs of substance use from parents, take advantage of friends' later curfews, or avoid disclosing whereabouts and activities.

Once your daughter is allowed to drive with friends or gets her own driver's license, however, your position on attending parties may require a whole new analysis. That is because it will be pointless to forbid her from attending parties; if she wants to go, she will find a way to get there. Lynne's daughter Mary Ann, for example, says:

"My mother thinks this is fifty years ago or something. Everybody goes to parties. If all I did is go to movies, I'd never have a social life and I'd be such a loser. So I just tell her I'm going to my friend's house, and then we go out. My friend's parents are so much cooler; they let us go anywhere we want and they don't freak out if we come home late."

This is another situation that calls for considering your daughter's age and being flexible. Otherwise, all you will accomplish by trying to control an older teenager will be alienating her and prompting her to sneak around behind your back, as Lynne eventually discovered. At this point, a better approach may be to make truthful disclosure and honest communication your priorities. If you know where your daughter really is and what she is really doing, you are in a better position to anticipate problems and help her to stay safe. By acknowledging and respecting her age-appropriate autonomy, you are also strengthening the mother-daughter relationship.

At this point, you might shift from, "Are the parents going to be home?" to "Let's assume the parents are not home. What will you do to make sure you're safe?" Remember that if you have allowed your daughter to get her license and drive a car, she probably has shown generally good judgment and trustworthiness. Now it may be time to let go a bit and have confidence in her applying these same skills in social situations. If and when she makes mistakes, at least you're prepared to respond to them.

Drinking

The Risks of Starting Young

For many parents, parties and the risks of drinking go hand in hand. However, those of you still anticipating or just entering the teenage years may be tempted to skip this section, thinking, "Thank goodness, we're nowhere near this issue yet." You might want to reconsider. Statistics tell us that the average age at which youngsters have their first drink is, astoundingly, only twelve and a half! According to MADD, half of sixth-grade students have been pressured to drink by classmates. Half of all junior high and senior high school students drink monthly. This is not surprising, given their perception that alcohol is legal, readily available, and harmless. In fact, according to MADD, 2.6 million teenagers did not know that it was possible to die from an overdose.

This is why it is important to convey to your daughter that the wine you have with dinner, the beer her friends may drink at parties, and the mixed drinks she may see you serve guests are in fact powerful, mind-altering drugs which, if abused, are potentially dangerous. Few girls appreciate that the earlier they drink, the more harmful alcohol can be. Teenagers who start drinking before age fifteen are four times as likely to become dependent upon alcohol as those who begin drinking after age twenty-one, and also are more likely to use other drugs. Of teenagers ages twelve to seventeen, 28 percent are currently considered problem drinkers (defined as drinking at least once per week and consuming five to twelve drinks on a single occasion).

New research suggests that the adolescent brain is more vulnerable than the adult brain to the destructive effects of alcohol—and the younger the brain, the more it is at risk. Neuropsychologist Scott Swartzwelder and his team at Duke University compared two groups of young people, ages twenty-one to twenty-four, and ages twenty-five to twenty-nine (because it was illegal to have subjects under twenty-one). They found that after three drinks, the younger group's learning was impaired 25 percent more than the older group's.

Anatomical changes occur too. Using MRI, Michael De Bellis at the University of Pittsburgh Medical Center found that young people ages fourteen to twenty-one who abused alcohol had hippocampi (brain structures responsible for many kinds of memory and learning) that were on average 10 percent smaller than the hippocampi of healthy teens. Moreover, the longer the alcohol abuse, the greater the shrinkage of brain cells.

Prevalence and Risks of Binge Drinking

Another study with rats showed that those who had binged as adolescents performed much worse on a maze-memory task, suggesting long-lasting damage in brain function. MRI testing of human teenagers bears this out. Those fourteen- to twenty-one-year-olds who abused alcohol had a 10 percent reduction in the size of their hippocampus compared to healthy teenagers. The other area of the adolescent brain most affected by alcohol is the prefrontal cortex, which regulates thought processes involved with planning ahead, thinking abstractly, and integrating information to make smart decisions. Thus if your daughter drinks heavily during her teenage years, she could be shrinking her cognitive functioning by 10 percent.

If college is in your daughter's future plans, you should also be aware that binge drinking is prevalent on campuses. A Harvard School of Public Health study found that 50 percent of males and 39 percent of female students reported binge drinking in the previous two weeks (defined as five or more consecutive drinks for men, and four or more for women). The costs of binge drinking are immense: 30 percent reported engaging in unplanned sexual activity as a result of drinking, and alcohol was involved in 95 percent of property and violent crimes on campuses, including date rape.

Temptations to Drink

The good news is that substance abuse is a highly preventable problem, especially if you begin to instill a healthy respect for alcohol as early as possible. The first step is probably to recognize the many compelling reasons for your daughter to experiment with alcohol. Teenage girls are typically curious, they want to be cool and to feel grown-up, and many want to perform better in dance and sports. Some enjoy taking risks. Without healthier coping strategies, teenagers may use alcohol or drugs to seek revenge when angry; deal with uncomfortable feelings such as depression, loneliness, and boredom; relieve anxiety; and escape from family conflict.

You may have noted that peer pressure is absent from this list. Contrary to what you may believe, the National Institute on Drug Abuse reports that only 8 percent of teens cite peer pressure as a reason to drink, and a 2000 *Newsweek* poll similarly found that only 10 percent of teenagers surveyed felt pressure from friends to use drugs or alcohol. Clinical experience bears this out. Teenagers do not usually feel coerced or pressured by others to try substances. In fact, a "do your own thing" attitude often prevails. But your daughter may drink to feel part of the group experience. Many a girl has lamented, "It's no fun being the only one not drinking. Everybody's laughing and having fun, and you're thinking, 'What's so funny?' "

It is always a reassuring sign of maturity, then, when your daughter admits, "Drunk people actually sound pretty dumb."

Educate Her

What can you do to prevent your daughter's early or excessive use of alcohol? Rather than issuing ultimatums (e.g., "If you take so much as one sip of alcohol, you will be grounded until you're twenty-one"), take the noncontrolling approach of teaching your daughter the facts about alcohol's potential harm, as described earlier. Also, talk about the risks of drinking and driving. Scientists explain that due to the ongoing maturation of the brain, after two drinks young people are ten times more likely than older adults to have an auto accident. This is because teenagers have exactly the wrong sensitivities to alcohol. Compared to adults who drink the same amount, they become far more impaired but less sedated. Thus, your daughter may feel more awake to drive, but is less capable of doing so safely.

You might also mention research associating drinking with academic, social, and family problems; being the victim of violent crime; and having earlier, more frequent, and unsafe sex. You can note disrupted sleep cycles, feeling ill, and gastrointestinal problems. If all this seems too abstract for your daughter, she may think twice when she hears that drinking can ruin her looks, give her bad breath, and cause her to gain weight.

Model Healthy Drinking Habits

Knowing the sobering facts (excuse the pun) and even appreciating your daughter's temptations will probably not be enough to teach her to make good choices. Along with articulating your values, your most powerful tool is your own drinking pattern, which is the most visible yardstick your daughter has against which to measure her own behavior. What are you modeling for her about the role of alcohol in your life? How often and how much do you drink? Do you share a bottle of wine at a restaurant and drive home? Do you always serve alcohol when you entertain friends at your home? Does your daughter see you intoxicated? Or do you demonstrate that you do not need to drink to enjoy social situations? Do you have religious or personal reasons for abstaining? If so, do you expect your daughter to follow your example?

Clarify Your Expectations

What are your expectations about teenage drinking? Whatever they are, don't hesitate to state them directly. For example, you might tell your daughter, "Our religion forbids drinking" or "I'd like you to wait until you are the legal age to drink" or "I expect that you will try drinking sometime during your high school years, but I never want you to get drunk."

Whereas some mothers believe teenagers should not drink because it is illegal, others think, "All teenagers drink; that's part of being a teen" or maintain, "I can't be a hypocrite; I drank when I was her age." It is not being insincere, however, to want your daughter to take a different path from the one you took as a teenager. You are now viewing drinking from an adult—rather than adolescent—perspective. You have the added wisdom of maturity, plus years of research that point out dangers not known in times past. Just as you may make an effort to improve upon the skills of your mother, it is legitimate to help your teenage daughter to make better choices than you did.

However clearly you say all this, however, it is important to recognize that your daughter still may not agree. Or she may appear to acquiesce but actually make different choices. In fact, at a time in her life when she may revere autonomy and go overboard demonstrating her separateness from you, she may decide to do something precisely because you are adamant that she not. As Theresa says, "Since my worst fear is seeing my daughter's lips touching a beer can, that's probably what I can expect."

In fact, after suspecting several times that Darcy had tried alcohol, Theresa arrived to pick her up at a party earlier than planned and found her obviously drunk. Says Theresa, "Of course, I completely overreacted. At that moment, I saw my daughter as the relatives whose lives were destroyed by alcohol. But when I calmed down, I could see that my whole outlook had changed. Instead of trying to prevent Darcy from drinking, which is obviously impossible, I have to help her to know how to drink responsibly."

Teach Responsible Drinking

If you agree with this philosophy, at some point when you believe your daughter is old enough you will want to help her develop the skills to drink in moderation. She is not born with this ability; it takes practice. She will need to learn to monitor closely her responses to alcohol, and become sharply attuned to changes in her body and mind that tell her when she has had enough to drink. Making this judgment helps her to stay in control.

Some parents believe that a sensible approach to drinking is facilitated by a matter-of-fact attitude at home, much the same way that doling out candy occasionally to a toddler prevents her from craving forbidden sweets later on. Thus they permit older teenagers to taste alcohol during special occasions—for example, to sip wine during holidays and religious celebrations, or to sample beer during a family party. In addition, these strategies may be helpful in teaching your daughter to drink responsibly:

• *Set Rules and Consequences.* According to MADD, one-third of 200,000 polled students reported that their parents do not set clear rules, and half said they are not disciplined routinely for infractions. You can decide to be one of the mothers who sets rules and follows through with consequences.

• *Discuss Substances Openly.* It is a myth that if you bring up the topic of alcohol and drugs you are putting the idea to experiment in your teenager's mind. Or that raising the issue means you don't trust your daughter. Talking about substances gives you an opportunity to offer information, correct misconceptions, answer questions, and impart values.

• *Differentiate Among Various Scenarios.* Help your daughter to make distinctions between the potential consequences of, say, sipping a beer at a small, contained party at someone's home, and doing shots while driving around in a car with older boys.

• *Arm Her with Coping Strategies.* Elicit your daughter's solutions for dealing with social problems. Can she attend a party where there is drinking and choose not to drink? Will she feel more comfortable holding a beer can? Will she take sips of alcohol or pretend to do so?

• *Anticipate Dilemmas.* Coach her to handle situations that may arise with her friends. For example, you might ask, "What if a party gets out of control?" or "What will you do if your friend drinks too much and gets sick?" or "What are the signs that someone may have alcohol poisoning?"

• *Use Role Playing to Stimulate Problem Solving.* When your daughter's rigid, black-or-white thinking prevents her from seeing the situation from different angles, prompt her to broaden her perspective: "What would you advise your younger sibling or cousin if she were in this situation?"

• *Ensure the Status of a Designated Driver (DD).* Lectures in drug education classes have apparently sunk in. Teenage girls regularly rely on designated drivers. However, your daughter may need you to clarify that when friends say, "I only had a beer (or two)" or "I stopped drinking hours ago," this automatically disqualifies them from the job. If a DD drinks even a teaspoon of alcohol, by definition he or she is no longer a DD. Assure your daughter that you are not questioning her judgment; rather, it is impossible for her or anyone to determine simply by observation if a person is impaired. Her friends may walk and talk just fine, but their reflexes and judgment can be way off, especially in traffic situations that require split-second decisions and instant maneuvers. No matter what, that is not a chance you want your daughter to take.

• *Develop an Informal Parent Network.* This invaluable resource allows you to trade information, gauge the relative safety of various situations, and share both driving and supervision of teenagers.

• *Share Constructive Ways to Cope with Unhappiness, Worry, and Anger.* Teach your daughter to find other, healthier ways to soothe herself, such as by being assertive, exercising, listening to music, using relaxation techniques, or talking to someone.

• *Welcome Teenagers into Your Home.* Provide a pleasant, enjoyable environment in which your daughter and friends can have some privacy and safely hang out together.

• *Monitor Your Liquor Supply.* Some advocate locking liquor cabinets to eliminate the possibility of teenagers fighting against temptation. A more compelling reason, however, is preventing your daughter from having to become a watchdog should her visiting friends propose trying your liquor.

• *Protect Your House When Away.* Many parents leave for brief vacations with peace of mind believing that their daughters will be safe while staying with friends. Then they are shocked to learn that teenagers still used their home to have a party in their absence. Take precautions to prevent this possibility.

• *Support Alcohol-Free Social Events.* Parents have become increasingly involved in creating, sponsoring, or supporting dance marathons, game nights, battles of the bands, and other events for teenagers in the community.

• *Monitor Music and Movies.* This is where your supervision of movies and music, as discussed early in this book, pays off. References to substances abound in the media. In one large study, 27 percent of one thousand surveyed songs (including 75 percent of rap songs) directly referred to alcohol, tobacco, or illicit drugs. Alcohol appeared in 93 percent of movies, of which 29 percent portrayed positive statements about substance use. A more subtle appeal is conveyed by the association of alcohol use with wealth or luxury in 34 percent of movies and 24 percent of songs. In contrast, only 14 percent of movies had characters who refused a drink, and only 6 percent explicitly addressed limits on consuming alcohol. One advantage of restricting the movies your daughter sees is that her chance of seeing alcohol use declines from 37 percent in R-rated movies to 31 percent in PG-13 movies to 27 percent in G or PG movies.

• *Be Consistent.* Your policies about alcohol—and particularly drinking and driving—should be clear and inflexible. For example, caution your daughter about accepting rides from anyone who has been drinking, not just teenagers. What should she do if the friend's father who is supposed to drive her home is drunk? What if her best friend's mother arrives to pick them up from school smelling of alcohol? Margot encountered just this situation: "When Jackie was in tenth grade, her best friend Evi's mom showed up at a school function obviously intoxicated. It was pretty awkward. After that, I couldn't allow Jacki to accept a ride with her, even if it was only to the movies or a soccer game. How could I be sure she hadn't been drinking? Jackie was embarrassed, but I came up with a lot of creative reasons for why I needed to drive."

Drugs

According to a 1998 University of Michigan study funded by the National Institute on Drug Abuse, 29 percent of eighth-graders, 45 percent of tenth-graders, and 54 percent of twelfth-graders used illicit drugs. Drugs are highly available not just to teenagers, but also to preteen girls. A mere click on her computer will whisk your daughter to Web sites devoted to describing and even glorifying the highs of specific drugs. She can just as easily get advice on cultivating, procuring, and copying their chemical formulas. Here are some thoughts on the drugs most often encountered by teenage girls.

Marijuana

Marijuana use is prevalent among teens; studies report 40 percent or higher rates of experimentation among high school seniors. Here again your own background will probably determine your reaction to your daughter's use of cannabis. If you smoked pot as a teenager, you may be more tolerant of your daughter doing so and less concerned about potential ill effects. What you should know, however, is that the marijuana circulating today is not the same as the marijuana of the 1960s and 1970s. Some studies claim that it is as much as 117 times stronger. Others report that marijuana is frequently doctored with other, more dangerous chemicals.

Your daughter probably needs to know that marijuana is not as benign as she would like to think. It is potentially harmful to her health. Smoking marijuana has been found to cause cancer, including lung cancer. Tetrahydracannabinol (THC) temporarily alters brain functioning, affecting perception, coordination, reflexes, and judgment. It changes the way girls sense things. Marijuana is also physically addicting, with one hundred thousand teenagers treated every year. Both short- and long-term memory deficits have been found. If all that isn't compelling, if your daughter is arrested for possession or distribution, she will confront legal problems and possible jail time.

Inhalants

Sniffing, with a reported incidence of 20 percent, has reportedly been on the rise among even younger teenagers. This is something to be aware of, since the use of household items makes this form of experimentation readily available. Teenagers have abused, for example, nail polish remover, spray paint, cooking spray, and paint thinner, all of which can cause unconsciousness or death. Signs of abuse include unusual breath odor or chemical odor, runny eyes or nose, and hidden rags or cloths.

GHB

Another drug worth mentioning is gammahydroxybuterate (GHB), a highly addictive chemical compound that depresses the central nervous system and causes temporary euphoria, hallucinations, and sleep without a hangover. Often prepared by kitchen chemists using caustic materials like paint remover or drain-cleaning agents, GHB can also burn the throat. More worrisome, since it is difficult to regulate the precise dosage for someone's size, even a fraction of a gram too much can decrease respiration and result in coma or death. Several boys in one community experimented with GHB and miscalculated the amount they ingested; they were kept alive on respirators in the local hospital, fortunate to recover.

GHB's properties and use have earned it the name "date-rape drug." Specifically, women cannot remember what occurred while they were high. In addition, because it is tasteless, odorless, and colorless, GHB can be added to beverages without girls' knowledge or permission. After the death of Samantha Reid, a fifteen-year-old freshman from Michigan who drank a GHB-laced can of Mountain Dew at a party, her mother was instrumental in seeking legislation to control its use. Girls have been increasingly warned to watch their drinks closely, not to accept a beverage from someone they don't know, and to alert someone whose drink has been tampered with. (See "Rave Parties and Ecstasy," page 286.)

Trouble with Substances

Hopefully, the closeness you have nurtured with your daughter and your efforts to arm her with good skills will protect her from making poor decisions about substances. But no teenager is immune. Every mother should at least be aware of the signs that her daughter may be progressing from rare experimentation, usually at parties, to more serious use.

When experimentation becomes social use, your daughter may intend to get high or drunk (i.e., trashed or wasted) more often. As a way of coping, she may look for situations in which she can use substances. Use of other drugs, such as pills, cocaine, and ecstasy, may follow. Eventually, if she becomes increasingly preoccupied with substances, regularly using on weekends and weekdays, and perhaps doing so alone, she will probably experience problems at home and in school. Finally, during the dependent stage, your daughter would need to use substances daily and would probably try harder drugs. It is likely that she would experience memory problems, and may begin to deal drugs, to steal, or to get into other trouble with the law.

The Warning Signs

You might be alert to the possibility that your daughter is abusing alcohol or drugs if she:

- Loses interest in her usual activities
- Portrays significant personality changes (e.g., more frustrated or irritable)
- Is excessively secretive
- Changes eating or sleeping habits
- Changes appearance
- Borrows or steals money
- Develops new friendship patterns
- Has new friends who make you uncomfortable
- Loses motivation or energy
- Seems confused
- Laughs inappropriately
- Acquires drug paraphernalia
- Frequently uses gum or breath products
- Has breath odor
- Begins using eye drops, incense, or candles
- Has trouble with the law
- Is chronically truant or tardy to school

How to Help

If your daughter manifests a few or more of the above warning signs, or if you find drugs or paraphernalia in her room, do not wait until a crisis develops to speak with her. Assume that on some level your daughter is sending a cry for help. Just as you did in discussions about sex and other hard topics, keep open the lines of communication by not lecturing, interrupting, or overreacting. Similarly, don't escalate the situation by becoming unduly angry, accusatory, or threatening. Support your daughter and her ideas by listening and minimizing your criticism. When you do chastise her, focus on her choices and behavior rather than on who she is as a person.

NOT

> MOTHER: You are making a total mess of your life, and you'll never amount to anything!

OR

> MOTHER: You're turning into a drunk like your grandfather! That's it, I wash my hands of you.

TRY

> MOTHER: Julie, you have made some really bad decisions.

OR

> MOTHER: I'm very concerned about your drinking. Let's talk about it.

This is a time when you may want to seek out the expertise and support offered by resources in your community. Ask for help from a trusted physician, clergyperson, or therapist. Find out where people you know got effective treatment. Or call your local Alcoholism and Drug Dependency Council, drug hotline, or crisis intervention facility. Many clinics offer services specially designed for teenagers and their families. Alcoholics Anonymous and Alateen are probably available in your area as well. Regardless of whether or not your daughter participates in these organizations, if you are concerned about her substance use take good care of yourself and get much-needed support and information by attending Alanon meetings. If your daughter is increasingly troubled or out of control, you may want to refer to the resources and programs described by Carol Maxym, Ph.D., and Leslie B. York, M.A., in their book, *Teens in Turmoil.*

Cigarettes

Although girls don't see it this way, nicotine is also a powerful, highly addictive, and potentially lethal drug. Yet, according to the CDC, 35 percent of teenage girls currently smoke. Moreover, the American Lung Association reports that 76 percent of teenage girls who currently smoke feel dependent upon cigarettes. Of those who tried to quit in the previous year, 82 percent were unsuccessful. The fact that the rate of smoking among high school students has gone up 32 percent in the past decade is no coincidence.

Tobacco is portrayed in 89 percent of movies, only 7 percent of which showed characters who refused to smoke. Perhaps more important, the tobacco industry has targeted teenage girls in their advertising campaigns, placing ads in magazines that link smoking to beauty, slimness, alluring fashion, sexiness, etc. According to recent studies, because the adolescent brain is more sensitive to nicotine, girls who are swayed by these powerful messages can become addicted after trying only a few cigarettes during several weeks of experimentation.

If you smell cigarettes on your daughter's breath, detect the odor of stale smoke on her clothing, or find matches in her pocket, you may well hear that she wore the offensive sweater in a smoke-filled diner and got those matches to light her new aromatherapy candle. Expect that it will always be someone else's cigarette that materializes in her backpack.

But despite appropriate wariness when you hear these explanations, it is still best not to overreact or accuse. Lynne's daughter Mary Ann, for example, is convinced that "if I even know someone who smokes my mom is afraid I am going to become a coke addict." Despite your daughter's denials and protests, it is wise to ask matter-of-factly how much she is smoking. Understanding what "Not much" or "I just tried it once" means, however, may require a process of gentle but determined inquiry.

If you conclude that your daughter does smoke regularly, set up incentives and realistic goals to help her stop. Encourage her by using positive reinforcement and rewards, which work better than punishments. You might also seek the advice and support of her physician, who can reinforce the considerable known health risks and suggest smoke-ending strategies. Help your daughter to be savvy about analyzing the media's outrageous and flagrantly manipulative messages about tobacco. And, most important, as you would do with any drug use, teach her better ways to reduce stress and cope with uncomfortable feelings.

Coed Sleepovers

In the good old days, when your daughter asked for a sleepover, she probably was proposing a traditional pajama party, with her girlfriends huddled together under cozy blankets on the couch, wearing fuzzy slippers and drinking hot chocolate while they watched endless repetitions of *The Princess Bride*. These days, however, she may mean a coed sleepover—a new form of socializing in which boys and girls hang out together all night, staying awake or sacking out during the early morning hours in adjacent sleeping bags or segregated areas of the home. Influenced by an increasingly unisex society and sexually saturated media, this get-together is appealing to ever-younger girls who are eager to socialize, experience excitement, and feel grown-up. For some, they are becoming routine weekend social events.

Parents are divided about their acceptability. While some insist, "What's the big deal?" others believe that permitting daughters to have coed sleepovers is sending the wrong message: "It's okay to associate socializing with boys and sleeping."

It is probably wise to think through your views before your daughter first requests a coed sleepover. As in most other issues, of course, consider her age. It is difficult to imagine a situation in which coed sleepovers would be appropriate for middle schoolers. Once teenagers can drive, however, it may be sensible to provide a safe, contained environment after special occasions such as sports events, junior or senior proms, or camp reunions. If you think the occasion warrants a coed sleepover, assess whether your daughter's emotional maturity and social skills would enable her to handle its unique pressures. Use discussions to anticipate together potentially confusing or threatening predicaments; are you comfortable with how she would handle them? If so, this may be a chance to recognize her readiness for more autonomy.

Should you agree to allow your daughter to hold a coed sleepover in your home, careful planning is your best strategy. Besides all the guidelines offered for hosting regular teenage parties, as described earlier in this chapter, you may want to obtain permission directly from the parents of all invited guests. In addition, consider if, where, and when guests will sleep. When you clarify in advance your specific expectations, there is less chance of misunderstandings. At bedtime, it is recommended that you separate boys and girls in different areas of the home, keeping doors open at all times. Needless to say, you must be prepared to stay awake all night to monitor the goings-on!

Rave Parties and Ecstasy

Rave parties, all-night gatherings with some form of electronic or technological music played by DJs, are a cultural phenomenon your teenage daughter may wish to experience along with an estimated 8 percent of other high school students. Teenagers typically wear loose, wide-legged flared jeans to enable them to dance comfortably, sometimes accessorized with pacifiers or water bottles to battle dehydration.

Dehydration is caused by dancing for long periods, but can be aggravated by the use of the drug ecstasy, which is associated with but not exclusive to rave parties. Having both hallucinogenic and amphetamine-like effects, ecstasy (whose street names include X, XTC, E, and lover's speed) is similar to cocaine and speed, which increase heart rate and blood pressure. Teenagers typically "roll" on ecstasy to achieve increased empathy, perceived insight, a peaceful feeling, heightened senses, and bliss. Because of decreased sexual inhibition and increased empathy, risk taking is prevalent.

The harmful effects are well known. Ecstasy causes brain cells to release a rush of the neurotransmitter serotonin. There is a short-term danger of overheating because serotonin helps regulate body temperature along with mood. Under the influence of ecstasy, body temperature can climb to 110 degrees, which causes blood to coagulate. Death can occur. Chronic use can cause long-term damage to the ends of serotonin-containing neurons, or nerve cells. If irreversible, or if cells grow back abnormally, brain functions such as the regulation of emotion, memory, and higher cognitive processes are compromised. Indeed memory deficits have been found in people who used ecstasy within the previous two weeks. There have also been reports of severe anxiety, paranoia, and flashbacks of psychological traumas, which can result in emergency room visits and subsequent depression.

In discussing the dangers of rave parties and specifically the drug ecstasy, ask your daughter what she has observed among users. Elicit her reservations or fears based on dangers she has heard about or seen herself. One fifteen-year-old who had experimented with ecstasy on a few occasions suddenly announced in therapy, "I decided I'm not going to roll anymore." When questioned about her change of mind, she explained, "I saw my friend Emilia do it last weekend and it was gross. She was all sweaty and she walked like she was completely wasted. It was embarrassing to listen to her because she sounded so stupid. I asked everybody if I looked like that when I did it and thank goodness they said 'No!' That's not the way I want to look."

Chapter 11

Making Her Way

LETTING GO

*I*f you have gotten this far along in this book, you've been working hard to develop the best relationship you can with your daughter. This collaborative approach to parenting has asked you to look critically at yourself, making adjustments as your daughter's age, circumstances, and your own imperfections have required. Undoubtedly this has not always been easy, but you persisted.

Despite these efforts, however, your daughter probably doesn't always respond as you would like. She may decide on the spur of the moment to skip school for a joy ride with an older guy to whom she is apparently attracted. Or in spite of how much you emphasize honest communication, when she calls home to tell you she is at her best friend's house down the street, you may see an unfamiliar or out-of-area telephone number on the caller ID. In some way your smart, sensible daughter will ignore a rule so basic and oft repeated you were sure it had been etched into her head.

Throughout these pages I've talked about ways to help her face up to these mistakes so that she learns from them and can improve the way she resolves dilemmas in the future. As her mother, you have helped her to reason better, consider her values, see a variety of solutions, and pay closer attention to her inner voice. All these tools help your daughter to fashion healthier relationships and increasingly take on the responsibility of protecting herself. Her growing repertoire of skills reassures you that you are making progress in the task of getting her ready for her life beyond your home. This faith in her abilities helps you to accomplish one of the main tasks of parenting a teenager, letting go gradually.

As you well know, however, no matter how well educated you are about her social world or prepared for potential hazards, she will eventually deal with problems you can neither predict nor remedy. As your daughter gradually broadens the scope of her social experiences, crises will inevitably occur. This is why I have emphasized the need to focus on your daughter's emotional education—teaching her basic problem-solving skills, refining her judgment, and giving her tools to cope with feelings—so she is capable of handling whatever new challenges come her way.

Letting your daughter go will require that you step back and quietly watch, perhaps holding your breath, as you wait to see how she reacts and conducts herself. This is the part of mothering that *you* may not feel ready for! But hopefully, as she progresses through the teenage years, you will see increasing evidence that your daughter is becoming a strong, capable young woman. For example, you may be astonished—not to mention relieved—by her astute observations and wise decisions. These are truly wondrous moments, affirming that your daughter's hard work and your persistent devotion are paying off. You just never know when they are going to happen.

A while back I had such an experience. My daughter, Laura, was a sophomore in high school when she proposed attending a camp reunion two states away. This, of course, prompted the predictable, sometimes heated, parent-teen discussions about what activities her friends were planning, the availability of their parents, the sleeping arrangements, the adequacy of supervision, etc. Only the transportation seemed straightforward; I would take Laura to the train, and her friend's mother would pick her up. Vice versa for the return trip.

In truth I was still somewhat uneasy about the idea of this coed gathering, but ultimately decided that because my daughter had demonstrated she was responsible and trustworthy, there was no way I could justify denying her this privilege. Plus a sleepover was truly a necessity for this unusual occasion. As is often the case, though, my uneasiness turned out to be misplaced. Rather than the unsettling scenarios I imagined, a whole different set of circumstances materialized that none of us could have foreseen when my daughter left home that Friday afternoon.

Apparently, after an uneventful journey and fun-filled reunion, her friend's mother brought her back to the station, as planned. But halfway from home, the Amtrak train on which she was riding caught fire and suddenly stopped. Amid the acrid odor of smoke, the shrieking of emergency sirens and mass confusion, my daughter was evacuated from the train in a completely unfamiliar station, in the middle of an urban neighborhood considered not particularly safe. Along with throngs of other frantic passengers, she was swept along darkened city streets, her luggage in tow, to look for one of the few taxicabs available on a Sunday evening.

When my daughter saw that television camera crews were filming this chaotic scene, she had the presence of mind to call home from a corner pay phone to alert us to what was happening. I was extremely grateful for that phone call, as I shudder to think of how I would have felt had I seen all this on the metro news *before* being reassured by her voice. Even now I can recall vividly how I struggled to keep my own tone normal, even exaggeratedly nonchalant, during that call. Not only didn't I want to contribute to or intensify my daughter's anxiety, but I also hoped my soothing voice would convey even better than my words my confidence that she could manage this situation.

Meanwhile I have to admit that I was anything but relaxed. After that call I was all too keenly aware that my young daughter, who had grown up in the quietude of the country and had minimal experience in urban areas, was traveling all by herself, at night, in an unfamiliar city. Moreover, unlike when she was at school, at a friend's, at the library, or any number of other places, it was impossible for me to reach her. (Among many unfortunate events of that evening, the cell phone she was using ran out of battery power.)

So all I knew was that she was somewhere in that city trying to get to another train station across town, where she planned to check the schedule and find the next available local train, buy herself a ticket and get directions to the correct track. She had also promised to look for another pay phone to call home again; I needed to know what time her train was due to arrive so I could pick her up at the station.

During the eternity it took for her to accomplish these steps, many questions and fears whirled through my mind. Along with mundane matters such as whether she had enough cash for both the taxi and the extra train, I worried if my daughter would have the wherewithal to keep herself safe. Had she learned the necessary street smarts during brief family trips and summer travel? Could she assess whom she should ask for information? Where would she choose to sit if she had to wait for a train? Would she be too trusting of strangers? Or, too scared to think clearly, would she heedlessly attach herself to the wrong individual? How would she react if, heaven forbid, someone approached her inappropriately? There was no time during that brief phone call to review these situations.

As thirty minutes turned into forty-five, as an hour became an hour and a half and then stretched, inconceivably, to two hours, my agitation knew no bounds. Yet there was literally nothing I could do except wait until I heard from her again. As any mother who has experienced this sort of helpless fright knows, even the most far-fetched, catastrophic possibilities can seem plausible. While watching the phone, nearly begging it to ring so I could know my daughter was safe, I remember thinking that since she was alone I might never know if anything terrible happened. Although this now seems absurd, the thought "I might never see my daughter again" actually crossed my mind.

Looking back I now think of this incident as most fortuitous. Unexpectedly, and under rather unique and challenging conditions, my daughter got the chance to test her courage and resourcefulness. Because this scenario had not been anticipated, our games of "What would you do if? . . ." had never addressed these particular problems. Handling them successfully required that she apply the coping strategies, judgment, and self-control she had learned in the course of previous experiences and predicaments.

Happily, as she traversed the city streets my daughter purposely sought the company of an older woman, whose demeanor and appearance suggested respectability. After a somewhat brief but reassuring conversation, she felt comfortable accepting the woman's invitation to share her cab to the second train station. Wisely, she reasoned this would be preferable to waiting alone on the street, and perhaps in vain, to find another empty cab. When she finally figured out how to operate the train's on-board phone to report her arrival time (which was, for her, a triumph in itself), we shared a collective, audible sigh of relief that the ordeal was nearly over.

Unlike this unplanned trial, most of the time when you let go gradually it will be deliberate. You allow your daughter to take one tiny step at a time along the road to independence, based on what she seems capable of managing. If she is adequately prepared, she will prove to herself (and to you) that she is mature and competent enough to handle herself. Most especially, both of you will trust her to rely on her inner resources when she is on her own. This process gives girls much-needed confidence to make their way in the world. In fact, their new assurance is self-perpetuating: Girls are then empowered to take on even more challenges, which further strengthens their trust in themselves and, in cyclical fashion, leads to greater accomplishments.

This is not to say that you and your daughter won't have your moments. From time to time, expect that she will boisterously reject your suggestions, doggedly rebut your logic, unashamedly lie, and obstinately contradict you. Remember, however, that she is still taking in your words. While she probably won't describe the minutiae of her social life, let alone her every transgression, this might actually be a good thing. Rather than depending completely on you, her inner voice will increasingly catch her poor choices, prompting her to make necessary changes and use better judgment next time.

By the same token, in your eagerness to mother your daughter, you'll probably worry too much, interfere, or say the wrong thing. In your reluctance to let go of what has been most dear to you, on occasion you'll go beyond what is appropriate for her level of maturity and hear yourself blurt out unsolicited advice ("Button your coat; it's cold!"), disapproval ("Are you out of your mind?"), or reminders reminiscent of when she was three ("Aren't you going to finish your milk?"). But because you have been making steady deposits of goodwill in your relationship, you and your daughter may better tolerate your missteps, perhaps enjoy a laugh together, and even grow from them.

On a final note, it seems that no matter how old your daughter, some maternal feelings never change. After a year filled with tense expectations, applications, and uncertainty, my daughter is now standing poised on the precipice of young adulthood, one foot on the path to college. I often think about how inconceivable it is that she is really packing up and pushing off in just a few short months. Along with a myriad of other feelings, including bittersweet pangs, great pride, and an awful sense of anticipated loss, I am also aware of a vague, uneasy sensation flickering in the back of my mind. Wouldn't you know it? As she heads to college, my daughter will be taking that very same Amtrak train.

Index

McDonald, Heather, 32
MADD (Mothers Against Drunk
 Driving), 253, 271–72, 276
magazines, teen, 62–63
malls, as hangout location, 265–66
marijuana, 72–73, 141, 279
maturation, inhibition of, 212
Maxym, Carol, 282
Mead, Margaret, 210
means vs. ends, 76–77
media, 44–45
 challenging the portrayals of young
  women in, 62–63
 correcting distorted view of
  physical appearance in, 57–58
 influence of, 221
 sexual messages in, 14, 36, 45, 252
menstruation, 8
mental health clinics, 136
Michigan, University of, 252, 278
middle school, 17, 38, 39, 44, 46–47,
 109, 182, 201, 208, 284
Milholland, Charlotte, 71
mistakes, 138–42
 clarifying your beliefs about,
  142–43
 learning from, 13, 77–78, 148,
  151, 157, 234
 see also trouble
models, fashion, 57
Monday morning quarterbacking,
 77–78
money management, 132
Monitor on Psychology, 85
mood swings, 8
mother-daughter relationships:
 acknowledging your part in, 89–91
 choice of friends as sign of trouble
  in, 200–201
 decrease in time spent together in,
  38–39

empathy and, 148, 203
evolution in, 12–13, 17–18
five basic premises of, 14–18
focusing on "trees" vs. "forest" in,
 20
following daughter's cues in, 13,
 122
friendship compared with, 197–99
indications of problems in, 142–43
maintaining connection in, 158,
 178–79
praise and criticism in, 64
reasons for daughter's challenges in,
 98–99
relative importance of mothers and
 friends in, 10–12, 14, 16, 34,
 94, 199–202, 230
separation and, 198
as shared experience, 21, 90
social life as major concern in,
 2–12, 94
as team, 13, 26, 89, 193
trust and, 187–89
 see also BRAIN; parenting
  strategies; talks, mother-
  daughter
mothers:
 appropriate expectations on part
  of, 29–31
 as authority figure, 198–99
 comparisons of daughter and
  friends made by, 65–66
 daughter's siblings compared by,
  66–67
 exchanging views between, 46,
  123–24, 129, 148
 fine-tuning of parenting by, 23–31
 identifying own principles of, 20
 information resources for, 32
 involvement and, 13–14, 24, 89,
  108–9, 193

For more information on Dr. Roni Cohen-Sandler's work or to schedule a speaking engagement, please visit her Web site at: www.ronicohensandler.com